D0787952

Muscle and Manliness

Sports and Entertainment
Steven A. Riess, *Series Editor*

OTHER TITLES IN SPORTS AND ENTERTAINMENT

The American Marathon
Pamela Cooper

Anything for a T-Shirt: Fred Lebow and the New York City Marathon, the World's Greatest Footrace
Ron Rubin

Black Baseball Entrepreneurs, 1860–1901: Operating by Any Means Necessary
Michael E. Lomax

Catching Dreams: My Life in the Negro Baseball Leagues
Frazier Robinson with Paul Bauer

Diamond Mines: Baseball and Labor
Paul D. Staudohar

The Fastest Kid on the Block: The Marty Glickman Story
Marty Glickman with Stan Isaacs

Glory Bound: Black Athletes in a White America
David K. Wiggins

Great Women in the Sport of Kings: America's Top Women Jockeys Tell Their Stories
Scooter Davidson, Toby and Valerie Anthony, eds.

Playing Nice and Losing: The Struggle for Control of Women's Intercollegiate Athletics, 1960–2000
Ying Wushanley

Running with Pheidippides: Stylianos Kyriakides, The Miracle Marathoner
Nick Tsiotos and Andrew J. Dabilis

Sports and the American Jew
Steven A. Riess, ed.

Muscle and Manliness

*The Rise of Sport in
American Boarding Schools*

AXEL BUNDGAARD

 Syracuse University Press

Copyright © 2005 by Syracuse University Press
Syracuse, New York 13244–5160

All Rights Reserved

First Edition 2005
05   06   07   08   09   10   6   5   4   3   2   1

The paper used in this publication meets the minimum requirements
of American National Standard for Information Sciences—Permanence
of Paper for Printer Library Materials, ANSI Z39.48–1984.∞™

Library of Congress Cataloging-in-Publication Data

Bundgaard, Axel.
Muscle and manliness : the rise of sport in american boarding schools / Axel Bundgaard.— 1st ed.
p. cm. — (Sports and entertainment)
Includes bibliographical references and index.
ISBN 0-8156-3082-4 (hardcover (cloth) : alk. paper)
1. School sports—Social aspects—United States. 2. Boarding schools—United States. 3.
Masculinity in sports—United States. I. Title. II. Series.
GV346.B86 2005
796.07'1—dc22   2005013558

Manufactured in the United States of America

For Elizabeth, Eric, Chris, and Mark,
who exemplify good character

Axel Bundgaard, professor emeritus of physical education at St. Olaf College, brings a broad background in sports and education to writing this book. His athletic prowess when he was an undergraduate studying history at Midland Lutheran College in Fremont, Nebraska, later won him election to the college's Athletic Hall of Fame. Over his career, he worked as a coach and athletic director, first at Wartburg College in Iowa, next at South Dakota State University, and then at St. Olaf College. He also served on conference and NCAA committees. Still later, Bundgaard drew on his interest in history to study the history and philosophy of sport. He developed and taught courses in these areas, while overseeing a curriculum as chairman of the Physical Education Department at St. Olaf. Early research for this book was reported in "Tom Brown Abroad: Athletics in Selected New England Private Schools, 1850–1910," an article appearing in the Special Centennial Issue of the *Research Quarterly for Exercise and Sport*.

Contents

Illustrations

Preface

HAVING BEEN A COLLEGE COACH a great deal of the time during my early professional career, I am more than familiar with the ubiquitous claims made by high school and college coaches to the effect that athletic participation teaches teamwork, sportsmanship, honesty, fair play, and other laudable virtues. My own subsequent study of sport caused me to question such claims. Research that appeared in the later twentieth century left me even more curious about how and where and when such claims may have originated. How did the association of character development with the playing of sports first come about? Although discussed by sports historians primarily in relation to sports at the college level, did this association begin at earlier levels of schooling? While historians have also discussed character-building through sports and recreation as employed by Protestant evangelicals and by social programs like the Boy Scouts and the YMCA, I was particularly curious about the origins of this association with respect to boys' sports in the school context.

It occurred to me that the earliest connection of sport with moral values was likely to have been in secondary schools where young males found organized opportunities for playing games. Although sport historians have found evidence of games-playing in grammar schools as early as the latter part of the eighteenth century, this kind of play centered on loosely organized frolic occurring irregularly when the schoolmaster permitted it. In the nineteenth century, boys in secondary schools, which were just becoming a part of the American educational scene, stepped up play-like activities to team-oriented games, mainly those of the bat-and-ball and kicking variety. Because much of this early schoolboy play took place in New England and mid-Atlantic private boarding schools, I decided that those schools provided the best place to pursue my research. The schools I chose were founded between 1763 and 1900. This book is based on material derived from archival searches at the following schools: Groton School, Phillips Andover Academy, St. Paul's School, Suffield School, the Williston Northampton School, Woodberry Forest School, and Worcester Academy. Information pertaining to other boarding schools came primarily from school histories and early twentieth-century sources.

As any historian knows, the search for primary source documents can sometimes be extraordinarily difficult. This was certainly true in my researches. Some early boarding schools were short-lived and left few records—for example, Adams Academy and Round Hill School. Others did not keep organized archives, especially before the Civil War. School newspapers, bulletins, and catalogs seldom appeared with regularity until after the Civil War—and even when they were produced, they often were not well preserved or were not kept at all. Thus, it became necessary to rely on secondary sources such as school histories. Most of these were written by those close to the scene, sometimes from personal recollection. However, not all school histories include information about athletics. Typically, such accounts tell about faculties, curricula, finances, and buildings. Sometimes student life, including athletics, is given little attention. Also, in some instances little sports playing went on, so school historians had virtually nothing to write about in this area.

Outside trauma created other obstacles to my search for materials. For example, on occasion fires raged through wooden-framed buildings, destroying what records might have been kept. The Hill School, in particular, had two disastrous fires in the nineteenth century, which completely destroyed the main building.

Some schools lacked staff members with the time or training to organize early historical materials. At the schools I chose to research and whose archives I visited, I was fortunate to have found helpful archivists and librarians who graciously assisted me in my efforts. Then there were those archivists with whom I corresponded and who willingly answered questions and sent me valuable materials: Frank Callahan of Worcester Academy; Edouard Desrochers of Phillips Exeter Academy; Jacqueline Haun of the Lawrenceville School; Paula Krimsky of the Gunnery; David Levesque of St. Paul's School; Barbara May of Woodberry Forest School; Kate Pinkham and Mary Leary of Governor Dummer Academy; Ruth Quattlebaum of Phillips Andover Academy; Mark Renovitch of the Franklin D. Roosevelt Library; Denise Spatarella of the Hill School; Rick Teller and David Anthony of the Williston Northampton School; and Laura Vetter of Episcopal High School. I must give special recognition to the assistance and interest shown by Doug Brown, master and archivist at Groton School. He helped me sort through Endicott Peabody's school records and personal files, and he willingly answered questions that came up over several years' research.

I am also deeply indebted to others who helped me in various ways. The late Fred H. "Ted" Harrison of Phillips Andover Academy encouraged me during my early days as I struggled to determine whether enough material existed to undertake a book. His own work on the history of athletics at Phillips Andover Academy left me with a feeling for the boarding school environment. Dr. William Baker, a sport historian at the University of Maine, also gave me strong encouragement in my early research and willingly critiqued an initial draft. Dr. Erling Jorstad, professor emeritus of history at St. Olaf College, also read an early draft and made helpful critical comments. I also wish to acknowledge the timely and gracious aid of many reference and interlibrary loan staff members in securing materials I needed. Finally, I am grateful to St. Olaf College for a sabbatical and for several summers of grant assistance in which to travel to some of these schools.

I am deeply appreciative of the impeccable work of my typist, Sara Robinson-Coolidge. She was faithful and always cheerful through an irregular schedule over several years and amidst the challenges of rearing babies and toddlers. Her husband, Austin Robinson-Coolidge, eased our anxieties many times by providing important and timely assistance on computer technology. Our good friend, Beverly Gorgos, proved invaluable as proofreader.

Lastly, I am indebted to my wife, Ann Wagner, author of *Adversaries of Dance* (Champaign, Ill.: Univ. of Illinois Press, 1997). Because I have been handicapped in recent years by low vision and other health problems, this book never could have been completed without her encouragement, editing skills, and analysis in the final chapter.

Introduction

FROM THE LATE EIGHTEENTH CENTURY through the first decade of the twentieth century, American boarding schools educated boys for university and college, assuming they would pursue vocations such as the church, or professional careers in such fields as public service, business, medicine, and law. Yet from the outset these schoolboys did not tolerate all study and no play. In this book, I have attempted to describe the origin and early evolution of their sports and athletics, particularly with reference to motivations and governing philosophies for such activity.

Although my initial quest was a search for the beginning connections of character development with sports, I realized that understanding these connections necessitated describing the evolution of sports programs in the boarding schools. The association of character development with sports points to a rationale or justification for having sports and athletics as part of a formal school program. Without such a program, there is only a rationale, either implicit or explicit, for not having sports. The presence of an organized sports program may result in several goals or benefits being heralded as the raison d'être for the program, one of which can be character development. In the boarding schools, this ideal emerged only after several decades during which there was virtually no play and then a few more decades during which the boys themselves initiated games and contests. This time lag is not surprising. The presence of infrequent and informal play, games, and contests does not typically yield claims of character development or moral virtue. As a rule, it is the presence of several elements constituting a highly organized program of athletics in a school that produces the assertion of character development through sports participation. That context includes coaches, practices, schedules, opponents, rules, and officials. Further, it is typically the adult leaders, not the boys themselves, who tout the moral benefits of athletic participation in terms of players' character development. Thus, the connection of character-building with schoolboy sports was tied to the evolution of the sports and athletics programs of the boarding schools. This book traces the early play, games, and sports from the absence of such activity in the late eighteenth century to an established pattern of school sponsorship of athletics by the early teens of the twentieth century.

During the decades when the boys initiated play, games, and sports, in a climate wherein the purpose of the schools focused on academic study, headmasters and masters typically did not countenance or encourage the boys' sporting activity. But from the mid-nineteenth century on, the attitudes and actions of headmasters slowly began to change as they struggled to absorb student-initiated sports into their classical curricula. The evolution in changing attitudes culminated in the early twentieth century, when all the boarding schools sponsored interscholastic or intramural programs, thereby attempting to accommodate an athletics-for-all philosophy. Attention in these years focuses on the values and rationales of headmasters as well as on their implementation of sports programs. This evolution from spontaneous play by the boys to highly organized, adult-sponsored athletics may be understood best as a continuum. Frolic, for example, probably constitutes the most fundamental nature of play; that is, a spontaneous and unorganized activity, motivated by pure fun, with no set skills or rules, and available to all wishing to participate. At the other end of the spectrum comes interscholastic athletics—highly organized, motivated by a desire to compete, with codified rules and enforcement, requiring sophisticated skills, and available only to a select few who successfully clear tryouts. In between these two extremes fall many degrees of organized sports, from a student-run club format to more formal games between schools, sometimes with masters playing.

A mix of terms permeates the narrative up to the Civil War era, as educators struggled with questions arising from the changing roles of play, games, and sports. What is play? What is exercise or gymnastics? Are games and sports the same? For the purpose of clarification, I am using the term *play* to bring to the reader all the early, unorganized games-playing, for example, marbles or tag. Early examples of ball games may be called either *games* or *sports*. Not all games are sports, but football, baseball, and cricket are all commonly referred to under either label. As these activities became more sophisticated in rules and more complex in skills, the term *sport* seemed more appropriate. The term *exercise* usually meant physical activity like walking or running in the woods. When used in the plural, however, it occasionally referred to games and sports, such as athletic exercises. *Gymnastics* usually meant physical activity using an apparatus. The term *athletics* had two meanings: first, track and field activities, mainly races run over certain distances; and second, highly organized sports sponsored by schools but excluding professional sports — its most common meaning today.

The process of defining terms meant that headmasters and masters had to rethink their valuing of study and play. For many people, the opposite of play is labeled work. Thus, participation in sports and games occurs in work-free time. For schoolboys, that meant time free from studies. Sports participation did not involve intellectual work, as did the study of Latin or Greek or mathematics. Therefore, the nature of playing games ran counter to the aims of early boarding schools. Even though early school masters could accept the necessity for some exercise — for example, a run in the woods to curb boyish spirits — with few exceptions, they did not plan for such time off from studies as a part of the school day. Playing games, which also occurred in study-free time, could have been viewed as actually immoral because it was time wasted. In the seventeenth and eighteenth centuries, Christian Puritan values held that time was to be redeemed, not idly wasted away. As well, some activities involving gambling seemed immoral in and of themselves. Consequently, mere acceptance of play and games by school leaders took some decades. Asserting the values of athletics as an integral part of the boarding schools' curricula required yet another significant step. As that transformation occurred, during the latter part of the nineteenth century, headmasters moved toward approving sports and highly organized athletics when they contributed to the development of both character and health. If, for example, playing football built manly vigor, then it was neither immoral nor a waste of time. With such a shift in thinking, headmasters had a rationale on which they could promote athletics as a legitimate school activity.

I have not defined the terms *health* and *character;* the headmasters and masters who used the terms did not define them. They did not need to. The notion of health seemed self-evident in the way one looked and acted, that is, with physical vigor. Moreover, the school masters all understood the second term as signifying manliness and conduct befitting a gentleman, that is, manly conduct. *Character development* meant moral education of the individual boy. For the most part, the masters and boys making up the nineteenth-century boarding-school population came from America's upper class and upper-middle class. For headmasters, that background carried an ideal and an obligation in terms of conduct. Hence, Exeter's school paper could publish an article in October 1895 titled the "Gentlemanly Side of Athletics." The true gentleman played with his own internalized code of conduct. When headmasters did write about character development, they had in mind principles to be acquired, for example, fair play or playing by the rules. Playing hard and not shirking one's duty were also critical values. Honesty was equally essential: cheating was absolutely unacceptable. Although headmasters specifically and implicitly touted such values, that did not mean that their charges were impervious to the temptations of the era in which they attended school. Yet when allegations of rule-breaking occurred, headmasters immediately clamped down on the rule-breakers in an effort to hold to the school's sense of honor and moral order.

Attention to the history of particular sports falls outside the scope of this book except insofar as the evolution of some team games is tied to the development of rules and order. I do not focus on individual sports for the same reason. In a few instances, I write about track and field meets as part of a school rivalry. But it is within the realm of team sports like baseball, football, and cricket that most of the early evolution and acceptance of schoolboy athletics occurred, particularly with reference to the sought-after qualities, for example, loyalty, honesty, and fair play.

I have organized chapters chronologically as far as possible. The first two chapters briefly review the English historical origins of the association of sport with character and the transfer of that association to early American boarding schools through their connections with the British public schools. Chapter 3 probes American schoolboy attempts to organize their sports in the pre-Civil War era, while the following chapter describes the rapid expansion of schools and their sports programs in the years after the Civil War. Chapters 5 and 6 are rather discrete entities. The former traces the development of gymnasia and provision for health and exercise during the winter months of school. The latter chapter treats the development of school papers and their role in fostering sports on campuses. Both discussions focus the reader on the middle to later decades of the nineteenth century. Chapters 7 and 8 deal with sport and moral education specifically, first in terms of the leadership of Groton's Endicott Peabody and second in terms of rules' infractions. Both chapters cover the years from Groton's founding in the 1880s through the first decade of the twentieth century. During that period, the spread of sports programs in existing schools and in newly founded schools, coupled with the transformation of headmasters' attitudes, meant that athletics were established as an integral part of the boarding schools' curricula by the advent of World War I. Thus, chapter 9 reviews styles of faculty leadership in the evolution of sport and athletics. Chapter 10 describes the implementation of sports for all, with emphasis on the differing motivations of faculty and boys.

I conclude in the final chapter that the masters' notion of character development through sports could have occurred in the Victorian American boarding schools because of their relatively closed environment and the degree of control exercised by faculty over their young charges. However, the headmasters and masters who lauded sports participation did not analyze their concept of character as manliness, nor did they think through the validity of their claims with respect to all boys who played, the frequency of their participation, the voluntary or required nature of their participation, and the degrees of competition in which they engaged. Thus the final chapter presents a conclusion that ends this book while suggesting a starting point for additional research.

Muscle and Manliness

1

In the Beginning

Puritan Values, Private Schools, and Play

Early Puritans and Play

WHEN THE FAMOUS sixteenth-century Calvinist theologian, William Perkins, reminded English Puritans of when and what they could play, he did not do so because play had emerged as something new in their lives. The British had engaged
in sporting activities for centuries. What concerned Perkins was his belief that
time spent in sports had gotten out of hand. Perkins feared the growing secularism
being displayed by the followers of French reformer John Calvin. In a treatise fo-
cusing on approved behavior, Perkins carefully delineated what sports, games,
and recreations are lawful for a Christian and what ends they are to serve. He asserted, "it followes that *Recreation* is lawfull, and a part of Christian libertie, if it be
well used. By *Recreation*, I understand exercises and sports serving to refresh either the body or the mind" (Perkins [1608] 1966, 46).

More specifically, early Puritans learned that lawful recreation included
games of "wit or industry," for example, running, fencing, shooting the long bow,
and the like sports, "wherein the industry of the mind and body hath the chiefest
stroke." By contrast, games of chance, such as dice, were not lawful recreation.
Those games that began with chance but required some skill for victory proved
problematic for Perkins. He concluded it was best to avoid such pastimes. In the
use of recreation, Perkins stressed moderation or temperance. One's time and af-
fections were to be primarily devoted to God. Lawful games and pastimes could
therefore only claim a modest portion of a person's time and energy (Perkins
[1606] 1966, 220–22). Beliefs in such strict guidelines for play and recreation inevitably accompanied Puritans to America.

After the initial settlement at Plymouth, Massachusetts, in 1620, a steady flow
of Puritans from England came in the 1620s and 1630s to settle in Boston and en-

virons. The leader of the Massachusetts Bay Colony, John Winthrop, established a General Court (legislature) for carrying out regulations and laws in the new settlement. One aspect of communal life that came under the conduct of the General Court pertained to play. When work and worship held primary importance in daily life, lawful rest and recreation served only to maintain health. As sport historian Dennis Brailsford elaborates, "The Puritan . . . found only sin and error in the people's customary play. He was not looking for signs of communal well-being, for the simple satisfactions of the game, for the happiness of the participants or the relief of the strains of their working lives" (Brailsford 1991, 18).

Thus, typical youthful behavior came under the umbrella of what was circumspect. Youth older than fourteen years old and strangers were targeted in particular. According to researcher Nancy Struna, the General Court decried those youths who took the "liberty to walke & sporte themselves in the streets or feilds," thereby disturbing the religious preparations of others on the Sabbath! In 1647, the General Court specifically outlawed shovelboard, and soon thereafter bowling as well as gaming, because "much pcious time" was wasted in these pursuits, and "much wast of wine & beare occasioned thereby." But sporting contests served one communal value: defense. In 1639, the magistrates organized the first military company in the colony, to include physical exercise, marksmanship, mock battles, and athletic contests (Struna, 1977, 6–8). Perhaps this edict marked the emergence of exercising through sporting activities and may have signified the beginning in this country of the still-current belief in the role of sport as a socializing agent.

The ages of men and boys involved in the military drill are not clear. Adolescence as a concept did not find its way into the literature regarding the development of youth until later centuries. Thus, early citations regarding adolescent play remain scanty and incomplete. Teenagers of fourteen to eighteen years in the seventeenth century would have been treated like adults. One of the known and lawful sports that boys and men would have participated in was shooting. Hunting provided food for the table and, thus, was considered productive. Other individual sports that attracted boys included marksmanship with the bow and arrow, fishing, and hiking in unexplored lands. Where sport was condemned, it was often because of its negative or harmful consequences as opposed to condemning the sport itself. Historian Carl Bridenbaugh noted that boys and young men played football in Boston's streets until 1658, when bystanders were being injured (Bridenbaugh, 1938, 117). Thus, the Boston selectmen declared a fine for "playing at football . . . in any of the streets, lanes, or enclosures of this town." In Salem, as well as in Boston, authorities also prohibited horse racing or "violent rideing" in the streets because it endangered pedestrians (Struna 1996, 69; 1977, 11).

Perhaps a specific sporting incident also signaled a change in attitudes. In the 1680s, John Dutton, an English bookseller, spent some time in the colonies visiting with many citizens and getting information about the American experiment. In his travels he visited Rowley, six miles north and a little east of Ipswich, one of the original, early settlements, where Dutton was staying with the Stuart family. One of the things he and his host, Mr. Stuart, did was to see "a greate Game of Football." The people of Rowley, "many of whom were clothiers," played against opponents from some other village not far away. The participants played in their bare feet, a practice Dutton described as "very odd." Then he realized that players were not "so apt to trip up one anothers [sic] heels, and quarrel as I have seen 'em in England" (Struna 1996, 74–75). Because the game was played on the sandy seashore just a few miles from Rowley, playing in bare feet was tolerable.

The Rowley game suggests some questions about the early beginnings of organized sport. The game took place upon a prearranged date, including location and time of the game. Yet mystery surrounds much of this contest. What method was employed to inform participants from both sides about the time and location for the contest? Was this an isolated game or one in a series? If the latter, was it always the same two sides competing? How were team members chosen? Who decided on the rules for play? Who settled disputes during the game? These and other questions hint at the complexity that surrounds the origin and development of organized sports in this country.

By the turn of the eighteenth century, strong Puritan voices still railed against alleged sinful behavior, as leaders saw citizens becoming increasingly secular. Cotton Mather, for example, decried, "sinful Company—keeping with light and vain Persons, unlawful Gaming, an abundance of Idleness." Cards and dice also wasted time. As well, church members misspent "precious time" in "publick Houses" (Mather 1702, 54, 90). The key lament was idleness. Hardworking Puritans could see no benefit in time ill-used. Sports playing for self-amusement certainly fell into this category. Yet among Boston's 7,000 inhabitants, not all adhered to this Puritan ethos. People from other denominations had also settled in the town. The Puritans could not command everyone to follow their theology.

Gradually more and more secularism also emerged. Youngsters not well versed in Puritan theology simply stayed away from the church and spent their Sundays in recreational pursuits. Struna writes that, "In an attempt to enforce uniformity," Harvard officials actually permitted sport on college grounds and forbade students from leaving campus (Struna 1977, 10). More significantly, in 1712, Harvard authorities bought a Cambridge orchard and set it aside for the recreation and exercise of the students. Specialized areas for play helped ensure the safety of passersby and also secured some separation of students from the general public. Presumably the space was to be used regularly. The overseers had earlier instituted a period of time, probably each day, for sport. Struna notes this time was a minimum of two and one-half hours after 1655 (Struna 1977, 9; 1994, 409).

Because educational authorities set aside hours for sport, the rationale must have fit guidelines for proper use of time. To lay out money for the purchase of space in which to exercise and recreate meant a concern for health—certainly a lawful Christian pursuit. Despite Harvard's example, the adoption of sports and physical training into American academies would move slowly. The more important goal for early New England Puritans was to educate their citizenry. Reading and writing took precedence over play and pastime, a stark contrast with English social rank and school traditions.

American Academies Contrast with English Schools

The value of education had emerged as one of the most widely held Puritan beliefs. In fact, by 1643, one estimate held that Massachusetts had one university-trained man for every forty families. Continuing the emphasis on education in America helped to ensure survival of the culture by having a learned clergy and a congregation who could read. As Larzar Ziff put it, "New England Puritans pioneered in the field of education as the means of shaping the individual to a psychological acquiescence in the norms of his community, to educating him . . . for citizenship" (Ziff 1973, 50, 68). In order to achieve these lofty goals, the Calvinists and non-Calvinists by the end of the seventeenth century realized that more than the basic skills of reading, writing, and arithmetic were necessary for a community that had launched into the commercial world of trading. Moreover, Harvard officials had complained that students came ill-prepared for the demands that the classical curriculum required. But the growth in secondary academies during the eighteenth century moved slowly. Usually, such schools began with a single headmaster and a few pupils. Many communities would contribute a plot of land for schools, but that was the extent of it as far as support was concerned. Sometimes a religious denomination would sponsor a school. Sometimes one or more individuals would serve as benefactors. For the most part, it became necessary for the boards of trustees or headmasters to charge tuition. Usually, only the sons and daughters of the growing upper-middle-class population were able to pay the tuition (Butts 1978, 5). Despite such drawbacks, in time academies dotted the countryside. Eventually, more than 6,000 academies were located throughout the country, often in thinly populated areas. However, by the Civil War most of these ventures had failed, victims of urban expansion (Sizer 1964, 12–13, 40–45).

Those academies that survived and thrived as established boarding schools helped to pave the way for the development of secondary education in America. They also developed and refined the theory and practice of athletics as a character-building educational enterprise in this country. But the ideal of the boarding school and athletics did not emerge as a unique American venture. Instead, it can ultimately be traced back to the Renaissance traditions of the English courtly gentleman and the British public schools.

As early as the sixteenth century, the English gentleman or courtier learned from the courtesy books, or education literature of the era, that he was to set an example for the common folk and befit himself as a governor of the realm. Accordingly, the gentleman was to become not only learned but also skilled in warfare and courtly sports, as well as in dance and music. Above all he was to be a Christian, to seek virtue, and to shun vice. The ideal held that this Renaissance *vir perfectus* exemplified the noble amateur in his physical performance. In his detailed analysis of this courtly tradition, Dennis Brailsford asserts that from Sir Thomas Elyot's *The Book Named The Governor*, published in 1531, "there is a persistent English belief in the character-building qualities of sport." As a Renaissance scholar, guided by Galen in matters of health, Elyot devotes several pages of his book on education to the kinds of sports and exercises befitting a young nobleman's son, who was expected to grow up and serve as adviser to king or prince. Concluding his discussion of "commendable exercises and pastimes, not repugnant to virtue," Elyot writes, "And hereat I conclude to write of exercise, which appertaineth as well to princes and noblemen as to all other by their example, which determine to pass forth their lives in virtue and honesty." The connections here are clear. Those in the privileged ranks of society were to demonstrate health, skill in appropriate pastimes, and good character (Brailsford 1969, 25; Elyot [1531] 1962, 88, 94; Wagner 1980, 136–39). In time, the schools that trained the sons of gentlemen could foster sports and character development.

Often founded by churchmen, royalty, or aristocracy, English public schools held a long-established tradition, including those like Winchester, founded in 1382, Eton in 1440, Rugby in 1567, and Harrow in 1571. Typically, such an institution was characterized as "an independent, non-local, predominantly boarding school for the upper and upper-middle classes." At these institutions, early play apparently focused on group games of low organization, some of which were thought too rowdy for gentlemen's sons (Ogilvie 1957, 8–10, 104). For example, Elyot declared football to be "nothing but beastly fury and extreme violence." He followed historical tradition in advocating sports that could befit a nobleman for war or peace, for example, riding, wrestling, hunting, and shooting with the long bow (Elyot [1531] 1962, 92).

The first English schoolman to support the game of football was a dedicated and innovative sixteenth-century schoolmaster, Richard Mulcaster. However, he wanted the game refined from the "thronging of a rude multitude, with bursting of shins, and breaking of legs." He organized the sport into a series of school teams; students played with less vigor and simpler rules. Mulcaster also suggested a "training master" who could take over the practices and have authority to command and to act as a coach and a referee (Ogilvie 1957, 68). Thus, he advanced a far-reaching view in the employment of a master to conduct the sports and exercise of the students. In contrast, in this country aristocratic sporting traditions did not hold sway in New England, and Puritan influence helped to retard the emergence of team sports in early academies.

The American academies that survived as boarding schools and are noted in this text, along with their founding dates, include the following: Governor Dummer Academy (1763), South Byfield, Massachusetts; Phillips Andover Academy (1778), Andover, Massachusetts; Phillips Exeter Academy (1783), Exeter, New Hampshire; Lawrence Academy (1792), Groton, Massachusetts; Milton Academy (1798), Milton, Massachusetts; Deerfield Academy (1799), Deerfield, Massachusetts; Monson Academy (1804), Monson, Massachusetts; Lawrenceville School (1810), Lawrenceville, New Jersey; Wilbraham Academy (1817), Wilbraham, Massachusetts.[1]

In the midst of the demise of so many academies just before the Civil War, how did the above schools manage to survive? Several factors seemed to apply. The technique of incorporation, rather than reliance on a sometimes single, transient teacher proved critical. Second, if not supported by a governing board, some schools leaned on their affiliation with the religious denomination that founded the academy, such as Wilbraham and the Methodist church. Not least, a few schools benefitted from large endowments. Some schools also survived by altering their character and student bodies, thereby becoming widely known yet exclusive college-preparatory institutions (Sizer 1964, 26, 44–45; McLachlan 1970, 43).

---

1. Monson and Wilbraham academies merged in 1971.

Despite the varying strategies for survival, these schools were all private institutions and required payment of tuition for enrollment. Thus, the American boarding schools, like their British counterparts, usually educated sons from upper- and upper-middle-class families. But unlike the British courtly and aristocratic traditions, the cultivation of sports skills did not belong to the New England Puritan gentlemanly tradition. American school masters had to struggle and sort out their perceptions of and values associated with play and games.

Conflicting Ideas about Schoolboy Play

Several historians, including Robert Henderson, Harriet Marr, Jennie Holliman, and Roxanne Albertson, have gleaned information about the play life of the academy schoolboys in the late eighteenth and early nineteenth centuries. It became apparent to these investigators that both positive and negative attitudes and interpretations existed about what constituted children's play. Holliman and Marr both assert that boys and girls have always played ball. Marr introduces the novel idea that children early on may have learned to throw and catch from tossing stones and fruit at each other (Marr 1954, 87; Holliman 1931, 64). Warlike skills, such as throwing missiles and swinging clubs, may have eventually evolved into bat-and-ball games.

But such games did not always meet with favor in the early academy settings. They were considered dangerous to both persons and property. A wayward fly ball could inflict personal injuries and also break windows, whether at a rural academy or in a town setting. In 1799, at Atkinson Academy in New Hampshire, the headmaster charged John Adams Smith, a grandson of John Adams, then president of the United States, ninepence for playing ball too close to the schoolhouse. At Deerfield Academy, students also faced fines for playing ball too near the school building (Marr 1954, 87; Albertson 1975, 2). At Wesleyan Academy (later renamed Wilbraham Academy), students could not scuffle, wrestle, or engage in any other kind of sport "during intermission" (Wood 1971, 13). The town fathers of Worcester, Massachusetts, passed an ordinance in 1816 prohibiting ball-playing in the streets in order to protect the town-dwellers' safety. Moreover, neighborhood games of men and boys, in large open spaces, created so much noise that they became "absolutely intolerable" to nearby residents, reported the *New York Evening Post* in 1828 (Holliman 1931, 64). Similarly, in about 1820, when Governor Dummer Academy was refurbished, new rules were issued, warning that, " 'No ball, stick or stone' was to be thrown by any scholar so as to endanger any of the Academy property" (Ragle 1963, 44).

In addition to concerns that games might cause property damage and loud noise, some games became proscribed on moral grounds. For example, Lawrence Academy in Groton, Massachusetts, in its "Bye-Laws" of 1794, stipulated several limitations. Article three sanctioned any student who violated the rules concerning no card-playing. It further stipulated, "And it is recommended to the Preceptor, to restrain the Scholars from all other improper games, more expecially within the Academy building. But they may amuse themselves with decent Athletick exercises." Precisely what was meant by *athletic exercises* is not clear from the text, but it is very probable the term meant wholesome sports that would provide healthful physical body exercise, in contrast to "improper games" such as cards, which would have been considered a waste of time, if not immoral (Frank 1992, 16, 18).

A few headmasters saw an advantage associated with the frolicsome nature of students. Most notable in this regard was the example set by Samuel Moody at Governor Dummer Academy, the oldest still-existing academy in the United States. During his years there (1763–90), Moody introduced swimming as part of school life. He believed that aquatics held physical benefits that enhanced one's lifesaving capabilities. On the spur of the moment, likely on a sunny and balmy day, Moody would halt class proceedings and lead his charges for a plunge in the nearby river. School historian John Ragle describes: "In seasonable weather and when the tide was right, his powerful voice would penetrate the confused hum of the classroom with the pronouncement that all should immediately depart for the swimming holes, the older boys to the banks of the Parker [River], the younger to a shallower stream nearby. What storm of splashing and spirited horseplay ensued can easily be imagined" (Ragle 1963, 21). Moody represents the first schoolmaster to take an active role either in teaching swimming or in encouraging other physical activities. Douglas Frank claims that Moody "set a standard by which preceptors and headmasters would be judged for generations" (Frank 1992, 4).

While teaching at Greenfield Hill Academy in Connecticut, Timothy Dwight, later to become president of Yale College (1795–1817), also encouraged games-playing and insisted on recess in both morning and afternoon. Apparently Dwight had nearly ruined his own health and eyesight from unrelieved study in earlier years. Thus, he advocated vigorous games-playing and systematic exercises for his pupils. As the grandson of Jonathan Edwards, Puritan stalwart and leader of the Great Awakening, Dwight, who was also a pastor in Greenfield, thus showed some relaxation from early and narrow Puritan guidelines on play and games (Marr 1954, 88; Ahlstrom 1975, 1:507–9).

But school leaders of the late eighteenth and early nineteenth centuries did not hold a clear vision of what constituted acceptable physical activity. It appears, though, that advocates saw sport as "healthful exercise." In the *American Journal of Education* in 1826, a writer proclaimed, "The time, we hope, is near when there will be no literary institution unprovided with proper means of healthful exercise and innocent recreation, and when literary men cease to be distinguished by a pallid countenance and wasted body." Some school leaders thought that "innocent recreation," which can be interpreted as simple and moral games and physical activity, renewed a tired mind and recreated an unconditioned body. Union Academy in Bennington, Vermont, for example, in 1834 encouraged "rational and innocent sports." Excluded were activities like dancing, which were thought to "dissipate" the mind, despite the fact that the physical body was exercised. Hence, dancing could not be characterized as rational or innocent (Marr 1954, 85–86, 89–90).

Little evidence exists that school leaders typically looked upon play purely as a joyful experience and valuable as such. Within the context of the early nineteenth century, American school leaders had to explore the values of play and games. According to Albertson, leading educators who attended the American Institute of Instruction in Boston on August 26, 1831, debated the question, "Ought, Athletic Games, combining exercise with amusement, to be united with Manual Labor in the education of youth, as a means of forming and invigorating the body?" The question was discussed "with much animation." However, Albertson found no unanimity of opinion existed. *Athletic games*, in the minds of many, meant health and physical development. For others, the term held possibilities as a medium in which to teach morality, particularly if the teacher participated to provide an example. According to Albertson, the term included running events, bowling, swimming, boxing, fencing, gymnastics, and a variety of ball games. Although the Lawrence Academy regulations referred to "Athletick exercises," writers in this era seem to have used the terms *athletic games* and *athletic exercises* interchangeably. Moreover, the terms covered a variety of physical activities, most of which remained "unsupervised recess activities" until a later time (Albertson 1976, 1, 9–14, 15, 19).

Thus, the beginnings of play and games in American academies proceeded in happenstance fashion, depending on the ingenuity of schoolboys, the attitudes of masters, and the regulations governing the school. Three of the eighteenth-century academies, which survived to become legendary, provide examples of this happenstance mix of early play with the academic focus of the schools. The three institutions were located not far from each other in a triangular pattern: Governor Dummer, Phillips Andover, and Phillips Exeter.

The Threesome Leadership

William Dummer (1677–1761), farmer, politician, and lieutenant governor of Massachusetts, provided in his will that his Newbury farm should endow what became the academy less than two years after his death. Three trustees carried out the terms of his will, which also bequeathed money to Harvard to endow professorships. Though founded in 1763, Governor Dummer Academy was not incorporated until 1782 (*American National Biography* 1999; Frank 1992, 4). Within sixteen months after the will was executed, the trustees opened the school. The appointment of Moody as the first master proved to be a fortunate decision. A Harvard graduate, he had studied the classics, mainly Greek and Latin, thus meeting Governor Dummer's request that the curriculum should emphasize those two languages. But intellectual development did not comprise the entire school day for Moody. As an "inveterate horseback rider and an ardent swimmer," Moody passed along to his young charges the joy of play and physical activity by personal participation. This heretical attitude of Moody even went so far as to introduce dancing into the curriculum and, worse yet, by a French dancing master! The boys must have loved this "infectious" and "impulsive" schoolmaster (Ragle 1963, 21).

Samuel Phillips Jr. attended Dummer and as a result harbored thoughts about starting his own academy. Succeeding in his dream, Phillips Andover began fifteen years after the founding of Governor Dummer. The first principal became Eliphalet Pearson, Phillips's classmate from Dummer. Pearson remained at the Andover Academy for about eight years before leaving to enroll at Harvard and gain an advanced degree. But, along with Samuel Phillips, he set the stern tone of Andover for "one hundred years" (Harrison 1983, 4). The school had been financially assisted by gifts from Samuel's uncle, John Phillips, who subsequently served on the Andover board. Not long afterward, Uncle John founded a school with similar philosophy in the town where he had made his fortune. The Act of Incorporation for Phillips Exeter Academy was signed by the governor of New Hampshire on April 3, 1781, six months after the Andover Academy had been incorporated. The constitutions of both schools stress attention to the minds and morals of the boys as the primary focus for instruction (Crosbie 1924, 13–14, 31–34).

By 1783, when Phillips Exeter opened its doors, Governor Dummer had been operating for twenty years and Phillips Andover for five years. During that time, as fragmentary evidence tells us, a smattering of ball-playing had begun to take place. One can imagine the frustrations of the young Andover boy, Josiah Quincy, only six years old, as he sat on a hard bench in the schoolhouse, much more interested in playing ball and marbles than in the content and rote memorization confronting him in the classroom. The climate of the school under Pearson was too demanding for young Quincy. In his own words, "I was an incorrigible lover of sports of every kind. My heart was in ball and marbles. I needed and loved perpetual activity of body, and with these dispositions I was compelled to sit with four other boys on the same hard bench, daily, four hours in the morning and four in the afternoon, and study lessons which I could not understand."

It seems likely that young Quincy did not play ball by himself but with classmates, if they had permitted a six-year-old to take part. When he mentions ball, he probably refers to a form of rounders that had rules that permitted three people to play the game and increased the number of them depending on how many wanted to take part. Yet, it is doubtful that the youthful Quincy's demanding schedule permitted him time to play much ball, because he was in class eight hours a day with homework in addition. Of course, the same predicament clouded play time for fellow students (Quincy 1867, 24–25).

The boys at Exeter also made overtures toward ball games. Marr points out that Alphaeus Packard, who entered Exeter in 1811, encountered a football-like game popular in the fall. He notes that the boys had been playing it for some time prior to his enrollment. Some attempt at having regular or ongoing teams reflected the academic focus of the school. The teams consisted of those who sat on the north side of the aisle in the Latin room versus those who sat on the south side (Marr 1954, 87)!

Andover boys may not have been so fortunate. The principals who followed Pearson adhered to the strict Calvinistic code of behavior. In 1808, under Pearson's lead, Andover Theological Seminary was founded. From the outset, the same board governed both schools. In the words of Andover sport historian Fred Harrison, "Zion reigned supreme on Andover Hill." Although the academy lads could go swimming in nearby waters, they were under strict orders to protect the safety of nonswimmers and swimmers (Harrison 1983, 4–6). The orders were issued by the board of trustees, a more significant exercise of control than an order by the principal himself.

Governor Dummer and the two Phillips academies led in academic and play life for schoolboys, but two other schools in the early nineteenth century began the incorporation of German gymnastics into the boys' lives. Physical development was actively fostered and integrated into the total curriculum, rather than being restrained or repressed. Despite the short life of Round Hill School, it provided a unique model of physical training.

The Addition of German Gymnastics

The idea of schoolboys boarding near or on the campus of a school, as at Dummer, sprang from the observations of European schools by two young Harvard graduates. Joseph Cogswell and George Bancroft shortly after graduation traveled separately throughout Europe, but mainly in Germany, studying in selected universities and, between terms, visiting schools. Both had attended Phillips Exeter Academy, and each came away disenchanted with the schooling he had received both there and at Harvard. After several years on the continent, both returned to Cambridge in 1821, filled with new ideas about secondary education. Neither knew exactly what course of action to take. Eventually they met and discovered their mutual concerns. With some urging from the president of Harvard and other friends, Cogswell and Bancroft took steps to establish a school in a tranquil environment far from the perceived evil temptations of the city. They found their idyll at Northampton in west-central Massachusetts. There they rented two houses located on the brow of a hill overlooking the village and the Connecticut River. On October 1, 1823, Cogswell and Bancroft opened Round Hill school with twenty-five students; the school soon grew rapidly as a result of positive reaction from the press (McLachlan 1970, 49–82).

The founders established a rigorous daily schedule; boys had little idle time that could potentially lead to immoral behavior. The two leaders intended their school to be a tightly knit community. They envisioned a place where boys lived in the same building as the instructors. The founders publicly stated in their prospectus that they would take responsibility for the boys' deportment and morals. Each day would begin and end with devotions; Sunday worship would be strictly attended. By attending a boarding school, the students entered an expanded familial fellowship with Cogswell, Bancroft, and other faculty members. The founders viewed the ultimate objective for their school as becoming a place to mold "Christian gentlemen and scholars," who in turn would eventually take their place in society as leaders, upholding a culture undergirded by the values learned at Round Hill and reaffirmed at higher institutions such as Harvard and Yale (McLachlan 1970, 83–86, 95; Cogswell and Bancroft [1823], 16–17).

Cogswell and Bancroft set about to attain their lofty goals through a curriculum that emphasized nurturing the whole child. Developing their plans from the ideas that Cogswell had most likely internalized while observing Emmanuel von Fellenberg's Swiss school at Hofwyl and Christian Salzmann's Schnepfenthal school in Germany (Geldbach 1976, 237–38), the founders intended that the curriculum would train all the faculties of the child—intellectual, moral, and physical. Within this framework, Cogswell and Bancroft emphasized a facet of education that would have profound effect upon schoolboys—athletic and physical activity. In the words of their *Prospectus*, "We would also encourage activity of body, as the means of promoting firmness of constitution and vigour of mind, and shall appropriate regularly a portion of each day to healthful sports and gymnastic exercises" (Cogswell and Bancroft [1823], 17).

In less than a year and one-half after the founding of Round Hill school, the co-leaders appointed a German refugee, Charles Beck, as instructor of gymnastics and Latin. He was probably the first physical education instructor in an American school, bringing his ideas from his training in Berlin under Friedrich Jahn, the "father" of German gymnastics. Upon his arrival Beck immediately established an "outdoor gymnasium," similar to the German Turnplatz, a playground used for gymnastics that graced the grounds of Turner societies back in Germany. In following the German system of gymnastics, Beck's outdoor gymnasium most likely included horse, beam, and bars, which the students could vault over, walk on, and swing from (Leonard and Affleck 1947, 87–92; Geldbach 1976, 238, 240).

The year after Beck came to Round Hill, a school circular appeared describing in some detail the program of physical training. Himself a classicist, Beck wrote or certainly must have approved statements that went beyond merely a gymnastics regimen. For example, the 1826 circular contained the following statement: "Games and healthful sports, promoting hilarity and securing a just degree of exercise, are to be encouraged" (Bennett 1965, 59). Significantly, more than just gymnastics prevailed, as the founders recognized the importance of fun for the boys. By June 1831, a publication, titled an *Outline of the System of Education at the Round Hill School*, specified more detail in the kinds of physical activity emphasized. "Riding on horseback, gymnastics, bathing, and dancing, are prescribed recreations, under the same regulations as the literary exercises; all other innocent, active amusements are permitted, but no sedentary games." The strong emphasis on vigorous and total body sports and recreations was further underscored by the lack of a manual labor requirement at a time when that proved popular. Cogswell and Bancroft permitted "all the labors of husbandry and gardening" but did not require them (*Outline* 1831, 13).

Twentieth-century historian Bruce Bennett found that Round Hillers took part in a surprising variety of sports, including swimming, ice-skating, sledding, hockey, archery, marbles, and a form of baseball, plus a semblance of football. Other physical activities included cross-country running, wrestling, boxing, horseback riding, hiking, and camping. Ballroom dancing included instruction and occasional balls held at the school with ladies from Northampton invited as guests. The wide variety of activities available to the boys points to the effort put forth by the founders and by Beck to develop the total education of the whole person.

Bennett was the first to point out that Beck, through the Round Hill curriculum, not only developed an exercise program that concentrated on the health of the students but also brought attention to the variety of sports that "promoted hilarity." Some of that "hilarity" emanated from the joy associated with playing team games, such as baseball and football. Bennett concluded that, for the boys, physical training provided long-lasting memories centered on the good times they had in their games and sports (Bennett 1965, 59–61).

The semblance of football and baseball that Bennett alludes to requires some amplification. It is possible that the form of ball and bat game played was called rounders. Ronald Smith and John Lucas point out that, by the end of the 1830s, a writer of a boys' book on sport had renamed the game of rounders as baseball. Yet written rules had actually appeared in a boys' book published in 1829, and youngsters had played rounders in America much earlier (Lucas and Smith 1978, 170–71; Henderson 1947, 146). Further, Harrison speculates that young Josiah Quincy in 1778 might have played a form of baseball. Alphaeus Packard, who entered Exeter in 1811, mentioned a "bat ball" being played. It may have preceded the game or name of rounders. Later, Andover graduate Dr. Oliver Wendell Holmes, class of 1825, acknowledged that he played Base Ball[2] in his college days at Harvard (Harrison 1983, 18; Crosbie 1924, 233).

Football, as the Round Hillers played it, likely resembled a folk game. No doubt, two teams of boys kicked a stuffed bag of some sort back and forth in a hewed-out open space. Each side attempted, in a free-for-all fashion, to propel the "ball" over a designated goal line. Their ball games seem to have resembled those

---

2. Holmes is not to be confused with his son, the famous Supreme Court justice, Oliver Wendell Holmes, Jr. Dr. Oliver Wendell Holmes (1809–94), Harvard graduate, later became professor of anatomy there as well as a celebrated poet in Boston, perhaps best known for his published writings as the "Autocrat of the Breakfast Table." For a discussion of the shrouded origins of American baseball, see also Menke (1978).

played at the Phillips academies (Lucas and Smith 1978, 229–30; Harrison 1983, 36–37).

On a more curious note, how did these team games emerge upon the grounds of an isolated school in remote central Massachusetts, when neither Cogswell nor Bancroft seemingly displayed any interest in baseball or football? Nor did Beck's background lend itself to familiarity with such team sports. One can only speculate that certain boys themselves instigated the introduction of these sports. Many grew up in cities where some semblance of bat-and-ball games took place. Those who came from the Boston area, for example, likely saw older relatives or acquaintances playing a football type of game on the Harvard campus. One is reminded that the ages of most Harvard students in the early 1800s did not exceed by much the oldest of the Round Hill students. For example, Edward Everett Hale, celebrated cleric and author, entered Harvard at age thirteen and graduated in 1839 at age seventeen. In the story of his growing-up years, he tells of playing football at Harvard (Hale 1893, 200). Emulation of this kind no doubt repeated itself at other boarding schools as games-playing filled a void in the life of the schoolboy.

In addition to Round Hill, a small New Jersey academy also instituted a program of German gymnastics. Dr. Isaac Brown, Presbyterian minister, founded his tiny school, later to become Lawrenceville,[3] in 1810 and nursed it along in the village of Maidenhead. The name of the town became Lawrenceville in 1815, and the change in the school's name naturally followed (Mulford 1935, 10–11). By 1825, the school published a revised curriculum borrowing heavily from the German tradition. Brown hired an instructor who had been born in Germany and graduated from the University of Heidelberg. Well versed in the German system of education, the new instructor may well have been "the experienced and judicious superintendent" Brown refers to in the following advertisement introducing gymnastics into the new curriculum. Previously, no boarding school outside of Round Hill had publicly proclaimed that it included gymnastics in its program of instruction. A detailed circular included a description of how gymnastics and exercise would be treated in the education of Brown's students, "Gymnastic [sic], and other interesting exercises, will be introduced, so far as useful, to invigorate the physical system, and develop the minds of youth; and to render their exercises

3. Isaac Brown called his school the Academy of Maidenhead. In 1837 the school was sold to the Reverend Samuel Hamill. He ran the school until he sold it to the legatees of the wealthy John Cleve Green, one of the first students. This transaction occurred in 1879; Hamill remained another four years to complete four and one-half decades as the school's leader (Mulford 1935, 35, 78–79).

both safe and salutary; this department is committed to an experienced and judicious superintendant." In addition, students had the opportunity to learn the "art of swimming" in an especially constructed "Bathing Reservoir, supplied with perpetually running water" (Mulford 1935, 21–22).

Brown's plan did have detractors. But the comments of one Reverend James W. Alexander, a visitor at the academy, helped his cause. Alexander wrote, "I cannot but think there is something visionary in the new-fangled gymnastics. Boys, if kept at it as part of their work, will soon be glad to exchange climbing a mast, and vaulting over a wooden fence, for climbing cherry trees and playing at ball. . . . Military exercises, if they could be introduced without the military spirit, would be a happy improvement in physical education and riding, fencing (to which you will add dancing), have stood the test of centuries." Alexander's startling astuteness about the physicality of man places him as a knowledgeable historian. The skills of riding, fencing, and dancing had been the European ideal for gentlemen and courtiers since the Renaissance, Calvinists and like-minded reformers excepted.

Brown certainly occupies a place alongside Cogswell and Bancroft in moving physical activity into the mainstream of the daily routine of schooling. His experiment proved to be a success, drawing new students and the approval of patrons. Local papers wrote, "The experiment, in the use of Gymnastic exercises, clearly illustrates their happy efficacy in affording agreeable and invigorating excitement, both to the minds and bodies of the pupils." The *Trenton Federalist* and *Philadelphia Post* also reported that the students had found the "bathing reservoir" provided "a salubrious and delightful amusement." By 1830, Brown added "horsemanship and riding in carriages" to contribute to the health and "cheerfulness" of his students (Mulford 1935, 24).

In 1837, the school, by now renamed Lawrenceville High School, was sold to Dr. Samuel Hamill, a young instructor who had joined the teaching staff three years previously. Hamill went on to be Lawrenceville's principal for the next four decades, continuing to foster the early emphasis on play and exercise (Mulford 1935, 35).

Thus, by the early nineteenth century, it was evident that schoolmasters struggled with how to contain and even to foster boys' desire for play and their need for healthful exercise to aid physical development. No grand design existed for the masters to follow. Either the boys instituted their own games and sports, or individual and forward-looking men like Moody, Cogswell, Bancroft, and Brown developed embryonic and unique programs at their respective schools. In the latter cases, the schoolmasters seemed to aim at the ancient dictum of developing sound bodies to foster sound minds. No specific associations of character-building appeared to be clearly spelled out. The ideal seemed more diffuse, as in the Round Hill objective to mold "Christian gentlemen and scholars." The more specific emphasis on character-building via sports awaited some mid-nineteenth-century developments in English public schools. The ideas from England were spread in part by the publication of a famous novel about schoolboy life at Rugby.

2

Tom Brown at Home and Abroad

WHEN *Tom Brown's School Days* appeared in 1857, some Americans already knew about Rugby School and Thomas Arnold. Just before Josiah Clark assumed the principalship at Williston Seminary, a board member wrote on April 7, 1849, that he wanted Williston and the new principal to emulate Rugby and Arnold; "In short, we would like to make Williston Seminary a Rugby school, and to find an Arnold for its Principal, who would exert upon its students the combined influence of a Christian Scholar, and a Christian Minister." During his tenure at Williston (1849–63), Clark spent the school year 1853–54 studying in Europe (Sawyer 1917, 107, 113).

Later, other headmasters took English and European jaunts. Henry A. Coit, the first headmaster of St. Paul's School, visited Rugby and Westminister about 1868 (Pier 1934, 77). After the end of the Civil War, Cecil Bancroft, who became principal of Phillips Andover Academy in 1873, in part attributed his subsequent ideas for reform to what he learned from his visits to Eton, Harrow, Rugby, Winchester, and several other English public schools during the summer of 1878 (Allis 1979, 239–40). Dr. William Poland, headmaster at Worcester Academy beginning in 1868, acknowledged that he had read Tom Brown and wanted "An American Rugby" as the ideal at Worcester Academy. To that end he checked out the biography of Arnold from the local library (Ward 1918, 68). In a much closer tie, Endicott Peabody, founder of Groton School in 1884 and its longtime headmaster, graduated from Cheltenham, another of the prestigious English public schools. His love of athletics began with his own participation at Cheltenham. In the summer of 1892, Harlan Page Amen, later to become headmaster at Phillips Exeter, visited "the great public schools of England," including Eton, Harrow, Winchester, Rugby, and Cheltenham *(Phillips Exeter Literary Monthly,* Oct. 1895, 10). Although not a traveler to England, Worcester headmaster D. W. Abercrombie, who served for thirty-six years beginning in 1882, was remembered by students as having "held up before us the magnificent ideals of the best public schools of England" (Ward 1918, 89).

Whether or not Abercrombie learned of the "ideals" of the English schools from Thomas Hughes's book remains unclear. However, many Americans certainly learned of Tom Brown from the widely read article in the *Atlantic Monthly* of March 1858 titled "Saints, and their Bodies." Written by cleric Thomas Wentworth Higginson less than a year after Hughes's book appeared, the article called for Americans to heed the importance of a healthy body. As a "muscular Christian" and sports lover,[1] Higginson aimed for manliness, an element he found lacking in American youth (Higginson 1858, 582–95). Thus, the times were propitious for American schoolmen to look to England, where Victorian masters valued games-playing in their public schools. They associated the ideals of manliness and "muscular Christianity" with team sports nobly played. This British development had evolved over centuries. A brief review of the evolution serves to point out that cricket and football had to achieve a certain order of rule and civility, plus cultural acceptance, before the desired values could be attributed to games-playing.

In the later eighteenth century (exact dates vary), Eton and Westminister met in cricket, possibly the first such engagement between two schools; they followed their own agreed-upon rules. Eton and Harrow began their long sports rivalry in 1805 with a cricket match, and Eton met Winchester in 1826.[2] Just the year before, in 1825, another rivalry began, that of Winchester against Harrow. It might have been more than a coincidence that the best Winchester cricketer, C. Wordsworth, had a brother, Charles, who captained the Harrow cricketers. The brother act could have facilitated the arrangement for the first-ever cricket match between the two schools (Mangan 1981, 31).

With these initial interscholastic matches, sport-loving schoolboys learned to be rule-makers. It eventually dawned on captains that an agreed-upon set of rules must precede each match or the contest would end in overheated arguments. Over time, the frequency of prematch discussions in these pioneering interschool

---

1. Higginson loved the sports available to him during the 1840s in his Harvard years, e.g., swimming, skating, and a kind of "loosely knit football." After attending Harvard Divinity School, he served churches in Newburyport and Worcester. During the Civil War, Higginson helped raise and train a Massachusetts regiment and attained the rank of colonel. In his postwar career, he was mainly a writer. See *Dictionary of American Biography*.

2. Caption in Panel K, The Museum of Eton Life at Eton College in Windsor, England, says cricket was played as early as 1700 but competition with other schools did not start until 1778, when Eton played Westminster. For variation in dates, see Gathorne-Hardy 1977, 52.

games led to the written codification of rules. Sport leaders also learned about the seriousness of prematch logistics. To compete with another school meant formal arrangements and required correspondence as to time and place of the contest, finalizing field preparations, and enforcement of rules during the game. Captains assumed many of these burdens in addition to the task of leading the team in strategy and in player selection. The early games still represented loosely arranged affairs, conducted wholly by students. Despite this casual atmosphere, these beginnings of interschool contests ushered in the modern era of English sport. The staging of contests between teams representing schools, towns, provinces, or even nations became the crux of modern sport. It all started with the advent of cricket, the first organized team sport in English society and in America[3] (Kirsch 1984, 28). The other popular team sport, football, proved problematic in its evolution.

From the time of sixteenth-century schoolmaster Richard Mulcaster, who had called into question the advisability of engaging in an unruly, violent game, football had received mixed reactions. Its wild character, devoid of a set of rules, made it no contest for the timid and no game for young gentlemen. Despite the advent of a few rules, football remained an unregulated affair, played only on special holidays through the eighteenth century. Even these occasions came to a halt when open space dwindled with the expanding nineteenth-century towns (Brailsford 1969, 20, 45–46, 120, 205, 252).

But public school boys found means to play their own styles of football. In the early decades of the nineteenth century, because schools had little contact with one another, each school established its own version of the folk game and instituted its own rules, usually in accordance with available space. Fundamentally, games hinged on the rushes or skirmishes between sides aimed at moving an oval sphere over the opponents' goal line. As rules developed, they focused generally on how sides could legally advance the ball. One region might emphasize kicking and feinting, while another might place more emphasis upon running and tackling. At Rugby, boys caught the ball with their hands and kicked it.[4] But it was a

3. George Kirsch claims that cricket was America's first modern team sport and that British Americans played it before 1776.

4. According to legend, in 1823, William Webb Ellis caught the ball and ran with it—for the first time! A plaque on the Rugby School ground commemorates this event. However, historian William J. Baker declares that well before 1823 boys were catching the ball and kicking it back. By the late 1830s, the running and tackling game had become common (Baker 1982, 120–21).

1. The author with a plaque at Rugby School commemorating William Webb Ellis. According to legend, in 1823, Ellis became the first footballer to run with the ball. Courtesy of Ann Wagner Bundgaard.

rough and tumble affair. One headmaster at another school exploded at what he witnessed on the playing field, postulating that the game of football was only for "farm-boys" and "butcher-boys." Aided by the prefect-fagging system, the public school boys organized their own game, despite the objection of headmasters. The self-rule of the students maintained a stranglehold on authority in the schools, not easily dislodged. Eric Dunning points out that no referees or linesmen existed, and there was no limit to the number on a side. As many could play as wanted to. Games were wild and rough mêlées! (Baker 1982, 120–21; Dunning 1975, 169–70).

However, this saga drew to a close near the end of the 1840s with the appearance of written rules for rugby and soccer. Moreover, Rugby football got a boost from Arnold, who specifically banned the traditional aristocratic sports in favor of school games, team games. To reach an agreement as to how to play football on the Rugby campus, students took it upon themselves to set down the first written rules. In 1845 three prefects, including William D. Arnold, son of the renowned headmaster, spearheaded the move to draft rules. Apparently, the motivation to write down the regulations came from what prefects learned in their formal and democratic assemblies with Dr. Arnold: the necessity for order. According to Dunning, William Arnold and his friends produced a tiny pamphlet titled *Laws Of Football Played At Rugby School*, which was approved August 28, 1845, by a sixth-form levee, printed, and distributed among the other (intramural) school teams. According to Dunning, this was the first set of rules in writing. The next year another set of written rules appeared. These rules focused on reducing roughness and minimizing disputes. However, the first "Laws" had specifically forbidden harmful footwear. "No player may wear projecting nails or iron plates on the heels or soles of his shoes or boots." The new legislation allowed for continued "manly" physical entanglement, but with less chance of incurring injury. Brute power counted for less, while dexterity and finesse counted for more (Dunning 1975, 171–74; *Laws Of Football* 1845, 15). A correspondent of the time wrote, "Weight . . . is no longer the greatest asset. Activity, pace and mind are now required. . . . No longer do the purely muscular and ponderous rise to the top" (Simpson 1967, 255).

Thus, from a wild and unregulated game, Rugby football developed into a scientific and strategic sport composed of fifteen players on a side or team (Simpson 1967, 254). The uniqueness of Rugby football, in Dunning's words, "served to bring the game into line with prevailing educational aims, thereby preparing the way for the eventual elevation of football, as one of the chief team games, to the stature of an educational value in itself" (Dunning 1975, 174–75). "Rugbaeans" had ushered in a new order for football with their pioneering efforts at putting rules in written form. Also, running with the ball, as contrasted with the older kicking style in soccer, established the fact that two styles of football existed. Yet not all schoolboys agreed with Rugby's rules.

By 1849, Eton students, not to be outdone by the Rugbaeans, drafted their own rules for football. They would have none of the Rugby format. Etonians disdained the use of hands; their rules set in place for the first time the essential feature of soccer—kicking and trapping with the feet. Consequently, the bifurcation of football took place. Neither school would accept innovations introduced by the other. Several times during the 1850s and early 1860s, meetings took place where student and alumni representatives attempted to develop a uniform set of rules, but to no avail. The depth of the rivalry between the "Old Boys" of each school prevented such a resolution. Rugby and soccer remained separate. The "Old Boys" from Eton and Rugby and other public schools were responsible for forming two national organizations to regulate each sport. "By this route," Dunning concludes, "the concept of 'character training' became central to the ethos which developed in British sport generally in the later nineteenth century." The cricket and football fields were where boys learned fair play, loyalty, and the like virtues (Dunning 1975, 175–76). Though long considered virtues of the aristocracy, they received renewed emphasis under Arnold at Rugby.

Morality, Loyalty, and Teamwork

One cannot leave the subject of "Old Order" school sport, especially Rugby, without chronicling the influential career of Arnold as headmaster during 1828–42. At Rugby, he fostered the ideal of the Christian gentleman. His methodology rested on chapel preaching and lessons assigned in preparation for confirmation. He wanted Rugbaeans to be Christian gentlemen, undergirded with a strong sense of morality. Lastly, they were to be intellectual. Rugby grew in stature because of Arnold's knack for projecting a picture of righteousness, which was necessary for the development of the school (de S. Honey 1977, 5,7,11; Bamford 1975, 67–68; Mangan 1981, 14–15).

According to John Chandos, Arnold thought it his duty to impart his value system to students. He did this through the prefect system, mainly the sixth formers (seniors). They became his moral agents, cloaked with considerable power and privilege. Arnold spent his energy teaching his view of Christian ideals laced with moral precepts. In return, students responded to Arnold with loyalty and obedience. Although Arnold had little interest in games-playing, his lieutenants played. Arnold undoubtedly trusted them to conduct campus games within the bounds of his idealism. He thought it better that the energetic lads played sports on school grounds rather than roaming the countryside poaching and acting in a generally rowdy fashion (Chandos 1984, 248, 259, 265–66).

Hughes, in *Tom Brown's School Days*, may or may not have captured the correct observation of Arnold's relationship to Rugby sports. But Hughes reveals Arnold's approval when he describes "the head of the eleven," old Brooke's enthusiastic observation to his team, "You all know that I'm not the fellow to back a master through thick and thin. If I saw him stopping football, or cricket, . . .I'd be as ready as any fellow to stand up about it. But he don't [sic]—he encourages them; didn't you see him out today for half-an-hour watching us? (Loud cheers for the Doctor)" (Hughes 1863, 138). Arnold might have chosen to ban games on the Rugby campus. Yet he did not. In Hughes's book, Arnold acts the role of permissive observer, just as early American headmasters would do.

Hughes also introduced an important aspect of sport-playing for the first time—the virtues of loyalty and cooperation. Being a team player meant something in Brooke's day. In earlier times, the team concept would have been far from the thoughts of players who ran in the rowdy world of old-order football. Brooke alludes to this new component, if obliquely. In front of his winning house team, the captain proclaims the reason his side won. "We've more reliance on one another, more of a house feeling, more fellowship than the school can have. Each of us knows and can depend on his next hand man better—that's why we beat 'em today. We've union, they've division—there's the secret—(cheers)" (Hughes 1863, 136). House players learned that loyalty and teamwork brought results. Team sports now carried a new mission!

Hughes himself had entered Rugby in 1832, at the height of Arnold's reign. When he began writing about Tom Brown in 1856, the word "team" had been in sport literature for only a decade (*Oxford English Dictionary* 1989, 692). But Hughes had a definite tradition of Rugbaean "semi-fictional reminiscence" to lean on. He may also have relied on earlier publications. In 1848 an "Old Rugbaean" reminisced about life under Arnold and an "heroic football match." In 1851, William D., the son of Dr. Arnold, wrote about an "imaginary account of the first football match of the year, in lush language with Homeric echoes." Patrick Scott writes that Arnold made the match an "epic set-piece in which the smaller side won because of its greater discipline and *esprit de corps*" (Scott 1975, 44–45).

Clearly, Hughes envisioned team games as a strong contributor to the educational mission of Rugby school. Subsequent interpretations have expanded on the novel as well as the meaning and contribution of games (Winn 1960, 71–72; McIntosh 1957, 185–86). Soon after the publication of *Tom Brown's School Days*, a favorable report by the Clarendon Commission served to move schoolboy sport into the mainstream of the public school environment. The playing fields became the locale where maturation, courage, and moral control were displayed. The values fit with the Victorian order and upper-class ideals of the mid-nineteenth century.

The Clarendon Commission and the "Cult of Athleticism"

Roughly corresponding to Queen Victoria's ascension to the throne in 1837, society shifted into a new culture eventually known as the Victorian era. Values such as duty, honor, and industriousness, all grounded in a deeper Christian belief, assumed importance for the Victorians, who made up the largest portion of the

British society. The evangelical Christian revival, begun in the eighteenth century, gathered force in the early decades of the nineteenth century and had much to do with the change in societal outlook. By midcentury, the evangelical fervor dominated public and private life, including the public schools (Newsome 1961, 7; Gathorne-Hardy 1977, 70).

Charges leveled at the schools in the middle decades of the century included accusations of poor teaching, excessive hours spent in games, an overly rigid classical curriculum, and an overabundance of slavish duties in the fagging system. Eventually this criticism led to the formation of the Clarendon Commission. In July 1861, the government appointed a Commission of Inquiry charged with investigating a select number of public schools. Named after its chairman, Lord Clarendon, the commission became the first agency to probe the machinery of secondary-school education. It concentrated on seven boarding schools—Eton, Harrow, Rugby, Westminister, Winchester, Shrewsbury, and Charterhouse—and two day schools, St. Paul's and Merchant Taylor's (Chandos 1984, 30, 320–23).

The commission had no intention of abolishing games; members saw some good in games-playing. The final report revealed these sweeping and positive assertions, "athletic games which, whilst they serve this purpose [bodily training] well, serve other purposes besides . . . the cricket and football fields . . . are not merely places of exercise or amusement; they help to form some of the most valuable social qualities and manly virtues, and they hold, like the classroom and the boarding house, a distinct and important place in Public School education" (McIntosh 1957, 178). Any doubt about the role of sports in the public school environment had been put to rest for the time being.

The Clarendon Commission had officially sanctioned the role for games-playing that Hughes had alluded to in his narrative between Tom Brown and the master concerning the game of cricket. With their reference to the formation of "valuable social qualities and manly virtues," the commissioners advanced the notion that athletic participation served the larger society. Games-playing had moved from being merely schoolboy fun to becoming a noble pursuit! Moreover, the importance of physical development was not lost.

Hughes fashioned Tom Brown as a model for all public school lads, that is, a young man with physical vigor, courage, and strength. In all likelihood, Hughes owed a great deal of his idealism to Charles Kingsley, author of *Westward Ho!* A country vicar who lived an active life, Kingsley preached a "healthful and manly Christianity" (Houghton 1957, 204). Eventually this new ideal became widely known as "muscular Christianity." In Tom Brown, Hughes affirmed Kingsley's

Christian ideal by capturing this spirit of manliness, a term that came to imply the opposite of effeminacy. The "ideal of Christian manhood was seen in the muscular Christian, defined by Hughes" (Newsome 1961, 487–88). As epitomized by Tom Brown, team sports focused not only on execution of physical skill but also on playing the game with honor and team loyalty. The days of rowdyism and brute force had long gone. Hughes had linked the pulpit and the playing field in a common purpose; "In *Tom Brown* the chapel and the football 'close' are united by identity of purpose as well as physical proximity. Muscularity and Christianity find a common field, and the foundation of true manliness is youthful pluck and vigor" (Haley 1978, 154–55). The ideal of manliness had moved from chapel exhortations to demonstrated prowess on the field of play.

But the nobility of playing the game did not override the joy of winning. As the team concept became idealized, more players could share in the triumphs due to their loyal and cooperative efforts. Old Brooke had this in mind when he shouted after his house team's football victory that their win came, not from superior skill, but from teamwork. So important was this element that old Brooke went on to declare that winning the game was worth more to him than the much-prized Balliol scholarship at Oxford (Hughes 1863, 136). An ideology surrounding games-playing had been ushered into the lives of schoolboys!

At midcentury, games-playing burst forth into a movement eventually labeled the "cult of athleticism." It encompassed a belief, implied in Tom Brown and affirmed by the Clarendon Commission, that team games served as an effective means of inculcating certain laudable character traits: "physical and moral courage, loyalty and co-operation and the ability both to command and obey." According to J. A. Mangan, the widespread acceptance of athleticism after 1860 "had extensive educational and social repercussions" (Mangan 1975a, 147; Mangan 1981, 1). Whereas students saw their sporting activity as a pastime full of fun and pleasure, public school leaders viewed athleticism differently. They saw value in sports-playing as epitomized in the conversation the young Rugby master held with Tom Brown. Cricket was more than a game; it was an "institution." Further, it was the birthright of British boys, just as was habeas corpus and trial by jury. "The discipline and reliance on one another which it teaches is so valuable I think, . . .it ought to be such an unselfish game. It merges the individual in the eleven; he doesn't play that he may win, but that his side may" (Hughes 1863, 381). According to historian Peter McIntosh, the substance of this conversation did as much as anything to foster the belief in the educational value of games-playing (McIntosh 1957, 185–86).

Throughout the public schools, manliness and healthful playing emerged as goals, supported by the resurrected Latin ideal, *mens sana in corpore sano*. In the words of Bruce Haley, "Whatever nurtured manliness as an ideal, it is certain throughout the late Victorian period most people, including many intellectuals, came to regard it as the most estimable male character trait." Moreover, the notion that strength of character was intertwined with sturdiness of body was widely held by 1860. By contrast, such a notion was seldom given voice in novels or periodicals of thirty years earlier (Haley 1968, 115). Not surprisingly, public school leaders discovered that games-playing presented a disguised but useful tool for controlling idleness and subsequent sexual misbehavior. Jonathan Gathorne-Hardy surmised, "That games and exercise could solve the 'sex problem' immeasurably increased their power in the school curriculum. Schoolmasters fell upon the answer with relief."[5] For example, Eton headmaster Edward Ware testified that games held benefits for moral training in that they served as antidotes to extravagant habits, drinking, and all kinds of vice (Gathorne-Hardy 1977, 156).

G. E. L. Cotton, former Rugbaean master, paved the way in the acceptance of the new attitude surrounding games. When he became headmaster of the nine-year-old Marlborough public school in 1852, he instituted new policies. Cotton became the first school authority to take sport from its pre-Clarendon setting and place it into a post-Clarendon time. Supposedly, while at Rugby, Cotton personified the master in the Hughes narrative who carried on the memorable conversation with Tom Brown. What Cotton actually did was to put the idea into practice. When he arrived at Marlborough he ended the informality of games-playing. Cotton and his masters lifted games from frivolous pastime to a place of importance in the lives of the students. For the first time, games "were embraced . . . within the framework of formal school objectives" (Mangan 1975a, 150; McIntosh 1957, 185–86).

Cotton did not have the development of manliness in mind when he took over the troubled Marlborough school. The initiation of a school-directed games program stemmed from a practical motive. As Mangan states, "he introduced a policy of 'involvement' to seduce the boys away from the Wiltshire countryside through the provision of better games organization and by the recruitment of young, athletic masters who won the pupils' affection through their prowess with bat and ball" (Mangan 1975a, 150). With these two elements in place—organiza-

5. For an analysis of the "sex problem" in the English public schools, see Gathorne-Hardy 1977, 144–80, and Chandos 1984, 284–319.

tion and coaching of sports—Cotton, perhaps unwittingly, set the stage for the modernization of schoolboy sport.

Mangan also observes that Cotton advanced the holistic view of man. In 1858, Cotton preached to his flock that, in studying and developing physical strength, they carried out God's purposes. Mangan quotes Cotton's exhortation, "Of one thing there is no doubt: that both intellectual and bodily excellence are only really blessed when they are a reflection of moral and religious goodness, when they teach us unselfishness, right principles, and justice." The headmaster exhorted his boy congregation to remember that games-playing contributed to manliness and could even help boys to apply themselves mentally (Mangan 1975a, 151). The linkage of athletics with desirable modes of behavior went far to move games under the curricular umbrella. Concurrently, boys were also organizing to build enthusiastic support for sports.

About the time Cotton introduced changes at Marlborough, an important meeting concerning schoolboy sport took place in February 1853 at Harrow school. Student leaders wanted to arouse more interest in sports and other "manly" exercises. The attendees formed an organization known as the Harrow Philathletic Club. Membership was restricted to thirty students elected from the fifth and sixth forms. Those chosen eventually represented the elite corps of the school. The club then "organized, coerced and flattered the bulk of the school into a complicated system of regimented games playing." Mangan claimed the club to be a most striking device for "both innovation and maintenance in the history of English athleticism" (Mangan 1981, 28–29). Thereafter, most public schools followed suit, organizing their athletics around the leadership of a council or an association. The idea gained popularity not only in England but also arose as the modus operandi for early American schools. With the growing popularity of games, the Harrow Philathletic Club came to be an influential and powerful organization.

The increasing emphasis upon a controlled and organized environment for the conduct of games-playing inevitably led to new practices and innovations. The codification of rules for cricket and football enabled the schools to play each other without lengthy pregame discussion over rules (Baker 1982, 121–22). Schoolboys practiced their skills and scrimmaged on a daily basis. School songs also emerged as an instrument for the development of allegiance to the school and its teams. The nonplaying boys did their part by singing lustily in support of their housemates. Clarifying and mythologizing athletic feats, songs built school spirit (Mangan 1981, 151; Mangan 1975b, 324–35). This establishment of sentiments and allegiance to the school served the headmasters well; such emotional attachment assured a loyal clientele and certainly a manageable student body. Headmasters had stumbled upon a forceful instrument for controlling the behavior and antics of their underlings: the use of athletics as a means of social control.

Perhaps the Cheltenham headmaster in 1870, T. W. Jex-Blake, summed up best the ever-present concerns of the headmaster when he exclaimed from the podium at a prize-giving celebration, "I have seen six games of Football in the playground, each with its right complement of twenty on each side: and nothing that I have seen this term has given me greater pleasure. If there were more in the playground there would be less of that lounging about the town, that dawdling dandyism which is so contemptible, and no more haunting of billiard rooms and places of still worse repute" (Morgan 1968, 108).

Such sentiments could not have been lost on the young Endicott Peabody, who attended Cheltenham before going on to Cambridge and eventually founding Groton School. Neither did this British linkage of character development with sport and health escape other Americans. But across the Atlantic, organized sports activities in American boarding schools lagged behind their English counterparts, although the same basic themes were present.

Victorian Values and American Boarding Schools

In the mid-nineteenth century, several prominent citizens, including Dr. Oliver Wendell Holmes and Ralph Waldo Emerson, castigated the pallid and weak appearances of American young men. Holmes, professor of anatomy at Harvard and celebrated poet, concluded that young Boston males of 1858 needed serious physical activity:

> I am satisfied that such a set of blackcoated, stiff-jointed, soft-muscled, paste complexioned youth as we can boast in our Atlantic cities never before sprang from loins of Anglo-Saxon lineage. . . . We have a few good boatmen,—no good horsemen that I hear of,—nothing remarkable, I believe, in cricketing,—and as for any great athletic feat performed by a gentleman in these latitudes, society would drop a man who should run round the Common in five minutes. Some of our amateur fencers . . . we have no reason to be ashamed of. Boxing is rough play, but not too rough for a hearty young fellow. Anything is better than this white-blooded degeneration to which we all tend. (Holmes 1858, 881)

Emerson also lamented the "sickly" scholars of his day: "Out upon scholars . . . with their pale, sickly, etiolated indoor thoughts! Give me the out-of-doors thoughts of sound men" (Brooks 1937, 253). Although he wrote decades later, Charles Francis Adams,[6] grandson of President John Quincy Adams, emphasized the joy of sport and the importance to a boy of physical competence. Recalling his life as a boy in the 1830s and 1840s, he lamented his physical inadequacy, which he termed being "muscle-slow." He enjoyed swimming but realized, "how irreparable has been my loss in not acquiring other muscular aptitudes." As an adult he recalled that he should have been taught "all sorts of games — skating, fencing, boxing, riding" (Adams 1916, 18). Other adults recognized the same need for boys.

Less than a year after the appearance of Kingsley's and Hughes's writings, Higginson declared that the "charm which all have found" in reading Hughes's book lay "simply in this healthy boy's-life which it exhibits." Lamenting the lack of "physical culture" in America, Higginson observed that, at the present time, American boys "are annually sent across the Atlantic simply for bodily training." As an exception, Higginson believed "the new 'Concord School' recognizes boating as an incidental." (This was a reference to St. Paul's, a new school in Concord, New Hampshire.) Although American clergy had been partly to blame for negative attitudes toward the body, Higginson saw the glimmer of hope for future improvement. If parents changed their attitudes and clergy became physically robust and manly, conditions could improve. In Higginson's opinion, saints needed to have bodies: "What satirists upon religion are those parents who say of their pallid, puny, sedentary, lifeless, joyless little offspring, 'He is born for a minister,' while the ruddy, the brave, and the strong are as promptly assigned to a secular career! . . . We distrust the achievements of every saint without a body; and really have hopes of the Cambridge Divinity School, since hearing that it has organized a boat club" (Higginson 1858, 584–85, 588).

By 1866 evidence of common usage of the term *muscular Christianity* existed within circles of clerics. For example, the Reverend Edwin S. Williams, in an address before the annual meeting of the St. Paul, Minnesota, Young Men's Christian Association, referred to the new gymnasium at Yale as the "Seminary for 'Muscular Christianity'" (Williams 1866, 27). In 1870, on his first trip to the United States, Hughes spoke to a group of Harvard students about muscular Christianity, pointing out that Tom Brown, after his Rugby graduation, had enrolled "in the brotherhood of muscular Christians" at Oxford University (Winn 1960, 67–68).

---

6. Adams's father, the son of John Quincy Adams, was also Charles Francis Adams but lived 1807–86.

Later in the decade, boarding school boys expressed their views about exercise and muscular Christianity. One disappointed Exeter lad wrote in the school newspaper about his hope for a gymnasium: "Gymnastic exercises ought to be provided in such a way that all students may reap the advantages of it. . . . We hope that our suggestion will in a short time bear fruit in the shape of a commodious building, in which the muscular Christianity of P.E.A. [Phillips Exeter Academy] will find every appliance dear to the true born athlete" (Crosbie 1924, 241). The year before at Williston, a lad had euphorically penned his opinion about the growth in athletics, writing, "The increased interest which has been taken in athletics during the present school year ('76–'77) is very gratifying, especially to those of us who believe in, and in our humble way try to follow, the precepts of 'muscular Christianity'" (*Oracle* WNS, Apr. 1877, 28). The subsequent expansion of muscular Christianity in America has been well-documented by recent writers.[7] For the boarding schools, it was but one element of Victorian values that crossed the Atlantic and affected the growth of athletics linked to character development.

America also received the ideal of the gentleman. In the view of Edwin Cady, this concept came to us as a configuration of "six main ideas." Background facts of birth and wealth combined with the acquired elements of character, courtesy, and cultivation; the sixth element was the function or role of the gentleman in society (Cady 1949, 19). Those who founded and led American boarding schools were heirs to this tradition. The schools aimed to produce young men who could take their place and serve with distinction in society. Although the ideal suffered detractors over time in the wake of mere surface imitations (e.g., the fop, the dandy, or the snob), the essence of the true gentleman was held up by headmasters for boarding school boys to emulate. According to this concept, character was critical. One was not born with character; indeed in the Calvinist and evangelical traditions, one was born with the inheritance of original sin. Thus, molding or forming good character in young boys was a challenging task—even more so if the surrounding culture was viewed as in disorder or in massive transition from the familiar to the unfamiliar, as with the nineteenth-century transformation in this country from rural-agrarian to urban-industrial economy.

Although character has always been a part of Christianity, particularly in the evangelical revival tradition of repentance and reform, the importance of character formation among boys seemed especially critical for white, middle-class, Protestant Americans from the mid-nineteenth century on. The church, the YMCA, and later the Boy Scouts all emphasized the development of good char-

---

7. See, for example, Putney 2001.

acter, although they formulated no clear definition of character (Macleod 1983). In addition, publishers issued numerous advice books on conduct and character for young men, many written by ministers.[8] For middle- and upper-class families, whose fathers spent their time in the rapidly expanding worlds of business, industry, and finance, the dilemma of how to educate their boys in the matter of character proved a matter of concern. Burgeoning cities threatened traditional values. James McLachlan concluded that the main reason for the rash of family boarding schools originating in the century stemmed from a growing dissatisfaction with the low standards of the fast-developing but unproved public system of secondary schools (McLachlan 1970, 195). For Victorian educators, who were guided by nineteenth-century schoolbooks, imparting knowledge was important but not more important than shaping character (Elson 1959, 434). Yet many school teachers were women. Indeed another of the threats perceived by many upper-class fathers was the growing "feminization" of society (Douglas 1977). As a consequence, the rash of boarding schools for boys, which emerged and flowered in the middle and late years of the nineteenth century in addition to those that continued from earlier decades, proved highly desirable. With their concentration in the classical curriculum, residential requirements, and all-male teaching faculty, boarding schools developed strong traditions of guaranteeing entrance into prestigious colleges and universities. Parents could trust headmasters to mold their sons with the desired character traits.

Although American boarding schools were distinct as part of American secondary education, some characteristics resembled or mirrored those of the English public schools. Besides the classical curriculum, some American academies retained the Gothic architectural scheme for their chapels similar to those in England. Many adopted English usage of the term *form* instead of *class* in identifying groups within the student body. Some writers made specific comparisons. Horace Scudder wrote in *Harper's Monthly Magazine* in 1877 that, "The fairest ground of comparison between this school [St. Paul's School] and the English public school is in the hearty boy-life which prevails at both" (Scudder 1877, 711). Indeed, Charles Francis Adams recalled in his autobiography that he should have been

8. For an example of conduct books by ministers, see Henry Ward Beecher's *Lectures to Young Men*. The book appeared in numerous editions and printings between 1844 and 1912. Beecher, who became a renowned preacher in Brooklyn during the latter half of the century, has been labeled "muscular Christianity's first national preacher" (Ladd and Mathisen 1999, 30–32). Beecher had a son and nephew who attended the Gunnery in the 1860s.

sent to a boarding school, and for a reason similar to what Scudder pointed to. In Adams's words,

> As a developing boy I peculiarly needed the influence and atmosphere of boarding-school life. I should have been compelled to rough it with other boys. . . .
>
> The absolutely ideal training would have been that described in *School Days at Rugby*. I ought to have been sent away from home and been rubbed into shape among other boys; I should have been made to undergo a severe all-around discipline; I should have been forced to participate in all sorts of athletic games. (Adams 1916, 17, 20–21)

By the time of Adams's school years, several more enduring academies had been founded.

To those schools started in the eighteenth century, along with those begun in the early nineteenth century, can be added the antebellum schools. Collectively, these schools constitute the core of the oldest continuous eastern preparatory schools and those that carried out early or successful efforts in developing campus sport. In addition to the schools discussed in chapter 1, they include Worcester Academy (1832), Worcester, Massachusetts; Episcopal High School (1839), Alexandria, Virginia; Williston Seminary (1841), Easthampton, Massachusetts; The Gunnery (1850), Washington, Connecticut; The Hill School (1851), Pottstown, Pennsylvania; and St. Paul's School (1856), Concord, New Hampshire.

Their similarities stem from the fact that they began as religiously based and private enterprises, and they managed to sustain themselves from small beginnings to become well-established boarding schools. Each school had its own pattern. For example, Worcester Academy was located in a town while St. Paul's was rural and isolated. The Episcopal High School was, for some thirty years, the only high school in the state of Virginia. Some schools, such as the Gunnery and Worcester, labored for a time with small enrollments, a reality that affected the rise of organized sport due to lack of participants and funds to sustain a higher level of sport competition. Except for the Gunnery, none of the schools had much encouragement for sports from headmasters. However, William Pendleton, first principal at the Episcopal High School (1839–44), loved to play a hockey-like game called "bandy." The West Point graduate, reportedly, could often be seen at the head of a throng of boys chasing the ball (White 1989, 13–15). Students generally instigated and directed their own play in these early years. Faculty intervention remained rare, usually occurring if some serious infraction took place, or, conversely, if a master had an enthusiasm for play, for example, Pendleton, Gunn, or Moody.

Sometimes parents intervened with their admonitions. In 1823, the mother of Elizur Wright wrote to her son at Lawrence Academy about not studying too much by candlelight for fear of diminishing his eyesight. But Mrs. Wright also had other concerns. "I am glad to hear that there is useful exercise that students may make a benefit to themselves." She went further, however, to predict that "kicking a football and many other trifling" amusements, "which have exercise as an excuse," will disappear from the scene in the future. That kicking a football remained popular is demonstrated by a letter in 1848 from one Laurentian to a friend, saying, "We have some good games at football now." In this sense, it seems apparent that the boys played football for the enjoyment, not for the exercise (Frank 1992, 38, 98).

Antebellum Sport

It might well have been that the first loosely organized team games, football games, took place at Lawrenceville about 1852. One former student, a retired army doctor, General Alfred Woodhull, recollected that "The ball itself was spherical, of black rubber, blown up through a movable tube and the air retained by a brass cap. This was bought by general subscription of a few cents apiece, and it belonged to the boys as a whole." The games took place with the student body, split in half, contesting against each other. Sometimes leaders chose the makeup of teams; sometimes self-selection prevailed. Woodhull went on to intimate that all Lawrenceville boys played, and, at times, the games reached unwieldy proportions because of the large number of players engaged in the soccer-like contests (Mulford 1935, 57).

By 1853, after the Lawrenceville boys took up football, the lads of Phillips Andover Academy, the "Cads" (academy students) were playing the "Theologues" (Andover Theological Seminary students) in baseball. The Seminary, founded in 1808, occupied space across the street from the Academy, so arrangements for a game were simple. The form of the sport, known as the "Boston game," seems to have been a combination of cricket and rounders (Harrison 1983, 18–20). About the same time, at the Hill School in eastern Pennsylvania, a student in the middle 1850s recalled what sports he and his classmates played: "The amusements of the playground were 'shinney' [a kind of field hockey], town-ball [similar to baseball], football, and later on, that scientific and fascinating game of cricket, whose most enthusiastic devotees were the boys from Germantown [Philadelphia], then the centre of patronage of this recently imported English sport" (Chancellor 1976, 239–40).

Other examples of informal sport in the 1850s come from the *Rural Record* of St. Paul's School in Concord, New Hampshire. A number of entries for early summer of 1857 point out that sports depended upon what equipment was available to the boys and sometimes occurred as a part of celebrations for special occasions. Like the Gunnery boys, those at St. Paul's went swimming. However, the *Rural Record* indicates that the boys used "a bathing hole," which was "in very good condition" on June 2, 1857. Whether it was natural or man-made is not clear. Although swimming in summer and skating in the winter are not surprising sports, the entry for July 31, 1858, notes perhaps an atypical sport: "The boys have taken quite a fancy to the exercise of fencing." No additional information is given, so one wonders where the equipment came from and who was teaching the boys. Safety concerns would have dictated the need for some instruction, at the very least.

The boat races to be planned for July 4, 1857, indicated some concern for both organization and safety. Four older boys were appointed "Commodores." They became the supervisors; no one was allowed in the boats without the supervision of one of these four. However, the boys did their own work of caulking and painting the boats so that they were in perfect order for the Fourth of July event. Presumably, the boys also named their craft. The one new boat was christened the "Niagara;" the other older boat was called the "Water-lily."

The celebratory nature of Fourth of July events is also indicated by other sports in which the boys participated. The entry for June 22 indicates that the boys had received a set of cricket balls and bats. Thus, they began practicing for a "grand cricket match on the 4th of July." The entry for that specific day reads, "There was a general rush of the boys to the rear of the bowling alley, which was the place allotted for firing the crackers. This kept the boys busy till ten o' clock when the Cricket Match was to come off. This was played between the two sides of the dinner table, some exchanges having been made to make them evenly matched." In the evening, after "orations and dialogues" by the boys, the boat race was held. The winning boat received "a bouquet of flowers from the hands of the Rector's Lady." Thus, special events involving public speaking, a cricket match, and boat races crowned the holiday for the boys. A special "prize" awarded by none other than the wife of the rector, the highest person in authority at the school, further distinguished the day and the boat race. The *Rural Record* does not record that prizes were awarded for outstanding "orations and dialogues." So, although the boys planned the sporting events, they were recognized and tacitly approved by the headmaster.

Entries in the *Rural Record* for 1858 and 1859 note that the idea of a cricket match and boat races on the Fourth of July continued through 1859. The entries indicate more boats and suggest that they were owned by individual boys. By July 2, 1859, a total of nine boats were seen on the pond. The *Record* implies that cricket had expanded as well. The notation for July 5, 1858, records that the "annual Cricket match" was played, beginning at ten o'clock in the morning and lasting for nearly three hours. Although it was only the second such contest, popularity had already decreed that it be called "the annual Cricket match." "It was the most interesting match that has ever been played here." Thus, initial success had grown rapidly. By the same holiday the next year, two Cricket Clubs had a match "upon the ground on Mr. Belknap's meadow. Several ladies and gentlemen from town were present." Clearly the initial game, which resulted from the gift of equipment two years earlier, had grown to some renown beyond the school.

The other special event that occasioned sporting activity proved to be the completion of the "Telegraphic cable" connecting the United States with Europe, which was noted in the *Rural Record* for August 6, 1858. St. Paul's students received a half-holiday to celebrate "the great news." The active boys tried a new game of "Hare and Hounds" or "Fox-hunt," in effect, cross-country running where the boys formed teams of hares and hounds. "It was a first experiment and was so successful that the game was voted the finest that ever was played." Success bred more of the same. On September 10, 1859, the boys had a game of "Fox and Hounds" that included a three-hour chase!

These few examples from the *Rural Record* at St. Paul's probably exemplify the kind of informal sports competition that occurred in the 1850s at the other boarding schools. That is, the boys played whatever was at hand, depending upon available space and equipment. Headmasters, like Coit at St. Paul's, did not organize the competition but also did not stand in its way. Also, as demonstrated by his wife giving a prize, the rector in some ways encouraged sports by rewarding winners. However, occasions for sporting competition did not exist on a frequent and regular basis. Limiting games and matches to special occasions made sports competition extraordinary, not ordinary or expected. Thus, no regular or systematic framework for organizing the special games and matches existed. The technique of forming teams by using two sides of the dinner table proved simple and expedient but did not provide a stable form of organization for teams. The technique recalls the similar strategy mentioned by young Packard at Exeter in 1811, when the north and south sides of the aisle in the Latin room were used to determine teams! These examples serve merely to point out that the nature and system of interscholastic athletic competition known for much of the twentieth century had not yet begun to evolve by the 1850s.

The move from informal, special-event contests to a modern, highly organized schedule of competition would involve a host of changes and advances. Coaching of teams, regular practices, scheduled games and referees—all would come in the future. They called for order, leadership, money, and facilities. The move to off-campus contests would bring additional requirements—school uniforms, travel, tighter rules, and keen rivalries. Emerging modern conveniences such as railroads, telegraph, roll presses, and sewing machines would aid in the transformation of sport. During the post-Civil War era, the modern sport structure would become recognizable. But organization started in 1859.

3

The Name of the Game

Organize!

THE AMERICAN CUSTOM of people voluntarily associating themselves in groups to accomplish a particular purpose had distinguished our society by the early nineteenth century. When Alexis de Tocqueville visited the United States in 1831, he remarked, "The Americans make association to give entertainments, to found seminaries, to build inns, to construct churches, to diffuse books, to send missionaries to the antipodes; in this manner they found hospitals, prisons, and schools" (Tocqueville 1945, 2:114). Schoolboy sports would be no exception. In America, the earliest organized teams developed from a club basis.

Clubs, a form of voluntary association, already existed in some colleges and in the cities along the eastern seaboard. George Kirsch, who makes a strong case that cricket emerged as America's first modern team sport, notes that in 1839 the St. George Cricket Club was founded in New York, followed by the formation of the Philadelphia Union Club in 1843. These beginnings mark the first modern sports clubs in the United States.[1] Both organized to promote their sport, and both used newspapers and periodicals to advertise. Club members helped to form other associations and to organize matches on an interstate basis, vying with clubs of other cities and even staging all-star matches. Surprisingly, perhaps, annual cricket conventions took place. By 1859, Kirsch estimates that between 300 and 400 clubs existed in the country. They were organized in twenty-two states, including more than 125 communities, during the antebellum years (Kirsch 1984, 28–29).

The club system also existed at the college/university level and in other cities. Harvard and Yale students organized boating clubs in the 1840s (Crowther and

---

1. Stephen Hardy notes that a Boston cricket club existed in 1809 but was short-lived (Hardy 1982, 130–32).

Ruhl 1905, 16–17). In New York City and Boston during the 1830s, 1840s, and 1850s, young men organized baseball, rowing, and yacht clubs. Spawned by new wealth and abetted by Victorian values, sport clubs were used by the elite of society as a way to set themselves apart socially from the rest of Americans. For members, maintaining a gentlemanly code of conduct was as important as athletic skill. After the Civil War, however, the popularity of baseball was such that men in Boston's working classes organized clubs (Hardy 1982, 132; Rader 1983, 41, 52–53, 108–9).

It would be no wonder that boys of boarding schools employed clubs to launch or promote their favorite sports. For the most part these were team games. Boys gathering on campuses where they lived together for months at a time found in team sport participation a venue for fun and developing friendships. In their zeal to bring campus sport into a manageable program, early student leaders were often inspired by collegians. For example, Joseph Sawyer observed that Yale's navy (boat club), organized in 1853, caused Williston boat enthusiasts to take notice (Sawyer 1917, 135). Up in New Hampshire in 1859, St. Paul's boys purchased a boat for $140, "stirred by the reports of rowing as a college sport" (Pier 1934, 147). The event, as well as the year, proved to be a milestone.

The Epic Year of 1859 and Following

The initial emergence of schoolboy athletics into an organized framework under the control of student sport leaders marked the year 1859 as pivotal. From then on, the context in which schoolboy athletics would operate began to take shape. Any student could join, especially if he held a special liking for a particular sport. Membership dues became the main source of funds for the operation of the clubs. Through these efforts, schoolboy sports eventually flourished as a vigorous and potent force on campuses similar to the cult of athleticism that took hold of English public school prepsters. Perhaps the following words of an unknown Andoverian, from the *Philo Mirror* in the fall of 1877, serve to illustrate the growing attention paid to organization and to the English model: "It would give us great pleasure to see the Athletic Association reorganized. The remark has come to us, if there is a school in this country that resembles Rugby, it is Phillips Academy" (Quinby 1920, 18). To be like Rugby School meant the inclusion of sports in the school life of the boys.

Headmasters found it fruitless to stem the tide of burgeoning campus sport led by students. Increasing references indicate the tacit approval headmasters or masters gave toward play. Often they did this simply by refusing to interfere with the organizing efforts of the student leaders. For example, Sawyer makes no mention in his history of Williston Seminary of any negativism on the part of Principal Clark when students first promoted the formation of boating clubs in 1859. In 1862, one year before his resignation, Clark had recommended that a system of physical training be adopted for all students. Thus, he may have visualized boating as a good form of exercise.

Similarly, as noted in chapter 2, Coit at St. Paul's School did not stand in the way when his students organized and staged their first cricket match on July 4, 1857[2]—this despite the fact that Coit himself took a somewhat dim view of the physical antics of his young stalwarts. Initially, St. Paul's students had created their two cricket teams by utilizing the "two sides of the dinner table." By July 4, 1859, the "sides of the dinner table" had evolved into permanent clubs. Organized, on-going club teams eventually increased the level of competition for what was at stake. Two years after the first match, players competed for a ten dollar "prize bat," awarded to the boy with the most runs scored. By August 20, 1859, student organizational efforts had led to the Olympian and Isthmian Cricket Clubs, basic record-keeping, and a prize at stake based on individual scoring! These two clubs remained the core of St. Paul's cricket competition until the game met its demise, to be supplanted by baseball in the early 1900s (*Record,* Aug. 20, 1859).

In October of 1859 at Exeter, the Phillips Club played a baseball game with a selected group of seventeen students from the school at large. It was the first evidence that a sport club had been organized on that campus. Master Brad Cilley wrote in his diary that he had refereed the game. He also recorded some of the hazards of the early game. "Two players were disabled and the game adjourned." The cause of injury apparently resulted from the then-common practice of throwing the ball at a base runner to put him out (Crosbie 1924, 233). Cilley does not record who requested that the game be adjourned!

At Williston, not one but three boat clubs were organized. One of them, the Iris, was under the sponsorship of the English Department.[3] The constitution of the Iris boat club contained a roster of thirty-one names, including those of two

2. Outside of St. Paul's, the Hill School was probably the only other school where the boys played cricket. School historian Paul Chancellor notes only that cricket was played during the tenure of founder Matthew Meigs, 1851–76. He does not say when Meigs's account was written (Chancellor 1976, 238–40).

3. According to Sawyer, the first organization of athletic sports occurred in "1858 or 1859." But he states specifically that the Iris club began in June of 1859. Its history is the best known (Sawyer 1917, 135).

teachers. Sawyer credits one of the teachers as the individual who "pulled the club into existence and kept it alive" (Sawyer 1917, 135). By 1860, the boys of the nearly twenty-year-old school had organized clubs in three sports: boating, baseball, and football. Still, in each case, the clubs fell by the wayside for reasons unexplained except in the case of boating. After a November 1860 act of vandalism, in which the boats were destroyed and the boathouse decimated, the boating club no longer functioned. "The navy ceased to exist." For the time being, boating became a sport of the past. Not until 1877 did enough interest evolve to revive the sport. Also in 1860, the Williston Football Club went through an organizational process of electing officers. No evidence exists that the club engaged in any formal contests. The Independent Baseball Club also organized with a staff of officers, but contented itself with playing pickup games among the members. Here again data remain scanty as to the extent it functioned as an active and ongoing organization (Sawyer 1917, 136). The outbreak of the Civil War may have disrupted plans for staging contests.

The introduction of organized sport as a school-sponsored activity in a boarding school also occurred in 1859. In contrast to student-organized clubs, school sponsorship meant official approval and encouragement by headmasters. At tiny Gunnery School, located in Washington, Connecticut, and not quite a decade old, baseball emerged early[4] with the enthusiastic support of founder Frederick W. Gunn. The headmaster loved sporting activities; as a result, his school's uniqueness rested on the point that "school work was regarded as less important than the moral and physical condition of the student" (Korpalski 1977, 1). This objective, certainly a departure from those of other boarding schools of that time, formed the basis for including sport as a regular part of the schoolday and was encouraged and supported by Gunn. For example, the Gunnery baseball team in 1859 traveled twice to engage a "brawny nine from Litchfield, composed largely of old 'wicket' players." Gunn led the team; he could play "thrower" and "catcher" equally well and was "famous for the unerring precision with which at long distances he hit the base-runner" (Deming 1887, 84–85).

Eligibility rules did not exist in these early days. Gunn's energetic participa-

---

4. According to archivist Paula Krimsky, baseball came to the Gunnery through the sons of Judge William H. Van Cott of New York. Judge Van Cott was "a member of the rules committee which developed the Knickerbocker rules in 1845 and became the first president of the National Association of Base Ball Players." This group originated in 1858 (Smith 1988, 53). Thus, the fact that Mr. Gunn and his boys were playing organized baseball in 1859 shows an early familiarity with the game.

2. First known picture of a baseball game in progress, taken August 4, 1869, on the village green in Washington, Connecticut, at the first reunion of the Gunnery. Frederick Gunn, the principal, is standing to the left in a white coat, holding his hat. Courtesy of The Gunnery School Archives.

tion, coaching, and encouragement marked the first instance of a headmaster's active involvement in organized schoolboy sports. Gunn's participation also led to more skilled play. In the words of one student, "Our proficiency must be ascribed rather to the master's insistence on faithful practice, and to his personal presence on that first base." But, in addition to Gunn, "a hard-handed countryman or two not usually members of the school" also added their prowess to the team (Deming 1887, 84–85, 87–88). The practice did not seem surprising at the time because the school team played country clubs with strong, grown men. Although Gunn was exceptional in fostering school-sponsored sport, masters at other schools gradually and voluntarily began to associate themselves with the sporting efforts of students.

The association of sports participation with health maintenance emerged as one of the principal reasons for faculty acceptance of sport. Headmasters increasingly became concerned about the general health of their underlings. But many did not know what to do about the problem. When Williston's Clark left a recommendation, "That the Seminary should provide some system of physical training for its pupils," he might have been influenced by his young master, Edward Hitchcock (Sawyer 1917, 156). When he left the school in 1861, Hitchcock became the first professor of physical education at Amherst College, also the first such post established in America. He had taken a deep interest in the physicality of man through his doctoral studies. His work at Amherst set an example for many teachers in subsequent decades.

Andover apparently had no such enlightened example as did Williston in Hitchcock. Headmasters and masters seemed quite unaware of the poor physical condition and recreational deprivation of the boys. A poem in the 1860s expressed the frustration felt by many pupils:

> From morn till sultry noon
> From noon till dewy eve,
> From eve's last lingering light
> Till silence crowned the night
> He toiled without reprieve.

Whether such student sentiments influenced their elders is not clear. But in 1859, Andover trustees authorized an expenditure of up to fifty dollars toward the purchase of exercise equipment to be placed in a makeshift gymnasium (Harrison 1983, 17). This equipment would, for the time being, provide a means for exercising indoors during the winter months when team games could no longer be played.

Headmasters also began to link physical activity, whether by playing games or exercising, with subduing the wild spirits of schoolboys. Claude Fuess, a onetime Andover headmaster and historian, saw the unruliness of students in the 1850s as resulting from the absence of organized sports. In his view, robust boys needed to give vent to their surplus energy (Fuess 1917, 287). Both exercise and sports-playing met this objective. Many other headmasters agreed. However, prior to the Civil War headmasters assumed their positions with little experience in games-playing. Enlightened supervision of the many play activities taking place on campuses would have been beyond their frame of reference. Some might have learned from the ideas espoused by Cogswell and Bancroft, the Round Hill founders, about the development of the whole person. But literature and research on the subject proved virtually nonexistent. Thus, conversation at get-togethers of schoolmen or an occasional article in an educational journal provided the only likely sources for understanding the play instinct in their young charges. As a result, many school leaders remained aloof from the playing antics of their students. There were a few exceptions, of course. Most notable of them was Gunn, who thought playing in supervised games helped to develop character (Deming 1887, 81). For the most part, though, antebellum headmasters had little precedent to rely upon when it came to organizing, supervising, or coaching a sport. Yet sporting activity was clearly on the way to permanent status at the boarding schools due to the unrelenting efforts of the boys themselves. In their quest for organization and permanent structure, they inevitably had to deal with money matters.

The Club System and Finances

The move from spontaneous, pickup games to sport clubs brought a sense of responsibility toward providing sport for all who wished to play. Club members made a commitment to their sport and took an active role in providing the structure whereby ideas could be advanced and the cost of operation be underwritten. Expenses brought more attention and concern to the club members than did any other phase of management. Dues paid by club members were intended to underwrite costs, but reality soon set in. Sport represented fun, but it did not exist in a vacuum. In today's terms, early student expenses seem minuscule. Yet not all boarding school students had unlimited resources. In early school publications, appeals for funds from students appeared with regularity. Eventually, club members could not meet the costs, thus forcing leaders of sports groups to resort to plans that encompassed a greater portion of the student body. For example, the newly formed Andover school paper, the *Phillipian*, carried this account as late as October 19, 1878:

> Every student in an academy like this should be interested in athletic sports. The very scholarly student often makes the excuse, that he don't [sic] understand the games, and really has not time for them. And so the physical sports are left to a certain class, who while they are perfectly willing to incur all the expense, are obligated too frequently to resort to the subscription list or hat-passing. The present Athletic Association is designed to do away with all this; to divide the expense of athletic games and exercise among the school; to give each member a lively interest in all feats of endurance or physical prowess (*Phillipian* 1878, no. 1).

In spite of such hurdles, the sport clubs served useful functions. They codified rules for their particular sport. They also scheduled contests, whether on or off campus; and they engineered the election or appointment of team captains and managers. Captains held an important role as coaches of the teams. The manager carried the responsibility of collecting funds and dispensing financial obligations. Notably, the clubs were organized for team sports, but only for a select few of these. Circumstances affecting the growth of particular sports included popularity outside the boarding schools, in colleges and society at large, as well as availability of space and equipment. In the case of cricket and crew, English tradition and attitudes of headmasters also affected the sport's prevalence.

Early Cricket versus Baseball

Although they were ultimately less popular than baseball and football, cricket and crew early on drew enthusiastic players. Both sports gained stature in selected areas of the country, either because of ethnic promoters or because of the proximity of suitable streams or lakes. Rooted in the traditions of English sport, American cricket flourished in cities where British Americans congregated. Enthusiasts organized clubs to promote their pastime. By 1859, it was reported that about 6,000 cricketers lived within one hundred miles of New York City and Philadelphia (Kirsch 1984, 28–29).

Unlike baseball, which had its foundation as a child's game, cricket existed as an adult pastime. The membership, however, did not overlook talented youngsters. Many clubs formed junior groups for those young men under the age of twenty-one years. Others added a third category—that of boys sixteen years and younger. By 1859–60, any Philadelphia boy who played bat-and-ball games knew cricket quite well. Of the 500 students at the Philadelphia Free Academy, 60 percent played cricket. At about the same time, boys at Philadelphia Central High School also took up the game, organized a number of class teams, and staged games among themselves (Kirsch 1984, 36, 40).

But cricket did not attain the widespread popularity for boys that baseball earned. Whereas cricket gained recognition in selected pockets of the population, baseball mushroomed in hamlets or towns. Only a few boarding schools accepted cricket as a campus sport. The game did not lend itself to the spontaneity of the moment where boys could assemble and easily start a game. For example, the cricket bat had a special design, not easily honed from a piece of wood. The ball, too, had a particular composition not readily fabricated. Probably the greatest drawback encountered by cricket advocates came down to finding appropriate space to develop a special "well manicured," grassy field (Edmonds 1902, 251; Kirsch 1984, 45). Space became increasingly scarce as cities grew. Therefore, cricket did not lend itself easily to staging pickup games. Baseball, on the other hand, could be played on almost any vacant space as long as the land was flat. Thus, pastures and empty lots served as ready-made diamonds.

However, the English sport was not unknown to boarding school boys. During its first decade (1851–61) and perhaps into the second, lads at the Hill School in Pennsylvania played cricket. Most of the players came from Germantown (a Philadelphia suburb), the hotbed of cricket in the Quaker City (Chancellor 1976, 240). Sometime in the decade between 1841 and 1851, boys at Williston Seminary played "wicket," an offshoot of cricket (Sawyer 1917, 90). From their location at Easthampton in central Massachusetts, the young Willistonians apparently had the game introduced to them by some youngsters who had witnessed or played on the Amherst College campus, located just a few miles to the east of the Seminary. Claude Fuess reported that an Amherst student wrote in his diary in 1847 that he participated in a "wicket" game in which his class overcame the juniors, scoring seventy-seven to fifty-three. Because several youngsters from the village of Amherst gravitated to Easthampton to attend Williston, they may have introduced the game to other "Willies." Unfortunately, as Fuess points out, how the Amherst collegians played "wicket" the young diarist does not describe (Fuess 1935, 142).

Sawyer gives us an inkling of the Williston version, probably a copy of the Amherst game. The trait that distinguished "wicket" from cricket centered on the type of ball used. The "wicketers" batted a large round ball similar to the Rugby football, as contrasted with a much smaller and harder ball used in cricket. The batsman took a position protecting one of the two wickets, two stumps set twenty feet apart and each supporting a wooden crossbar. Like in cricket, a bowler attempted to roll the big ball from his position near one wicket into the other wicket. In protecting the wicket, the batter struck the ball, and if successful he ran to the other wicket and back, while opponents fielded the ball and threw to the bowler, who in turn attempted to knock down either wicket before the batter returned to his original position (Sawyer 1917, 90–91).

Cricket received its most serious attention at St. Paul's School. A little more than one year after the school's opening, cricket assumed its place as a campus sport. Because gentlemen in Philadelphia played the game, which also had a long English tradition, the austere rector approved of holding the match. Coit, the nonathlete, supported the efforts of the boys in sporting endeavors because cricket and rowing represented clean sport and good exercise. As well, they did not encourage "vulgar shouting" (Pier 1934, 82). The following incident serves to illustrate the low regard that Coit held for the undisciplined, raucous game of baseball. "While some boys were playing a scrub game of ball. . . , he [Coit] appeared,

3. Students of St. Paul's School on the cricket field, about 1890. Headmaster Henry Coit advocated cricket over baseball. Courtesy of St. Paul's School Archives.

walking across the field, and said, 'Who is the captain?' William Blair replied, 'I am, sir.' Dr. Coit said, 'William, here is a letter from a Concord Baseball Club challenging St. Paul's to a contest. Please write and tell them there is no baseball nine at St. Paul's School, that cricket is the ball game of this school. 'Yes, sir,' said Blair ruefully" (Pier 1934, 84).

Although cricket enjoyed popularity in some sections of the eastern United States during the antebellum period and immediately after the war, the game did not gain prominence with schoolboys beyond the campus of St. Paul's School. The game may have been too slow for exuberant American teenagers, who were just beginning to thrive on the action found in sport. By contrast, baseball was garnering supporters in the postwar years, due in part to changes in rules from earlier decades.

Subsequent to the 1853 "Boston" style of baseball matches between the "Cads" and the "Theologues" on the Seminary campus at Andover, there appears to have been a period during which haphazard arrangements for matches between the two groups occurred. For organized sport to flourish, however, standardized rules needed to be accepted by all players. The National Association of Base Ball Players, founded in 1858, eventually led to the structuring of baseball beyond a local basis and resulted in the nationalization of rules. Essentially, it meant adoption of the rules set down by Alexander Cartwright in 1845, a change from the "Boston" style of play (Baker 1982, 139–40). For example, the "Boston" game had permitted "plugging" or throwing the batted ball at a base runner for an out. Under the new rules, batters had to be "tagged" out, or retired by caught fly balls (Rader 1983, 109).

The codification of rules helped to bring more attention to the game at independent schools. Baseball now could be played within one town or school without time being wasted in discussion as to what rules should govern play. Baseball thus moved from a child's game to a sport for young adults, requiring little equipment and using almost any open space, with minimal landscaping required. As a result, more teenaged youngsters gained experience in playing the game. Some of them gravitated to boarding schools where baseball became the popular team sport for spring, mirroring football in the fall. In contrast to the ease with which baseball could be played, crew, like cricket, required more costly and particular environments and equipment.

Crew for Collegians, then Prepsters

Crew gained prominence in certain sections of the eastern United States in prewar years. It had its roots in the elite private rowing clubs that developed mainly in cities such as Boston, New York, and Philadelphia. But, like cricket, the sport of rowing originated in the English penchant for boat racing (Rader 1983, 71; Betts 1974, 37; Crowther and Ruhl 1905, 5–6). Crew emerged as an American college sport by 1843, when seven Yale juniors purchased a boat and thereby set in motion the tradition of rowing at the New Haven college. Soon other students obtained boats; this led to intramural challenge races during the summer of 1844. In addition, Harvard students, augmented by the Chelsea club regattas of 1842 and 1843, also took up rowing. In 1846, a Boston rowing club challenged the Harvards to a race on the Charles River, surprisingly won by the Crimson and which sparked enthusiasm for the start of crew as an intercollegiate sport at Harvard (Smith 1988, 26–27; Crowther and Ruhl 1905, 16). Spearheaded by Harvard and Yale crew enthusiasts, competition between their rowing clubs became an annual event.

Soon students in other colleges organized boating clubs, spawned by a noteworthy event in 1852. Recorded as the first intercollegiate athletic contest ever staged, the Harvard and Yale boating clubs met in August of that year in a specially arranged match on Lake Winnipesaukee in New Hampshire under the sponsorship of a New England railroad magnate, James N. Elkins. Organized as a promotional event for the Boston, Concord, and Montreal Railroad, the race was watched by an "estimated one thousand spectators," including Democratic presidential candidate Franklin Pierce. The Crimson won by several lengths. Perhaps this initial Harvard-Yale boat race created an interest in rowing for schoolboys. Whatever sport the collegians took up, it seems that the boarding school lads tried to emulate it, particularly the sporting trends that took place at Harvard and Yale (Smith 1988, 3–4, 27–29).

To St. Paul's School goes much credit, not only for first instigating rowing as a schoolboy sport, but also for sustaining it. Only at boarding academies was there the likelihood that crew could survive as a secondary school activity. Several schools, including St. Paul's, bordered on or were near suitable water—a reality that enhanced the opportunities for establishing clubs.[5] Also encouraging the sport were the middle-class Victorian families whose means contributed to the purchase of racing sculls. Moreover, many St. Paul's boys came from homes in the Philadelphia and New York area, where boat racing was prominent. Thus, locale as well as context affected the popularity and permanence of crew, just as with cricket. Although several boarding schools eventually formed clubs, crew never gained the popularity of the more traditional field sports.

"The First Organized Football Club"

Not all early schoolboy sporting efforts can be attributed to boarding schools. One notable exception occurred at the Latin School of Epes Sargent Dixwell, a private institution located in Boston. The first evidence of organized football grew out of the novel experiences of kicking a ball during recess and after school by the small band of boys who attended Dixwell's school. Gerrit "Gat" Miller, a New York lad, entered the Dixwell school in 1860 at age sixteen and immediately became a star of the nearby Boston Common playground, the locale for their informal scrimmaging. It seems likely that he and his schoolmates gleaned the rudiments of Association football, fundamentally soccer, from their observation of Harvard students playing the game, even though it had been banned on the Harvard campus in 1860. Miller and his classmates may have witnessed the mock burial of

---

5. For example, Groton School, about twelve years after its founding in 1884, initiated boating on the Nashua River, approximately three-quarters of a mile from campus. To the south, Choate School took advantage of the lake resulting from the dammed-up Quinnipiac River and began rowing about 1910.

football by Harvard sophomores soon after the ban went into effect (Scudder 1924, 7–13; Lovett 1906, 81–97; Smith 1988, 68).

What rules that Miller and his friends may have garnered from witnessing the Harvards at play must have been of the elemental kind. The codification of soccer rules in England did not take place until 1863. Not before 1871 did standard rugby rules emerge following the formation of the English Rugby Union (Baker 1982, 121–23). The advanced stages of soccer/rugby football in the United States had not reached the point that necessitated a standard set of rules; games remained rough-and-tumble affairs. Thus, pickup games took place between Dixwell boys and the informally organized, combined teams from Boston Public Latin School and the Boston English High School, as well as from the Roxbury and Dorchester high schools. Unwritten rules were passed down from game to game.

Frays of this sort apparently produced frustration for Miller, who in the fall of 1862 organized a team of twelve Dixwell boys, two from Boston English High School and one from Boston Latin School.[6] Through his outstanding managerial skills as an innovator of plays, as a coach, and as an organizer of practices, Miller headed a team that devastated opponents. Playing on the Boston Common, the newly named Oneida Football Club of Boston had no goals scored against it in its three years of existence. In the meantime, the Oneida Club and their various and sundry opponents, with the leadership of Miller, eventually devised a simple set of rules that included no lines other than those scratched on the ground marking the goal and boundary lines. Two avenues led to scoring: running with the ball over the goal line, or kicking it over, an offshoot of the Rugby school rules. They had no time-outs, no playing intervals such as a quarter or a halftime. The teams played their games in constant action (Scudder 1924, 11; Lovett 1906, 92).

Winthrop Scudder's claim that the Oneida Club goes down in sport history as the first organized football team in this country seems well taken (Hardy 1982, 112). Even though the Oneida Football Club had a short-lived existence (1862–65), Miller and his teenage teammates set the mode for playing football and eventually other team sports. The context in which games took place needed to be structured. Scudder astutely observed that Miller realized the best football could be played only through organized teams (Scudder 1924, 11). Starting with

6. Authors Winthrop Scudder and James D'Wolf Lovett both played on the Oneida team. Scudder was from the Dixwell school; Lovett from Boston Latin. For the association of Dixwell boys with Harvard men, see Hardy 1982, 112.

the need for agreed-upon rules, organization for Miller meant team practice, including rehearsal of skills under guidance, development of predetermined coordinated movement patterns, and arrangement for contests.

Fortuitously, the Oneida Club had space enough on which to play football. The Boston Common became their field. If this space had not been available free of cost to the participants, Miller could never have organized a team that sustained itself even for three years. This reality points to an obstacle that other city schoolboy athletes faced for several decades — lack of a field on which to play football and baseball, cost-free and owned by a sport-sponsoring agency (the school). Boys in boarding schools, thus, had an advantage because the pastoral location of many of their schools provided room for playing fields.

Clearly, the doors were beginning to open for teenage boys to take part in sport, especially for those in boarding schools. Negative attitudes towards games and sports had all but disappeared. Exuberant participation developed healthy bodies and kept boys out of mischief. Being occupied in sports worked to diminish idleness and attendant evils. American boarding school headmasters were beginning to realize, just as had English headmasters before them, that controlling an energetic and active group of youthful males, housed twenty-four hours every day in a pastoral school setting, required measures other than enforced study and class participation. Headmasters discovered with a sigh of relief that worries about control lessened considerably when the boys had time, space, and equipment with which to play. But, because of the hesitation and inexperience of most headmasters, it was up to students themselves to initiate and carry on campus games.

Thus, those doughty school chaps of the mid-nineteenth century put into motion a roughly hewn framework, a club system, for the conduct of school sports. Still, it would be a rough-and-tumble journey for some decades before any stability surrounded an expanding and highly popular program of club and interscholastic athletics. A look at the development within individual schools during the postwar decades can serve to complete a picture of progress despite pitfalls at particular institutions.

4

Postwar Surge

More Schools, Sports, and Schedules

THE EXPANSION OF SCHOOLS and competitive sports in the later 1860s and 1870s followed a probable hiatus of activity during the Civil War years. Available evidence suggests that whatever games-playing occurred among the school sports clubs that had been formed in the 1859–60 period probably did not continue to any notable degree during the first half of the war decade. For those boys who remained on their school campuses between 1861 and 1865, clubs may have functioned with some contests on a local, intramural basis. But, if Exeter and St. Paul's were typical of northern schools, the war fever invaded boarding school campuses. On the Exeter grounds, the boys too young for war formed clubs for military drill. Writing his centennial history in 1883, Charles Bell recalled, "When the Southern Rebellion broke out . . . in 1861, the great body of the students, in common with the youth of the entire North, formed themselves into drill clubs, and practiced the rudiments of the military art." Of the Exeter students old enough for military service, Bell wrote that "a considerable number" left to join the Union Army. Similarly, the *Rural Record* for February 1, 1861, and May 10, 1861, notes that St. Paul's boys were "practising military drill." The May entry recorded that a drill sergeant from town came out to lead the boys "in military movements" (*Record*; Bell 1883, 80). Nonetheless, sporadic entries of campus cricket matches, along with croquet, music, and dancing, continue in the *Rural Record* through the war years. The entries simply suggest the reality that young schoolboys needed recreational, physical activity in spite of the wartime atmosphere. However, that pattern proved very different in the South. Episcopal High School in Virginia closed its doors entirely on May 3, 1861. It did not reopen till the fall of 1866 (White 1989, 23, 59). For both North and South, the postwar years gave rise to an expansion of competitive sports and the establishment of new boarding schools that had sports programs from the outset.

The fact of surging competition after the cessation of civil hostilities followed logically from early efforts to organize teams in the prewar years. But the degree of organization had to expand as did the component elements involved. To have organized teams on a club basis, the boys needed the tacit approval of headmasters, if not the active encouragement of the latter. Playing fields for team games and ponds for boat races had to be kept up. Equipment had to be secured and maintained. Whether or not club teams practiced is unclear from the available literature. The shift from intramural to interscholastic contests after the war meant additional elements to be considered, including the necessity of regular practice. Not all headmasters who approved of sports on campus also favored off-campus travel for team play. Scheduling games with another school could become complicated, depending on the distance. Athletic coaches were not yet regularly in the picture, so the boys had to secure the money for uniforms and travel. Sometimes horse and wagon prevailed over trains. Thus, time and weather had to be considered. As well, school teams had to be formed from club teams, a process that could vary in complexity and time consumed. Not least, both schools had to agree to the same set of rules. In sum, the beginnings of interscholastic sport and the spread of athletic competition among newer schools presented formidable challenges to the boys in the decades immediately after the Civil War.

The expansion and complexity of sports, contests, and schedules varied by schools, depending upon attitudes and actions of headmasters, on size of enrollment, on available play space and equipment, on location in relation to nearby schools who could be opponents, on local tradition, and on the experiences and desires of the boys themselves. To better understand the postwar expansion, this chapter is organized with short sketches on a school-by-school basis. Yet, despite individual differences among the boarding schools, they all continued to hold team sports in common. However, the team sports were limited to those played in the out-of-doors. The gymnasium had not yet made its entry on the campuses of most boarding schools, and basketball as well as volleyball had not even been invented. From 1865 through the 1870s, the new sports that flourished with widespread popularity were baseball and football.

The Phillipians Lead

In 1864, in his first year at Andover, James B. Wells taught his classmates the rudiments of baseball. A former player on the Brooklyn Actives Baseball Club, Wells, along with his team cronies, laid out a roughly hewn baseball field to be used mainly for practice. It was Andover's first baseball field. To gain some status they named themselves the Actives, a name borrowed from Wells's former team. Before long the seniors at Andover organized themselves into a baseball club, the Resolutes. Soon the juniors assembled a team, named the Alerts. These three aggregations comprised the nucleus for campus competition (Harrison 1983, 21–22).

Soon after the enrollment of Wells, Archie Bush entered Andover and spearheaded the drive to organize a school baseball club. With that, Andover launched its first all-school athletic team. Bush, a Civil War veteran, along with his cousin, James McClure, gained baseball-playing experience on junior amateur teams and possibly during their army days; the two served as coaches and managers. With their leadership and encouraged by the decision of the trustees to lay out a playing field, the Andover school team in 1866, now enjoying its own practice space, took steps to schedule games with off-campus teams. Apparently with the blessing of the principal, the austere Samuel Taylor, Bush scheduled a game with Tufts College in late June. For the first time an Andover team traveled off-campus, facing Tufts at Medford, located near Boston. Staged on a hayfield, the Bush-led team overwhelmed the collegians, scoring thirty-five to four. This momentous event represented not only the first out-of-town contest for the Andoverians but also the first organized contest for Andover against another team representing an educational institution. Interestingly enough, the Tufts game took place close to commencement. Taylor, a stern disciplinarian over his 250-plus students, had relented on his policy of no off-campus activity because classes were not affected. For the most part, though, Andover students had to be content with interclass contests and an occasional off-campus game held during vacation time (Harrison 1983, 24–25).

The formation of these Andover baseball teams led to the introduction for the first time of an intramural program involving a series of campus games between clubs. The club with the best record earned the school championship. Out of this arrangement emerged the school team, composed of the best players, which then played off-campus teams, as initiated with the Tufts contest (Harrison 1983, 27; Quinby 1920, 139–41). In effect, Andover institutionalized sport by this pattern of organization, but the pathway was not always smooth.

A rebellion in the spring of 1867 by Andover seniors sent the school into a frenzy, dampening any pursuit of the club baseball championship. One gorgeous New England spring day, five seniors left the campus and classes to enjoy themselves. Two, Bush and a friend, traveled to Boston to watch a "league baseball game";[1] the other three went boating and swimming at a nearby pond. The autocratic Taylor immediately expelled the recalcitrants, an action that caused a campus uproar. To show their disdain for Taylor's action, nearly one-half of the remaining forty-two seniors went by hired carriage to the neighboring town of Lawrence for an evening dinner at a hotel. Upon their return to the campus, they too felt the heavy hand of the irate Taylor. The "rebellion" reached national prominence through the press, forcing the board, at a special meeting, to pass a resolution supporting Taylor's action. Consequences came harshly to the expelled students because, without the principal's recommendation, their applications to Yale or Harvard would not be honored. Other colleges refused to accept incomplete work from the rebels, forcing many to do summer study in order to prepare for special-admission examinations to Harvard. Bush pursued this course and went on to become a campus and religious leader, as well as baseball star, during his career at the Cambridge institution (Harrison 1983, 26–28).

Somehow the "rebellion" dampened the spirit of the Andoverians for baseball. The game lagged, prompted by Taylor's edict that halted any future off-campus games, a ban that existed during the remainder of Taylor's regime. Between 1867 and 1871, baseball sputtered along, being played mainly by several club teams but not by a school team. It appears that the fervor for the game depended upon how enthusiastically the students wanted to play.

Within a year after Taylor's death in the spring of 1871, baseball emerged again the following fall with considerable spark. Spearheaded by the new Phillips Baseball Association, which represented the entire student body, funds flowed at the rate of twenty-five cents per member, a donation to carry out the agenda of the organization. Although not exactly a membership fee, the action of the officers to generate funds through student donations represents a first whereby a sport team could be logistically sustained. Hitherto, players themselves had to defray their own costs, much of it for train travel to off-campus games such as the contest the Bush-led team played at Tufts and those against independent Boston clubs.

The appeal for donations did not exactly meet with overwhelming student approval. Harrison quotes the editors of the academy magazine, the *Philo Mirror*, for November of 1871: "But one thing must be said: If the school wish [*sic*] to have a

---

1. Harrison does not explain his term *league baseball game*. Stephen Hardy notes that Boston's first baseball club originated in 1854 and was followed by three others in the next three years. Other amateur clubs continued to form in the postwar years. Presumably, it was a game among some of these clubs that Bush and his friend went to watch (Hardy 1982, 132).

nine they must *support* it; the small sum of *twenty-five cents* was voted by the school—only about fifty of the whole school paid. True we think the Treasurer ought to be blamed for want of activity. Some have told us that they were not called upon. What we want is enthusiasm in the school" (Harrison 1983, 29). Despite the criticism of the treasurer for not performing well, the editors still implored their readers to show more zest for the school baseball team. It would not be the only time that such exhortations appeared in school papers.

Undoubtedly, the need for funds for baseball grew out of the renewed effort to schedule outside teams. One of the tasks of the new baseball association focused on the reestablishment of a school nine. A special committee had the responsibility for organizing the school team; it also faced the formidable task of finding suitable opponents. The committee found itself facing a new phase of adolescent activity in the world at large: the art of communication. It would be a new era, that of boys from one school negotiating with those from another school over terms agreeable to both parties: date, time, officials, and acceptable rules. This phase of institutionalized sport had not been encountered before. Few schools similar to Andover existed, and those that did for one reason or another failed to muster the necessary leadership to launch into the unknown that accompanied the establishment of a baseball team. Despite these handicaps and bolstered by renewed interest in the game, the committee found a pool of potential baseballers around which to organize a team. The school team always had a ready opponent in the seminarians, housed across the street. Apparently, the committee in charge lacked the necessary expertise to find academy opponents on a consistent basis. Instead the leaders looked for competition to amateur club teams from neighboring communities such as Lawrence, Danvers, Methuen, and occasionally Boston.

Membership on the school team included some further responsibilities. To be a representative of Phillips Academy and to carry its fair name admirably meant that the team needed to practice diligently in order to perform well and "maintain Phillips reputation" (Harrison 1983, 30–31). It dawned upon student leaders that the successful support of a school team took perseverance and serious attention to a growing myriad of details associated with a purposefully designed sports program. Phillipians discovered that being selected to membership on the school team demanded more than just honor and playing an occasional, casual game. It also meant being serious about pursuing the development of baseball skills and fostering a disciplined mental attitude. Writers of the *Philo Mirror* article in the fall of 1871 had clearly stipulated that the school nine had to learn to "run bases, especially from home to first, and also to take care not to get scared when they play a better club than themselves" (Harrison 1983, 29).

According to Harrison, the years between 1874 and 1878 signified an important change in the development of the athletic program at Phillips Academy. As more Andoverians gained experience in conducting the fiscal affairs associated with their athletic organizations, student leaders could argue their cause for school athletics more cogently and with confidence. Bancroft, successor to Taylor, also provided a sympathetic posture. That helped the Phillipian athletes immensely; with his administrative approval, they, at least, had some moral support. Still, challenges remained for the student-led program. With their autonomy came the continual tasks of raising funds, scheduling, transporting teams, and selecting captains to lead and coach the teams. Moreover, the sports program expanded—football emerged as a rival for equal time and attention (Harrison 1983, 32).

Early football also had its student leader: Thomas W. Nickerson. In 1874 he entered Andover and in a short time enticed students onto the field to learn the rudiments of rugby football. Eventually, he formed a team. From Boston, Nickerson learned the rugby game, likely from his boyhood excursions over to the Harvard campus in nearby Cambridge. College football had been on the scene, beginning with the Rutgers-Princeton game on November 6, 1869. In the following years Harvard, Yale, Columbia, and Cornell students formed football clubs and scheduled games with one another (Smith 1988, 69–74).

Fortunately for the Andoverians and for Adams Academy, the first interscholastic football opponents in America, the wrangling between colleges over rules did not filter down to the schoolboy level. Adams Academy, located in Quincy, just south of Boston, and Phillips Andover sent students to Harvard; and both academies' sport-leaders benefitted from dialogue with Harvard footballers, so crucial in the beginnings of the sport. "It is reasonable to assume that the interchange of ideas between the schools and the college was not only verbal but also visible," observed Harrison (1983, 45).

When Andover and Adams squared off in October of 1875 for the epoch-making first football game between two secondary schools, they played under Harvard rules, which included running with the ball, a feature of rugby. The two academies became the first secondary schools to officially adopt the rule setting the number of players per side. Because the eleven on a side in the Harvard-McGill series of 1874 came about as a temporary decision, Harvard did not officially adopt the rule of eleven per side until later, when Yale won the argument for eleven instead of fifteen on a side (Harrison 1983, 45–46; Smith 1988, 77).

The first interscholastic football series between Andover and Adams Academy proved to be a fortuitous arrangement. Both schools had similar goals and objectives. Although only seven annual games took place between the two schools (1875–82), these yearly frays helped to solidify a developing student-led football system. When Phillips Exeter students fielded their first rugby football school team in 1878 and joined the other two academies in interscholastic competition, a triumvirate resulted that aided in nurturing and sustaining football interest. Students, both players and nonplayers, could look forward each year to contests among one another. Unfortunately, Adams Academy, apparently because of dwindling enrollment, could not continue the series after 1882. But during the seven years of annual contests, Adams won five of the games. Despite its illustrious relationship with the famous Adams family, the academy finally had to close its doors in 1908 after thirty-six years of existence. But in its short involvement with football and baseball, the school's sport leaders played an important role in strengthening schoolboy athletics (Harrison 1983, 46–47).

As supportive as the trio of academies were of each other, their contests meant only two games in football and not much more in baseball. In seeking other opponents the Andoverians, in a brilliant bit of negotiation, scheduled games with the Harvard Freshmen. As a result, a strong rivalry continued over decades, with the football series lasting into the 1950s. The Andover-Harvard football relationship rendered further evidence of the strong tie between the two institutions. Andoverians also scheduled games with freshmen teams from Tufts College, Massachusetts Institute of Technology, and Yale. In 1880, Andover played nearby Lawrence High School, one of the earliest accounts of a public high school fielding an athletic team. This contest proved to be one of the first between private and public high schools (Harrison 1983, 49, 77, 85).

The Exonians Follow Suit

In the meantime, thirty miles to the northeast, student leaders at Phillips Exeter Academy also encountered roadblocks in their efforts to bring baseball and football onto the campus. Although the Exonians did not have an autocratic Taylor to contend with, Gideon Soule, the longtime Exeter principal (1838–73), did little to encourage the recreational life of his students. When he retired, Exeter had an enrollment of about 160 students, who clamored for play space out-of-doors and for an exercise room indoors. They kept a keen eye southward to see what their Andoverian brethren might be doing to upgrade their sporting activities.

Just as it had at Andover, baseball received considerable attention from Exeter boys. As early as October of 1859, students had organized themselves into teams, according to master Cilley, who had refereed. But they played the style of game wherein runners could be hurt by having the ball thrown at them for an out (the New England style of game). Soon the more modern game was introduced to the campus. George Flagg ('62), the Archie Bush of Exeter, led the way in orienting schoolmates to the New York style of baseball, assisted by Frank Wright ('62), another student baseball enthusiast (Crosbie 1924, 233–34). In the new style (the New York game), the playing field took on a diamond-shaped configuration, doing away with the former rectangular-shaped field. Bases were set ninety feet apart. The game was now played in innings, instead of ending the game when one side scored twenty-one runs (Smith 1988, 53).

The first organized campus baseball club appeared at Exeter in 1865, but classes played only against each other. Off-campus competition did not take place until 1875, nine years after the Andoverians had invaded Tufts College. The Eagle Club from the town of Exeter served as the opponents on that memorable day, with the Exeter boys prevailing by a score of twenty-eight to twelve. At this juncture, Exeter launched its athletic program, featuring games against off-campus teams, much like what occurred at Andover. In 1878 the baseball team entered into competition with Andover and with Harvard Freshmen (Cunningham 1883, 282–83). Even more importantly, Exeter and Andover had joined in annual athletic contests that continue to this day.

Unlike those at Andover, the boys of Exeter took an active interest in boating, although there appears to be no indication that crews representing the school raced outside teams. In 1864 five members of the class of 1865 procured a four-oared boat and apparently raced no one, but instead experienced the joy of oaring as a group on nearby Fresh River. The year following, several members of the class of 1866 also obtained a boat, which they used for the same purposes. Strange as it may seem, no races were staged between the two crews. That abstinence from racing did not last for long, however. In June 1878, the Exonians staged their "first regatta" with four crews competing, using two boats. By 1880, class races had begun (Cunningham 1883, 282, 284).

Football at Exeter remained an interclass, loosely played affair until well into the 1870s. In 1875, the Exeter sport leaders called together the student body for the purpose of organizing an athletic association, "in order to more thoroughly protect, support, and unite the various athletic interests of the school." This preliminary step led to a permanent association, which constituted itself in December of 1878. In that year the association adopted a constitution that took charge of baseball and football interests and determined the captains of the respective teams (Cunningham 1883, 269–70). Urged on by the editors of the school paper, Andover students also organized their first athletic association (Harrison 1983, 62–63). Rarely, by this time, did one school take a step in the advancement of athletics without the other following suit in a short time.

The advances taken by both schools in 1878 to place athletics under the control of an umbrella athletic association set a precedent that became the mode of organizational control of athletics at other prep schools. The change reflects the action taken twenty years earlier at Harrow in England, when the leading prefects founded the Philathletic Club. The schoolboy athletes had discovered that sports did not exist in a vacuum. Funds, discipline, and even some philosophical musings would be needed to keep the growing myriad of sporting endeavors on an even keel. At both Andover and Exeter, football, baseball, and additional sports such as wintertime gymnastics, as well as track and field events now, to some extent, developed with direction and purpose.

The Andover-Exeter Rivalry

This long-standing rivalry between Phillips Andover and Phillips Exeter attests to the enduring quality of schoolboy athletics. The early history of the rivalry also demonstrates the vagaries and tenuousness such an arrangement can have. Efforts on the part of Exeter students as early as 1865 to arrange a game with Andover had proved fruitless due to the opposition of such a proposal by Soule, then the Exeter principal. Negotiations for contests between the two schools in baseball and football continued tentatively. After all, no one was sure of what such an arrangement would lead to. No precedents existed to guide sport leaders. Despite the advent of the telegraph and railroads, no assurance could be placed upon reliability of these forms of communication and transportation. In other words, could commitments be kept? Many unknowns appeared. But in the main, it was the opposition of Soule and Andover headmaster Taylor that held back negotiations. To show their disgust at Soule's opposition, the Exeter baseball leaders led a mock funeral procession to a nearby lot where they buried their bats and ball in a crude coffin. Nor did the Exeter boys receive much encouragement in their efforts to simply upgrade baseball at the school. The president of the trustees wrote in 1871, "As for a ball ground, it is the last thing that I would provide for the students." The trustee was not, however, simply cantankerous. He went on to describe the injuries that had occurred to Cambridge baseballers. Moreover, he questioned whether Exeter boys ought to associate with "rowdy clubs all over the country." Eventually, the students did get the ball field they had agitated for, a nine-acre piece of ground, which became the scene of games-playing for many years (Crosbie 1924, 234–35).

Both schools went through a change of principals in 1873. To these two new leaders goes credit for establishing a favorable climate enabling their respective schools to meet annually on the playing field. A renewed spirit and vision emerged on the Andover campus with the appointment of Bancroft as principal. He brought to campus a freshness that overcame the stagnant years of the Taylor regime. At Exeter, an unsympathetic principal had dampened the efforts of student leaders to upgrade athletics, especially with regard to the appeal for a gymnasium. When Albert Perkins arrived, also in 1873, he proceeded with a hands-off policy with respect to steps taken by Exonians in furthering the cause of school sports.

Thus when Perkins and Bancroft began their principalships, a more conciliatory attitude prevailed toward student athletic endeavors. When both schools inaugurated athletic associations, students carried the brunt of responsibility for conducting the affairs of the associations. It could be that a faculty member might have monitored proceedings, but it appears likely that any such interference was minimal. With some semblance of order in place, negotiations again emerged between student leaders of both schools to play a baseball game. On May 22, 1878, a memorable day in the history of schoolboy sports took place. It marked the first organized interscholastic game between the Andover and Exeter academies. The modestly trained Exonians upset the proud, well-drilled Andover nine, scoring eleven to one. However, several days later the Andover team, playing on their home turf, avenged the defeat by edging the visiting Exeter team, ten to eight. Thus began the long-standing rivalry between these two well-known and respected academies (Harrison 1983, 32–33).

Football quickly followed baseball competition between the two schools. Exeter accepted a challenge from Andover and on November 2, 1878, traveled to the rival campus. The Andover eleven overwhelmed the inexperienced Exonians by one goal and five touchdowns to nothing. Whereas Andover had played several outside teams prior to this epic game, Exeter had only a picked team of the best players whom the captains elevated from interclass contests. But Exeter school loyalty demonstrated itself, with eighty classmates accompanying their team. This demonstration of support signified the beginning of overwhelming student interest in the athletic exploits of their fellow students. Until this time no sporting event had caught the attention of fellow students as did the games between the two emerging rivals. In a short time, a majority of boys from both schools attended en masse the annual football games. In the future, the Andover-Exeter rivalry would draw capacity crowds of several thousand interested spectators, especially in football (Harrison 1983, 50, 90). Harrison labels it, "the oldest continuous independent school rivalry in the country." It likely represents one of the oldest continuous secondary school rivalries, public or private (Harrison 1983, 76, 448).

The St. Paul's School Experiment

A well-to-do Boston physician, George C. Shattuck, attributed his desire for a boys' school to the exhilarating experiences he had appreciated at Round Hill School early in the century. Firmly believing in the pastoral scene as a site for his school, he wrote, "Physical and moral culture can best be carried on where boys live with and are constantly under the supervision of the teachers, and in the country. The English public schools of renown, such as Eton, Rugby, Harrow, Winchester, and others, with their extensive play-grounds, show the advantages of such a situation. Outdoor exercise is thus secured" (Shattuck 1891, 15). On June 4, 1877, the *New York World* described St. Paul's and compared it to Rugby School in England, a perception that reinforced what Shattuck had in mind and what Coit affirmed. Yet the headmaster proved no strong advocate of interscholastic athletics. The heart of St. Paul's program was organized intramurals, that is, a club system.

Within a short time after the cricket clubs were formed in 1859, agitation arose over the absence of a suitable playing field. Approaches to Coit netted a substitute area, but one still inadequate in the eyes of the cricketers. Only the persistence of Richard H. Dana III, a fifth former, brought results. He met with Coit twice with a plea for another field. Dana had his eye on a piece of farmland owned by the school, located just below the campus. Rather than giving an abrupt denial, as was the case the first time Dana made his request of the stern headmaster, on this second visit Coit relented. If the headmaster favored any sport, it was cricket. He came to think of it as the campus game and, therefore, concluded it needed a field. Thus, he promised young Dana that he would take the matter to the board of trustees. In the summer of 1868, land on the "southwest end of the Belknap Farm," which the school had recently acquired, was turned into a playing field. The cricket close (playing field) of fifteen acres came to be known as the Lower Grounds (Pier 1934, 79–81; Heckscher 1980, 72–73).

For the next twelve years, St. Paulites played only cricket as an organized game on the campus. For another sporting diversion, the boys rowed on a nearby pond and had informal races. In 1871 boating enthusiasts took a bold step and appealed to the headmaster for the right to establish boating clubs. In reply, one can imagine Coit with pontifical overtones: "I will consent to the division of the boys into two rowing clubs." Races would have to be confined to the campus small ponds with no public announcement and not on "a distant sheet of water, accessible to the public" (Heckscher 1980, 73). Writing in the *Horae Scholasticae* for May of 1871, a student reporter took pains to note that boating was not intended to rival or supplant cricket: "We think that cricket and boating . . . will mutually assist one another, and that we will be thus providing an outlet for the nervous energy and enterprise of those boys, . . .who take no interest in ball, by creating in the School a love for this, one of the noblest, healthiest and most exciting of all athletic sports." An annual Race Day began on June 7, 1871, and the event became a regular part of the spring sport pageantry *(Horae* 5, no. 1: 3–4; 5, no. 3: 11).

The earliest account of football on St. Paul's campus occurred in October of 1871. The start of the gridiron game may have been in answer to an appeal that appeared in the school paper in May of that year. A disgruntled lad complained that, "Base-ball has not been encouraged, because it was feared that it might supplant cricket. Thus our amusements have been very limited . . . there has been hardly anything to do" *(Horae* 5, no. 1: 3). Once begun, discord reigned within the ranks of the footballers. Unfortunately, some did not bring with them a written set of rules. Amidst a sea of verbal interpretations, players argued over the intentions of rules. Such vehement confrontations caused enough disruption to prompt a campus pundit to publicly declare that arguments could now be set aside in light of a meeting of minds. "It has always been observed," he wrote, "that our football games have been marked and hindered by endless disputes concerning the rules. To avoid this, a football convention was held and a code of rules laid down." It would not be the first time that schoolboys wrangled over rules and not always with the amicable spirit displayed by the St. Paul gridders. Interestingly, their code of rules recalled the spirit of Tom Brown and team play; according to the *Horae Scholasticae* for October 1871, "Any boy who loses his temper, and willfully punishes another player, shall be considered unfit to play" *(Horae* 5, no. 4, "Football").

Continued obstacles impeded progress in the development of athletics. The growing conflict between cricket and baseball adherents festered for a number of years. It would be the most troublesome confrontation in the school's athletic program during the last half of the nineteenth century. As newer boys came to St. Paul's each year, bringing with them increased experience with baseball, the rise of the diamond game was inevitable. But the game encroached upon cricket. In the spring of 1874, one scribe reasoned that, "Although base ball is so popular, there can be but little doubt that had not cricket been unfortunately checked in the rapid progress it was making, by the war, it might now be holding the place that base ball occupies." This reasoning led him to think that cricket's long-standing tradition in England, as played by "many of her greatest men" at Rugby and Eton, justified its continuance as the principal campus sport in the spring (*Horae* 7, no. 4: 32). It mattered not to the St. Paul's pundit that baseball had thrived as a game played during the lulls in fighting during the war. Some boys saw themselves as being close to the English tradition, at least its athleticism. Others chafed under this belief because it "mortified them to think that their school was aping the English in its athletics when all other American schools were being thoroughly American" (Pier 1934, 147). As a result, baseballers kept alive the burgeoning diamond game.

As early as July 4, 1861, teams of the Union and Crackaway clubs had played a game even though the cricketers had staged a match the same day. Many cricket advocates saw this as an alarming confrontation. However, apparently nothing came of it. St. Paul's historians do not mention whether the two baseball clubs sustained themselves beyond 1861. The *Rural Record* makes no such mention, but on March 4, 1865, records that "Base ball is being revived." The entry for September 13 notes that two "Base Ball Clubs, the 'Alert,' and 'Fearnought'" played. The presence of no further entry suggests that, again, these clubs proved to be abortive affairs. In June of 1873, two baseball clubs again were formed, the "Doric" and the "Pythian." If members fancied that they were the first baseball clubs organized in the history of the school, they were brought up short by the student scribe who had read the *Rural Record* for 1861 and knew about the July 4 contest (*Record; Horae* 6, no. 6, "Items"). Still, the rebirth of baseball clubs followed the nationalistic fervor that surrounded baseball. In the 1880s this spirit strengthened. Baseball games drew boys away from cricket in alarming numbers. This phenomenon perturbed Coit so much that he prohibited absolutely the playing of baseball. Pier observed, "The action was necessary if cricket was to survive" (Pier 1934, 147). Only when the Coits, Henry and his brother Joseph, had died and no longer influenced the retention of cricket, did the game disappear from the campus. That occurred in 1903, and ended one-half century of cricket at St. Paul's. It also sounded the sport's demise in American boarding school athletics.

There were other hurdles to be cleared. After football enthusiasts settled their differences, crew members shortly thereafter faced a problem of severe proportions: how to pay for the two new boats ordered and now on campus? In the *Horae Scholasticae* for April, 1872, a rowing fan chided his friends and club pledgers to meet their promises. "In addition to enthusiasm we need money; and an appeal is made to those who have not already contributed, to come forward with their subscriptions" (*Horae* 6, no. 1, "The Boat Clubs"). Apparently funds came in. But the next spring, lack of funds hampered efforts to purchase boats for the second crews in each club. Any agitation for the formation of second crews met with the refrain that many boys did not have a great deal of spending money and to insist that they put more in the coffers would be asking too much (*Horae* 6, no. 5: 37). Thus, crew for a time remained a sport only for the more affluent.

Along with the appearance of football, hockey was being adopted by the boys. A news item in the *Horae Scholasticae* for December 1874 carried the story that "Hockey and football are the two great fall games, and this year an unusually mild November has allowed us to enjoy them to the uttermost." This seems to indicate that the St. Paulites played some form of shinny or bandy, games that had originated in Scotland and Wales. Apparently, the games could easily be transferred from land to ice. Because the school writer takes note of the mild autumn, it does not seem likely that ice had coated the nearby ponds hard enough for skating. But despite the informal nature of their playing, boys in hockey also clamored for rules, if for no other reason than for their own safety. "We ought to have a regular set of rules for hockey, just as we do for football; for we have noticed a great deal of unfair play, and careless handling of shinnies" (*Horae* 8, no. 3: 27). The term *shinnies* undoubtedly referred to the sticks.[2] When handled without control, hockey sticks could be lethal weapons. But the game persisted and was also played as ice hockey.

The emergence of cricket, boating, hockey, football, and baseball led to an extensive sports program in the latter two decades of the nineteenth century. It centered on established sport clubs that remained the backbone of a lively intramural program. St. Paul's student sport leaders scheduled off-campus hockey and cricket games with New York City clubs and Canadian clubs only during vacations. Despite these excursions, the events did not topple the exceptionally strong intramural system, which remained the core of St. Paul's athletics well into the twentieth century.

Worcester Academy—The Struggles of an Urban School

A faithful few on the Worcester Academy Board of Trustees kept the thirty-year-old school alive during the troubled times of the 1860s. In a momentous and risky decision, the 1869–70 board purchased the defunct Federal hospital located on

---

2. *Webster's New Collegiate Dictionary* (1974) lists *bandy* as a game similar to hockey and considered its "prototype." *Shinny*, "also shinney," is defined as a "variation of hockey played by schoolboys with a curved stick and a ball or block of wood." The term *shinny* also refers to the stick itself.

Union Hill in the outskirts of the city. The neighborhood of the old location was becoming "increasingly noisy and run-down" (Small 1979, 41). The pressures of urban blight forced the move; any expansion in the original location would have been economically unwise. By a stroke of good fortune, accompanied by prayers of the reverent and faithful Baptists who wanted the school to continue in order to train future ministers, the move to Union Hill saved the academy.

The change of location represented one of the first instances of a private educational institution moving to a new location away from urban deterioration. The academy gained a larger building in which to house its operations, and for the first time the school provided living quarters for students. It continued its coeducational policy and housed both girls and boys in the same building. Later, however, this policy came under review. By the spring of 1881 the "female department" had been closed and one result was a large increase in male enrollment (Small 1979, 54). In the meantime, besides obtaining a new building, albeit some eighteen years old, the board acquired land, allowing for future expansion in the open spaces now available. The purchase also included a barracks building, to the rear of Dale General Hospital, which had been used as a temporary care facility during the war. This wooden structure then became the academy's first gymnasium (Small 1968, 12).

The transfer to Union Hill not only made possible the establishment of a gymnasium, but also enabled the students to play baseball on both an informal and formal basis. For the first time outdoor play space became available. Within three years after the move, students in 1873 arranged three baseball games against men from the Worcester Free Institute of Technology; all games were played on the academy campus. All three were won by the academy boys. A new chapter in the history of Worcester Academy had begun, with students arranging and staging their first formal athletic contests (Small 1968, 13).

Pedestrianism (walking) caught on as a form of physical activity, thanks in part to Principal Leavenworth, who walked six to twelve miles daily, thus setting a noble example for the students to follow (Small 1979, 51). Not since the days of Cogswell and Bancroft at Round Hill and Gunn at the Gunnery had a headmaster or principal so exemplified the pursuit of physical fitness for students to follow. Eventually, walking became formalized into contests.

Although an urban school without the pastoral scene, Worcester Academy had one advantage that other boarding schools did not have. Situated in a city, the school had exposure to civic buildings erected for the benefit of its citizens. One of these was Mechanics Hall in downtown Worcester, a sizable edifice that housed large groups for any single occasion. One such instance took place with the introduction of a "Pedomania." Contestants from the academy, Worcester High School, and Worcester Technical School vied against one another in the mile walk, the mile run, and the five-mile walk "go as you please." Historian Cloyd Small adds, "with most running in their stockings" (Small 1979, 51; 1968, 13). This notable event, held on April 17, 1879, marked the first indoor sport contest involving secondary schools. Track and field, also called athletic sports, had not yet emerged as a school contest. The walking and running in head-to-head competition involving three schools signaled a new and novel structure in sporting activity—an athletic event involving more than two teams simultaneously! Within a few years the Boston Athletic Association sponsored its initial invitational indoor track meet for secondary schools, including both boarding schools and public institutions, at Boston's Mechanics Hall. It became an annual March event for several decades.[3]

Football also emerged at Worcester. Much like the kicking melees at Andover, St. Paul's, and Exeter in previous years, the football occasions at Worcester amounted to no more than informal skirmishes. But the game gained plaudits from its aspirants. An early enthusiast in October 1879 exclaimed, "Few games are more exhilarating and there is none in which *all* can engage so largely, as that of football." The all-inclusive game had additional merit according to the columnist. Since, in his view, the benefit came from the "zest" of play, he urged schoolmates, "don't stop to consider the probabilities of victory, but play for the exercise and fun" (Small 1968, 13). A true amateur had spoken!

During the spring of the same year baseball aspirants had encountered a serious problem because they played on some land not owned by the school. The owner of the field had decided to plough half of the diamond in order to raise potatoes, thus ending baseball playing for the spring. Apparently, the outcry of the baseballers at this turn of events eventually got the attention of authorities. By the latter months of 1880, the trustees approved the sum of five thousand dollars to purchase the lot, and from then on the players had no further interruptions (Small 1968, 13).

The flurry of student-instigated sporting activities at Worcester Academy during the 1870s indicates the importance the school's relocation had upon athletics. Outdoor space plus a new sense of camaraderie among students, enhanced by dor-

3. Mechanics Hall in Boston was built in 1881. The Boston Athletic Association was founded in 1887 (Whitehill 1968, 179).

mitory life, led to the advent of play and exercise. One school editorial writer caught the effect of the sporting fervor. As he reflected upon the continuing need for athletic facilities, he pronounced, "Athletic sports now form such an important adjunct to educational institutions, that the total absence of a gymnasium or of the more interesting out-door sports, has a remarkable effect upon the attendance, and even the enthusiasm a student should show in the class-room" (The Academy 6, no. 1: 4). To the writer, the renewed spirit on the campus in just a little more than a decade since the move directly correlated with the development of school athletics. The time had come that, if Worcester teams expected to be successful against off-campus opponents, they needed to start with some semblance of organization. By 1883 students had formed a baseball association. Buoyed by the success of the group against an occasional off-campus team and accomplished "without practice, hardly organized, and under other most unfavorable circumstances," the baseball association, with its team now practicing regularly, looked forward to greater success in an expanded schedule (Academy 6, no. 1: 4).

By November of the same year, Worcester gridders, caught up in the resurgence of football fever and enthusiasm, also envisioned success now that they had become organized. An association had been formed and officers elected. Most important, "An eleven has been selected of those who seem to be the best fitted for that position." Having an organization and a team, the boys realized their priorities. "All that we need is to have some systematic method of practise [sic]," observed one student sports writer, "and not go in for a general and useless tussle." Wiser heads had come to the conclusion that to have effective teams there needed to be a properly formed structure to meet their desired ends (The Academy 6, no. 2: 5).

The remarkable progress made by Worcester students in establishing an organized athletic program within fifteen years of the Union Hill move in 1870 testifies to the hold that sport had upon schoolboys of the era. It provided a sample of the rapid growth of school athletics, constituted and energized by the lads themselves.

Episcopal High School—The War and After

Episcopal High School had been closed in May of 1861 and had housed troops during the Civil War. When the war ended, the trustees of the Virginia school faced a most daunting task—how to reopen the school, find a new principal, and do this with no money. According to school historian John White, the trustees finally decided upon a Confederate veteran with unique qualifications. To wit, he actually had money in the bank! William Fowler Gardner assumed the reins as principal in 1866 and served for four years. Eighteen boys studied with him that first year of the reopened school. But the ravages of the war proved overwhelming for the new principal and veteran. For the school to flourish it awaited the lengthy tenure of Launcelot Minor Blackford, also a veteran but with some experience as a schoolman. He took over in 1870, when enrollment was down to twelve boys, and served until 1913 (White 1989, 23, 54–60).

The new principal, though not an athlete himself, had been a Confederate soldier and realized the need for sports for his boys. He started track at the school the year after he came. On December 19, 1871, earlier than the walking races at Worcester, Blackford staged "Prize Foot Races" along the Leesburg Turnpike. The following November, he initiated a 700-yard "Steeple Chase" with three classes of competitors. From these beginnings, a full-fledged track and field program emerged. A schedule of events held on "Athletic Day—Session 1877–78," for example, lists ball-throwing, wrestling, flat races, hurdle races, long jump, high jump, hop-skip-and jump, and a "potato race." The motto printed at the bottom of the program reads "Non Sine Pulvere," translated as "Not Without Toil."

In the later 1870s football emerged at the school. In March of 1878, Black-

4. Launcelot Minor Blackford, a confederate veteran who served as principal of Episcopal High School from 1870 until 1913, rehabilitating the southern school and fostering sports. Courtesy of the Episcopal High School Archives.

ford wrote, "Football has been quite the rage." Boys got their own uniforms, but the principal bought them a rugby football for seven dollars and a rule book for ten cents. This enthusiastic support for the game indicates the widespread popularity of football among schoolboys from St. Paul's in Concord, New Hampshire, south to Episcopal in Alexandria, Virginia.

In addition to encouraging the continuation of baseball, Blackford also introduced other sports to the campus. Mention of a "Tennis Club" appears in the catalogue for 1882–83, and two years later a "La Crosse Club" is noted. For unknown reasons, the latter sport apparently existed for only one year and then did not reappear until the 1963 catalogue.

It seems likely that Blackford's emphasis on sports for the Episcopal boys reflected an American trend as well as the British example. White notes that the principal "continued to go to England in the summers, as he always had done, mainly to observe the practices of those English principals whose conduct of their schools was modeled after that of the famous 'Arnold of Rugby.'" Blackford's goal, like Arnold's aim for the boys, would have included their sports participation and was to develop "first Christians, then gentlemen, and then scholars." Though not labeled a muscular Christian, Blackford's approach surely fell within that broad concept. Developing character became uppermost in the education of boys (White 1989, 72, 75–77, 79–80).

Williston Seminary—Some "Firsts"

Baseball remained the only sport that Williston students sustained during the immediate years after 1865. For some unexplained reason the Willistonians could not muster enough enthusiasm to form clubs in football and boating during 1860–78. Certainly the blame could not be laid to Marshall Henshaw, the wise and esteemed principal serving 1863–76. Henshaw traveled to Europe in 1870 for a sojourn. Sawyer provides no evidence as to what Henshaw saw or did during his leave of absence (Sawyer 1917, 184). Yet, it seems inconceivable that Henshaw would have ignored visits to the English public schools. Surely he witnessed the wave of athleticism that stirred the British lads.

The advent of baseball as a campus game may have been spurred on by the Harvard-Yale series, which began "in 1865." Sawyer implies this connection and stipulates the year. But it would seem more likely that the primary impetus could have come six years earlier from Amherst College, a school with which Williston had close ties. In 1859, Amherst and Williams College played the country's first intercollegiate baseball game, in Pittsfield, Massachusetts. Certainly, as baseball at Amherst gained momentum and acceptance, nearby Willistonians would have felt the lure of the game as they previously had with wickets (Sawyer 1917, 190; Smith 1988, 52–55).

The Williston campus had just enough open space to play the diamond game. It became a simple matter for students to gather quickly and play their class games, highlighted by a series between the players enrolled in classical studies and those enrolled in the English studies curriculum. By November of 1872 baseball had gained considerable popularity at the school. One student columnist wrote, "This deservingly popular game has commanded more attention at Williston, and afforded more pleasure to a greater number of students this term than any preceding one for a long time." But the boys had to play among themselves. Apparently, Henshaw, like Taylor at Phillips Andover, held tight to the regulation that students could not leave campus to compete. Students complained bitterly at this stranglehold, charging that the rule was detrimental to the development of the sport at Williston (*Supplement to Mirror* WNS, 1872, no. 1). The next spring, in May of 1873, another scribe sounded the same complaint, blaming enforcement of the rule as a hindrance to more dedicated practice and improvement on the part of the baseballers. Finally, by November of 1875, two and one-half years later, the faculty and Henshaw had relented on their policy of "no out-of-town play"; the Willistonians took part in a tournament in nearby Northampton (*Oracle* WNS, 5, no. 1: 41). Baseball at the school had mushroomed into a sport for both the spring and fall seasons. Apparently, with the advent of an expanded program, the baseball enthusiasts, "Taking a hint from the boating men," also formed an association in 1877 to manage the affairs of their growing enterprise, led by "active and go-ahead men" (*Oracle* WNS, 5, no. 3: 38).

In that year, the "boating men" attempted to reorganize crew as a campus sport after a decade and a half of dormancy. But again rowing failed to gain a foothold, mainly because scheduling races with other schools proved too difficult. Challenges sent to Hopkins Grammar School in New Haven, Connecticut, and to St. Paul's school went unanswered. With no competitors from these two schools, "the crew went out of training for this season." Unlike the St. Paul's program, the Willistonians apparently were not content to structure an intramural program and race among themselves. The hunger of rowing enthusiasts for legitimizing crew as a school sport may have been greater than could be satisfied. The problem of whom to schedule in off-campus contests plagued the managers in the early years of organized sport. Probably the most serious obstacle centered on the lack of contestants in the immediate area, which, of course, could have minimized length of travel. The Willistonian "boating men" had quickly discovered this problem (*Oracle* WNS, 5, no. 3: 39).

The development of football proved sporadic, perhaps in part due to the war. According to the centennial edition of the *Holyoke Daily Transcript-Telegram*, "The boys had formed a football team in 1860, but this new game of playng [sic] at war halted all thought of chasng [sic] a football." The "Williston Guards" drilled "and continued an active force" from 1862 until General Robert E. Lee's surrender. Nonetheless, in the fall of 1864, after a hiatus from organized sport for four years, the Williston students formed a football team made up of seventeen boys, who played a single and remarkable game against Wilbraham Academy at a public park in Springfield, Massachusetts. Wilbraham outscored Williston eleven to two. But the game was significantly labeled the "first recorded interscholastic contest" (*Holyoke DT-T*, June 6, 1941, 21). However, Wilbraham Academy historian James P. Wood makes no mention of this historic event in his work, *New England Academy: Wilbraham to Wilbraham and Monson*, nor does David Sherman mention it in an earlier *History of the Wesleyan Academy at Wilbraham Massachusetts*[4] (Sherman 1893; Wood 1971). But Sawyer does record it, observing that football was played "somewhat in 1864–1865." There were "few bothersome rules" and lots of vigorous physical activity. "The only game played with another school was lost to Wesleyan Academy" (Sawyer 1917, 190). By all accounts, the 1864 clash between the Williston and Wilbraham footballers indeed marked the first off-campus interscholastic athletic contest on record between two secondary schools. However, a permanent football program did not materialize until the late 1870s.

Among Williston football advocates, one of them pleaded in the school paper for the game to be adopted as a school sport. He exhorted, "Now that an interest has been taken in football, it may be best to say a word in its behalf. There is no game better calculated to strengthen and toughen the whole body. It is played at a time of year when the weather is cold enough to render baseball impossible, and so gives us the advantage of a more bracing atmosphere" (*Oracle* WNS, 6, no. 1: 29). Apparently, his words did not go unheeded. The following year, 1878, also a pivotal year for the Phillips academies in football, the Williston students formed a football team. The gridders in their opening season attained only modest success, splitting two games with Hopkins Grammar School and losing to the Amherst College eleven. It was not unusual for contests to be staged between boarding

---

4. Unfortunately, both historians of the school say little about student life, including athletics.

schools and colleges. Available opponents proved rare, especially for teams in midwestern Massachusetts (*Holyoke DT-T,* June 6, 1941, 22).

In 1879 one of the earliest forfeits on record in boarding school athletics took place at Blake Field in a contest with the Amherst eleven. The Willistonian captain confronted the Amherst leader with the complaint that an Amherst player wore shoes with spikes, "contrary to the rules of the game." The Amherst captain must have been taken back by such an accusation, for football rules had not yet been universally codified affecting all teams, college and secondary schools alike. Surprisingly, the Amherst captain accepted the ruling; the forfeit gave Williston, even though tainted, its first victory over a college team. However, a year later the Willistonians defeated Amherst in a legitimate contest, one touchdown to nothing. A columnist in the school paper claimed it to be the "first recorded victory of a preparatory school over a university eleven" (*Holyoke DT-T,* June 6, 1941, 22; *Oracle* WNS, 8, no. 1: 11).

With football gaining prominence on the campus, "go ahead" football leaders successfully moved the baseball team into a spring season only. Despite the school's isolated location, suitable space remained scarce. Even in a small hamlet, land had its price. One cannot guess what views were held by Henshaw, James Whiton, or Joseph Fairbanks, principals during the immediate postwar decades, regarding the expansion of play fields for athletics. Whatever the ambivalence, the football association managed to usurp the campus field for the rapidly developing grid team, which also had uniforms for the first time in 1879. A student scribe recorded, "This is the first year the eleven has ever had suits, and now that football is so firmly established in Williston, there is no reason why the eleven . . . may not win new laurels for the Sem" (*Oracle* WNS, 8, no. 1: 12). Not only did the game provide another form of recreation and involvement for the student body, but it also drew the attention of the alumni, who saw other advantages. One such enthusiastic graduate attending Amherst College wrote to the school paper in 1879, "We have watched with interest the great increase of attention which has been paid to foot ball, at Williston, this fall. Certainly the tide of popular favor is fast setting in that direction, and colleges are looking to fitting schools for a supply of materials for the game from year to year" (*Oracle* WNS, 8, no. 1: 17). Already, sports at the secondary school level had attained the reputation of being a breeding ground for college players. This development relieved college leaders of the task of introducing aspirants to the rudiments of the game, as had been the custom in earlier years. Some boarding school boys, though, were playing well beyond the rudiments of the game.

The introduction of at least two innovations that affected future secondary school sports also took place during these early days of Williston athletics. The line plunge in football apparently first came into play in 1881. The Williston captain, Nicholas Goodlett, concluded that if he could make a direct run through the "man-to-man skirmishes" in the line, he could carry the ball a fair distance. Because advancing the ball in early football concentrated on running around the line where the skirmishing took place, defensive backs favored positions that aligned them to meet the challenge of the end run, leaving the area behind the skirmishers unprotected. Goodlett therefore shifted into a position near the snapper, where he could take a quick handoff and burst through the line into the open field before outside defenders could react to impede his progress. In Goodlett's own words, describing this surprise play, "As a running halfback, I stole up beside the quarterback, who would hand me the ball, and I would find my own hole while the rushers were struggling among themselves" (Goodlett 1928). Eventually, the wedge play became a popular mode of advancing the ball, leading to the excessive pushing, punching, and hacking of shins that almost led football to its demise (*Holyoke DT-T*, June 6, 1941: 22). Subsequent rule changes, such as a scrimmage line and "the down" rule, saved the game (Smith 1988, 85–88).

Another innovative sport skill also developed at Williston. The school's baseball pitchers were the first to pitch the curve ball for any secondary school nine. Until 1872, rules permitted only an underhand, straight arm delivery. In the early 1870s, after the rule changed, Yale pitcher Hamilton Avery developed and successfully pitched the curve ball. Playing left field on "Avery's great Yale team in 1875 was Charles Francis Carter," a former Willistonian. Avery tutored Carter in the knack of pitching a curve. Carter returned to Williston and cornered the captain of the seminary baseball team, Frank Blair, to teach him his newly acquired skill. Along with his pitcher, Blair, in turn, trained their catchers in the art of retrieving the tricky pitch. Blair and his teammates then went on to enjoy much success with their new secret weapon in the spring of 1876 (*Holyoke DT-T*, June 6, 1941, 22; Blair 1940).

The Gunnery—Required Baseball

Because Frederick Gunn believed so firmly in the value of sport for exercise and character training, it is hardly surprising that he "encouraged and almost compelled every kind of rational exercise as part of his scheme of character-building." Other headmasters would move in this direction later in the century, but the headmaster at the Gunnery preempted them by decades. In requiring his boys to belong to a nine, Gunn made provision for the less skilled as well as the gifted, though modern readers might not like the attribution of "clumsy nine." The latter title applied to a team made up of large but inexperienced boys who sometimes comprised a nine of their own rather than play on the same team as the younger boys. However, "to gain a place on the first nine of the school was a Gunnery boy's hottest ambition." They went through "incessant" practice and training, according to former student Clarence Deming's recollections. Playing each weekday evening throughout the summer on the village green, they chose up sides and contested until darkness ended the game. They continued at noons, during short morning recesses, and even on Saturday evenings. Finally the school nine was chosen after this long sifting process. They played perhaps "a half-dozen regular matches with country clubs." Though they rarely lost on the village green, when they did, the local audiences "grew grim as bereaved mourners at a funeral." The girls who kept score wept, and a "thick gloom settled on the town" (Deming 1887, 81, 84–86; Korpalski 1977, 29).

Such was the importance Gunn attached to baseball that school would be let out for almost any excuse when a game was to be played. According to Deming's memory, "During the summer term of 1865 . . . out of six matches played, four came off on extemporized holidays." When baseball became prohibited on the village green, about 1877 or 1878, Gunn turned his farm into a ball field. Upon completion of the grading, he remarked that the diamond might not be the best, "but that at any rate the spectators would have a beautiful view" (Deming 1887, 88; Korpalski 1977, 29). Baseball, however, was not the only game at the Gunnery.

In fact, Deming recalls that football dominated the school in the winter months, perhaps as far back as the late 1850s. Early play was rough and tumble, but became "a well-regulated, civilized affair" by 1863. The game seems to have been a soccer-like football, not the modern American game by that name. But it became a very popular game with the boys and some village residents. "All through the long winters, in snow and in slush, under sunshine and cloud, young and old, including not a few grown-up citizens of the village, took part in the contests." Unlike early baseball, football games appear to have been enthusiastically played in an intramural fashion. As with baseball, Gunn himself played vigorously with the boys (Korpalski 1977, 28).

In these postwar years, the pull of sports at the Gunnery proved so strong that "old boys" made efforts to return for reunions. The gatherings of 1869, 1870, and 1872 brought back many who wanted to recall the joy of schoolboy play. Gunn himself, though much older, entered into the play and festivities on those reunion occasions with his "familiar zest." Deming recalled the headmaster's motivation for the school's sports, which as boys they only pursued for fun:

> The master's deep plan of character-structure, now revealed to our maturer sight, was masked then. For, though he relished the fun with the foremost of us, underneath all his encouragement of sports ran his deep conviction that they strengthened not merely muscle and nerve, but character as well. To him the shock of the foot-ball melee, the emergencies of a close base-ball game, the self-restraints, the skill, the pluck that sports of the field enforced, were tests of boy-fiber which, often renewed, constructed a muscular character as surely as a muscular body. (Deming 1887, 100–102)

Lawrenceville and Hill—Another Rivalry

It seems plausible that cricket may have caught on at Lawrenceville because of the near location to Philadelphia. But no Coit existed at Lawrenceville to give the push necessary to sustain the game. Even if it had been played, cricket at Lawrenceville never reached proportions of heavy schoolboy involvement; an earlier account by a former student claimed that no "exotic cricket" was heard of "except in books about English boys." After the war, any cricket-playing lost its place to baseball. "We have a long list of nines, running back to 1866, when baseball came into fashion and took the place of cricket," recorded a school writer (Mulford 1935, 57, 76).

Baseball became the first organized sport at Lawrenceville, with a rush toward forming campus teams occurring just after the war. One Lawrenceville alumnus reported that the "game was in full swing" by 1865, maybe even earlier. He had seen Lawrentians, as Princeton men, playing the game. For example, W. F. H. Buck, class of 1868, became the first Lawrenceville grad to captain the Princeton nine. Records indicate that Lawrenceville captains were named beginning in 1872, but team members were not recorded until 1879. Records also remain incomplete as to who the Lawrentians connected with for contests. During the period 1866–72, intramural club contests may have characterized the baseball played on campus, although the earliest reference to a game off campus appears in 1869 (Mulford 1935, 75–76).

Close on the heels of early baseball came football. Apparently the gridiron game as played by the Lawrentians took on the same style as when it was first introduced about 1852. Then the only rule was "to kick, kick hard and run fast." Through the next several years the game continued to be played in this rudimentary fashion. William S. Gummere, class of 1867, learned his skills well in this context. Later, as a student at Princeton, he was elected captain by the college gridders, making him the first in the history of Princeton football. Even more importantly, Gummere captained the Princeton Tigers against Rutgers in the first intercollegiate football game, November 6, 1869 (Mulford 1935, 57, 75; Smith 1988, 69–72). Lawrenceville football went on to produce many notable players who gained fame at Princeton.

With the appearance of Jotham Potter as Lawrenceville master in 1877, athletics assumed a different emphasis due to his mentoring. Potter's direct involvement in the sporting life of Lawrenceville lads represents a pioneer relationship; masters and boys played together. Such play would be a way of coaching the players, who had no experience in the finer points of football. This is not to discount the contributions of Gunn at the Gunnery, who also played with his boys. But sports were more organized in Potter's day. He came to Lawrenceville with considerable experience in rugby at Princeton. This fact made him unique; masters with sport experience hardly existed at the time. Mulford's analysis claims that "with him [Potter] athletics in the modern sense began." By 1886, Lawrenceville was competing successfully as part of a prep school league in baseball (Mulford 1935, 75–76, 262).

Not long after the founding of rival Hill School, situated north and west of Philadelphia about sixty miles, boys there began playing shinney, town ball (a form of baseball), football, and cricket. The latter sport, despite the large number of students from Germantown, a hotbed of cricket, failed to continue as a leading campus sport. Nor did shinney evolve into ice hockey. The Hill School football would have been informal, loosely organized, as it tended to be at the other schools at that time. Indeed, historian Paul Chancellor describes football in the 1880s as "nondescript." Besides the early sports, the boys enjoyed themselves during free time, swimming and boating in the summer and skating in the winter on the nearby Schuykill River (Canal).

Matthew Meigs founded his school in 1851, intending to develop a family boarding school, considered by some as the first of its kind. But Meigs was no autocrat like his contemporary, Taylor at Andover. For example, Meigs recognized play as essential in the life of a youngster. In the words of Chancellor, "There was to be work and rigor. . . , but there was also to be play." He pays tribute to Meigs, a nonsportsman, for his sensitive and visionary view of schoolboy education, which included simple games and recreational activities. Chancellor also notes the paucity of documents and descriptions about the Hill School's sport program in the twenty-five years under Meigs (Chancellor 1976, 9, 239–40). Though Chancellor does not say, it may be that early records were destroyed in the fires of 1884 and 1890.

Under his son, John Meigs, who took over the leadership in 1876, sports became organized and interscholastic competition began. Surprisingly, tennis became the dominant sport when baseball played that role at other schools. The Hill nine was not organized until 1885. Football teams had "only sporadic competition" with off-campus teams. But a gun club and a bicycle club apparently flourished in the late 1880s (Chancellor 1976, 239–40).

Today, Lawrenceville and the Hill maintain an athletic rivalry bordering on the intensity of the Andover-Exeter series. The rivalry began in 1888 in baseball. It was about 1897 when the football contest with the Hill "began to be considered the big game of the season." After the 1905 football game won by Lawrenceville, relations broke off, not to resume until 1916 or 1917, depending upon which school historian has made the correct determination (Mulford 1935, 262, 283, 285; Chancellor 1976, 245).

5. The Hill School's baseball team of 1889, with ten players and one manager. Note the catcher's mask and chest protector on the ground. Courtesy of The Hill School Archives.

St. Mark's and Peddie—Sports-minded from the Start

These two schools, both founded near or at the end of the Civil War, had little history that did not include some aspect of organized sports from the start. That fact testifies to the growing interest in and acceptance of games-playing by headmasters and masters of the era. At St. Mark's, begun in Southborough, Massachusetts, in 1865, it is interesting to note that a baseball club originated in the first academic year, along with the Missionary Society. In fact, the diamond game proved so popular that it was played both spring and fall until 1883, when the fall season finally gave way to football. Other early evidence of baseball's popularity included team uniforms in school colors that were matched by the triangularly shaped "foul flags" of "magenta silk fringed with gold," which were mounted on "walnut sticks with brass tops." In early play, no gloves or masks were used. Even after gloves had been introduced, school historian Albert Benson writes that some boys considered that wearing gloves made them appear too suggestively effeminate. They preferred to suffer bruises instead. Benson also asserts that St. Markers can claim credit for inventing the catcher's mask. The great game of each season was the contest with Harvard Freshmen, and it was in that game of 1875 that the St. Mark's catcher wore a protective covering made from a fencing-mask, fitted up by the local blacksmith "with large holes cut in it and the front reinforced by heavy copper wire." Thus, to St. Mark's belongs the "glory of saving innumerable American noses" (Benson 1925, 35, 41–42, 64–65).[5]

The other early organized sport at St. Mark's was crew. A boat club had been formed in 1870. Members received a challenge from the nearby Framingham Boat Club to a four-oared race on the Framingham pond. In preparation, the St. Mark's boys went into a two-week practice period and even had a training table, though one of their number could not see that their food differed any from that of the rest of the school. On the appointed date, the entire school "came down by train to see our efforts." Despite the school's cheering and the intensity of practice, the boys lost by about two lengths but had their pictures taken anyway. The date of

5. Exeter School historian Laurence Crosbie claims that an Exeter man, Frederic W. Thayer ('72), invented the baseball catcher's mask when he captained the Harvard team. However, St. Mark's historian, Albert Benson, writes that St. Mark's catcher, W. A. Howe, had actually been practicing with a mask during the winter of 1875 and wore it in the St. Mark's–Harvard freshmen game in April of 1875. Thus, "the invention and the demonstration of the practical value of the mask" actually belong to Howe and St. Mark's. Thayer's mask was not tried out until the winter of 1876 (Crosbie 1924, 234; Benson 1925, 64–65).

6. Phillips Exeter baseball team in 1883. A catcher's mask hangs from the right elbow of a boy wearing a white neck scarf. An Exeter graduate who went on to play for Yale is generally credited with inventing the catcher's mask in about 1876. However, St. Mark's also has a claim. Courtesy of Phillips Exeter Academy Archives.

the race is in question, but Benson postulates about 1872 as "the first one with outsiders in the history of the School" (Benson 1925, 42–43).

Although football proved popular at other schools much earlier, the gridiron game did not catch on at St. Mark's for several years. By 1877, though, the school paper, the *Vindex*, began calling for a school eleven. Benson provides additional commentary from the paper, whose writers offered advice freely after one game, probably played on January 7, 1878, in which the Harvard Freshmen beat the newly organized St. Mark's boys: "Too much bunching was done by our men. Some people say that there is not much in football but a struggling mass of boys and a leather ball which excites them to great fury. But entering into it, and sympathizing with either side, one finds it as exciting as possible. Canvas shirts were used by our men, which the Freshmen could not hold on to." A few years later,

Benson reports, though without dating the document, a code of rules for football was printed and sold for five cents a copy. Further evidence of increasing interest came from an article on training, "in which the value of oat-meal is strongly emphasized" (Benson 1925, 70–72).

Although founded one year before St. Mark's, Peddie School, which opened as the New Jersey Classical and Scientific Institute, included both men and women at the outset and only a few boarding students. The first year's enrollment totaled 105 students, which included the primary department, that is, those younger than twelve years. But school historian Carl Geiger points out the significance of this total number of students by comparing it to a total of only 205 college students at Princeton in 1865. All but twenty of the new school's students came from Hightstown, New Jersey, where the new school was located. Moreover, the Baptist associations in the state endorsed and supported the fledgling school. By July of 1866, after two years of operation, the school's total enrollment included 69 women and 108 men. But enrollment dipped later in the decade due to a lag in construction of the main building. Given this unusual mix of factors—in contrast with the situations at the other early boarding schools—it is amazing that Peddie fielded a baseball team in the fall of 1870 (Geiger 1961, 16, 17, 19, 26).

In their first game, the Peddie diamond enthusiasts played "a Freehold team." Geiger does not specify whether this was a town team or a school team. For the next fifteen years the Peddie boys played occasional games "against various clubs in nearby towns" but did not engage in interscholastic competition until 1885, when they beat Freehold Military Institute and lost to Rutgers Prep. According to an editorial in October of 1885, a student writer described the playing field as challenging. Left field was obstructed by trees and shrubs, ensuring "a three-bagger at least" when hitting the ball in that direction. In addition, "briars and weeds" grew all over the field, "making it difficult to field a ball." Despite such less-than-perfect playing conditions, the next year Peddie entered the league with Lawrenceville, Princeton Prep, and Rutgers Prep. Although the term *league* suggests that the team was sponsored by the school, that was not true. The boys had to raise their own money for uniforms. Thus, they resorted to various strategies, including a lawn party with Glee Club singing and a variety show, to acquire the necessary financial resources (Geiger 1961, 121–22). As was the case with the other boarding schools, Peddie's sports programs flourished or lagged depending upon the leadership of headmasters. Peddie's days would come later when Roger Svetland took over and held the reins for thirty-six years.

Lawrence Academy—A Lesson in Focus

Although founded back in 1792, Lawrence Academy did not develop a thriving program of athletics as the two Phillips academies had. Several reasons seem to have accounted for this absence; they serve to point out that for athletics to thrive at the boarding schools, both stability and focus were necessary elements. At Lawrence, a review of its principals indicates that the leadership changed hands every one to five years from the founding through the early part of the twentieth century. From its founding until 1899, the academy served both boys and girls. The academy was not always a boarding school, and it suffered from serious fires as well as periodic financial woes during its early history. At one point, in 1880, the board of trustees voted to close the school until its indebtedness had been canceled and sufficient income received to insure continuance. In the same decade, Lawrence authorities experienced a struggle with identity, as public high schools drew increasing numbers of students and Groton School was successfully launched just a short distance down the road (Frank 1992, 7, 160, 202, 399).

Nonetheless, Lawrence mustered some attempts at sports in the 1870s. A playground of sorts had been provided by 1878. But the school paper lamented its small size; apparently, a ball could easily be thrown from one end to the other. The school's first baseball team was formed that first year; sadly, the team lost two games and then "gave up the ghost." However, players won four games the next year and more in 1880 before an abortive ending. The Lawrence nine traveled to Exeter that year, a first. "With the score 6 to 4 at the end of the eighth inning in favor of P.E.A., the game was called 'to enable our boys to catch the train." Yet, before the demise of baseball at the end of the decade, Lawrence beat a Groton team thirty-eight to two, even with headmaster Endicott Peabody playing first base for Groton. Ironically, Peabody also served as a trustee of Lawrence Academy!

With baseball lagging in the fall of 1880, interest in football temporarily grew. However, the football game played in the fall of 1880 proved so chaotic and rough that it was forbidden by the school authorities. Moreover, they also banned baseball, because the lawn and shrubs had been so mangled during play. The substitute game proposed by the trustees was croquet! Not until 1901 did Lawrence field its first regular football team (Frank 1992, 145, 172–73, 208).

As will be shown in chapter 7, the stability and goals of neighboring Groton School from the outset permitted an extensive offering of sports and games for its boys. The contrast of Lawrence with Groton, and with other boarding schools where sports thrived, suggests that a flourishing program of athletics required stable leadership, consistent and clear focus, substantial numbers of boys in residence, and sufficient, ongoing, resources.

The Boys Had Led

By the 1880s about a century had elapsed since the beginning of American schools. During that time, sports had moved beyond Puritan prohibitions to a place of prominence on most of the campuses. This brief review of individual schools demonstrates that, in the two decades after the end of the Civil War, boarding school boys had continued their organization of sports so that interscholastic competition began, particular rivalries evolved, athletic associations and clubs provided financial resources, and some innovations in team play and equipment could be credited to the boys. All of this happened despite the fact that not all headmasters encouraged the boys' sporting endeavors, not all fields and facilities were in the best of shape, and not all treasuries were flush with monies. With the exception of the Gunnery, it was the schoolboys themselves who had persevered over the decades, thereby transforming sports-playing from the realm of the occasional and the haphazard to the status of being organized and permanent on their respective school campuses. Although the results of their efforts were most obvious in the universal popularity of baseball and football, yet cricket, crew, and other sports made appearances, sometimes substantial inroads, on various campuses by the 1880s.

But for all of their efforts, the boys had concentrated on what could be developed most easily, that is, team sports that required outdoor fields, which incidentally were the games emphasized by college men. What came next was the need for an indoor facility in which to exercise, especially during winter months. In advocating that and other needs, school papers became particularly important. As sports became permanent throughout the school year, the inevitability of faculty control loomed on the horizon. With that would come a developed rationale for the importance of athletics in the boarding schools' curricula; with the rationale would also come challenges in implementation of a sports program to meet the needs of all boys. That saga continues in the remaining chapters.

5

Muscle and Manliness Indoors

PLAYING FOOTBALL AND BASEBALL provided fun and wholesome exercise in the out-of-doors. But on cold and rainy days boys had little to do other than study. Winter activities like sledding, ice-skating, and tobogganing brought outdoor fun and exercise, yet they could result in occasional hazards and accidents and sometimes had to be curtailed due to severe weather. Not surprisingly, the boys began to clamor for an indoor facility in which they could exercise, building muscle and manly vigor, not only in bad weather during fall and spring but also during the long winter months. Although securing a building was far more difficult than simply laying out a playing field, the boys eventually won over headmasters and boards of trustees. It was rare that the initial request for an exercise room or gymnasium came from the headmasters, but a few did lead the way, motivated by their educational philosophy and recognition of the need for an outlet for surplus energy.

Within two years after the founding of Round Hill School in 1823, Charles Beck, a German immigrant, set about establishing a gymnasium. It was an outdoor facility, similar to the *turnplatz* popularized in Germany, where Beck had received his gymnastics training. A plateau down the hill from the two buildings that constituted the school was chosen for the gymnasium's location. Despite the fact that this gymnasium lacked a roof and walls, George Shattuck, a student and later founder of St. Paul's School, claimed the Round Hill facility as "the first gymnasium in this country" (Bennett 1965, 58–59; Shattuck 1891, 15). Its existence testified to the educational philosophy of Round Hill founders, Cogswell and Bancroft, that bodily exercise was essential to schoolboys' physical and moral development. Similarly, in the later 1820s, Lawrenceville School in New Jersey underwent a curricular revision to emphasize gymnastics (Mulford 1935, 20–23). The founder, Brown, had also caught the fervor of European educational philosophy, though it is not clear if he had any contact with Cogswell or Bancroft. Whether Brown prescribed a portion of the campus or nearby land to carry out the newly emphasized gymnastic exercises also remains unknown. One can only surmise that the activities occurred outside in favorable weather. Several decades would go by before indoor exercise rooms came into vogue.

The restlessness of a cloistered student body of young boys could mean trouble for a traditional, non-sports-minded headmaster. Periods of poor weather and general boredom with studies usually led the students to call for recreational activities. But at Episcopal High School in Virginia, it was Principal Blackford who first iterated the need. In one of his early letters to trustees after he took over in 1870, he wrote an impassioned plea: "A playroom, in a separate building, for cold and wet weather, is absolutely necessary for the proper conduct and discipline of the institution, and the comfort and well-being of pupils." Episcopal boys suffered from the fact that their former playroom, "known as the boys' parlour," had been destroyed "by the enemy during the War" (White 1989, 75). Even late in the century, one school historian pointed out, the Phillips Exeter principal attributed the fundamental cause of student misbehavior in past administrations to the absence of suitable "outlets for physical energy rather than the presence of original sin" (Williams 1957, 88). Eventually, administrative leaders and boards of trustees came to realize the necessity of providing gymnasia. However, school leaders did not justify the establishment of gymnasia solely on the basis of adult theories about diffusing surplus energy. Spurred on by the persistent requests of boys, many boards of trustees simply heeded student pleas for a place in which to exercise (Harrison 1983, 17; Fuess 1917, 487; Crosbie 1924, 241–42).

In the early 1850s, the Andoverians exercised in a wooden building located behind the Seminary, a facility they shared with the "Theologues." Apparently, use of the building's scant apparatus served well for the students' physical needs at the time. One Phillipian wrote, "To the daily use of this Gymnasium in 1853–54 I have been wont to attribute improved health while at Andover and years afterward in a constitution not naturally robust" (Fuess 1917, 486–87). Early attempts by school authorities to provide indoor space rested on efforts to clear a little-used room. But, in the case of Andover, students themselves had to provide some of the funds for the facility to be outfitted as a gymnasium, because, the trustees reasoned, the facility was especially for students' enjoyment. In 1865, authorities at Phillips Andover released a long-standing brick building to the "Gymnasium Committee" to be used as a gymnastics room. A delay of two years, for some unexplained reason, occurred before the "Brick Academy" became operational, the "first milestone on the way to a full program of physical education and game sports" (Harrison 1983, 17, 57–58).

Not to be outdone, the Exonians improvised their own exercise room in the 1870s, using space above a restaurant located near the campus. Students could muster only minimal equipment such as rings and bars. However, that arrangement did not last long, for apparently the owner decided to use the space for a pool room! The students continued to exhort the administration for a gym, but it was some years before the clamor would be quieted. During the interim, a running track "was built under the main recitation building in the winter of 1880," apparently as a stopgap measure. Not appeased, an unhappy student wrote bitterly over a decision to use school monies for the establishment of an endowed professorship in the English department. He castigated the authorities: "if some of the money had been invested in a gymnasium it would have been disposed of to an infinitely better end" (Crosbie 1924, 241–42).

The makeshift gymnasium at Andover does not constitute the first gymnasium at a boarding school, although a strong case can be made that it housed the first gymnasium in a building set aside solely for the purpose of exercising. However, from what can be gathered in the scanty literature on the subject, St. Paul's School set aside space for physical culture almost from the beginning. An historical account in the school paper, *Horae Scholasticae*, informed readers that during the early years, in the "old school," that is, the summer home of the founder, Shattuck, "the masters and all boys lived here, and there were connected with it [*sic*] a school-room and a gymnasium." Despite headmaster Coit's sparse background in physical culture, it is to his credit and probably with the urging of Shattuck that he approved such an arrangement. It is probable that the space was a small room, for the student body in those beginning years was not large. However, by 1867, Shattuck had given money for an addition to the gymnasium. The bottom story housed bowling alleys, and the upper story was divided into two rooms. One was a "play room" while the other served as storage for "the apparatus and collections of the school" (*Horae* 34, no. 1: 24; Shattuck 1891, 78).

But what did the St. Paul's boys do in their exercising regimens? No leadership could have been expected from the masters, who were Coit and perhaps one other man. We can hazard a guess that Shattuck's two sons, George Junior and Frederick, may have led their classmates through exercises that they had learned from their father. Although such an indoor arrangement for exercising provided a wintertime alternative to sleighing and skating during the New England winters, these arrangements in general proved unsatisfactory due to poor heating conditions, limitations on space, or a lack of adequate gymnastic equipment. Students demanded space specifically set aside and equipped for gymnastics. Only a specially designed building could fill such criteria.

The First Gymnasium Buildings

In 1863–64, Williston Seminary took a giant step toward giving full recognition to the needs of students for exercise. In that year, the school erected the first free-standing gymnasium on any boarding school campus. The cost came to $20,000. The background leading to its construction provides for interesting speculation. Hitchcock, a Williston graduate of 1845, taught at the school between 1850 and 1861. Subsequently, he emerged as one of the early schoolmen to advance the need for physical training during his long career at Amherst College. Available evidence does not indicate to what extent Hitchcock might have convinced the Williston board and the principal to build a gymnasium. It seems, however, more than a mere coincidence that the trustees took the step to erect a gymnasium at the time they did. The special newspaper supplement published on the centennial anniversary of Williston, June 6, 1941, indicates that the school founder, Samuel Williston, had had his attention called to the need for an indoor facility to continue military drilling in the same vein that a special student unit had carried on during the early years of the Civil War. But Samuel Williston had also learned of the success of the Barrett gymnasium at Amherst College. It seems the combination of these two factors probably influenced Williston authorities to undertake the erection of a gymnasium building. School administrators intended that the new edifice would "contribute largely to the physical, mental and moral improvement of the pupils" (*Holyoke DT-T*, June 6, 1941, 21; *Log* 1941, 81). These were the basic precepts of muscular Christianity that had been extolled earlier in the century at Round Hill and Lawrenceville.

Although it was not specifically elaborated in this Williston statement of purpose, the very erection of such a facility bespoke the new thinking that health and strength, in tandem with character, completed the ideal of manliness. The architectural grandeur of the building, modeled after "an ancient government building in Florence, Italy," served to emphasize the importance of what went on inside its walls. The two-story gymnasium with its imposing tower dominated the Williston campus and the surrounding pastoral scene.

Called "the first preparatory school gymnasium in the country," the building contained an "exercising floor" plus bowling alleys. Exercise equipment included vaulting horses, chains, bars, mats, "and all other imaginable equipment." For the earnest, the gym was, by 1890, equipped with "bath tubs" and a "sprinkling room." As early as 1865, the euphoria of having a specially built gymnasium led to gymnastic exhibitions that proved so popular that tickets were required for attendance (*Log* 1941, 77, 82–83; *Williston Seminary Catalogue* 1890, 26–27; *Holyoke DT-T*,

7. Williston Seminary campus, about 1880. To the right is the gymnasium, built in 1864 with a tower modeled after a building in Florence, Italy. The photograph is from a portfolio titled, "East Hampton Illustrated," published by the Linotype Printing Company of New York. Courtesy of The Williston Northampton School Archives.

June 6, 1941, 21). Unique for the time, the gymnasium included a recitation room designed as a place where the instructional materials for the teaching of anatomy, physiology, and hygiene would be located (Sawyer 1917, 171). Soon other schools followed with gymnasium buildings.

Authorities at the new St. Mark's and Peddie schools included gymnasia in their plans. Peddie had to wait five years before a gymnasium became a reality as part of its five-story building dedicated in 1869. By contrast, St. Mark's founder, Joseph Burnett, located his school in a home near the center of Southborough, Massachusetts, several miles west of Boston. Adjacent to the house stood a large barn, the upper story of which was partitioned off for a gymnasium. The space contained rings, bars, climbing rope, ladder, and pulley weights. Measuring about forty feet by fifteen feet, the room served "as a refuge in stormy weather" until the trustees could build "a large structure." Thus, from the school's beginning St. Mark's founders set aside space for physical development (Benson 1925,

8. Interior of Williston Seminary's first gymnasium, about 1880, taken from a portfolio of photographs titled, "East Hampton Illustrated," published by the Linotype Printing Company of New York. Gymnasia of the late nineteenth century, before the invention of basketball, typically were filled with apparatus for physical training. Courtesy of The Williston Northampton School Archives.

21). For Peddie, its temporary quarters from 1864 to 1869 apparently did not conveniently provide space for physical exercise as had been the case at St. Mark's. However, when the school moved into its newly constructed building, students climbed to the fifth floor to a room set aside for the regimens of physical development. All student, faculty, and staff activities took place in this one huge structure, which the *Hightstown Gazette* for October 28, 1869, characterized as "the finest school building in the state." Not least among its features was the "top floor center," which had been "designed" as a gymnasium (Geiger 1961, 28–29).

To the south, in 1877 trustees at Episcopal High School eventually heeded Blackford's pleas and supported the building of a gymnasium to replace the earlier "play-room." Blackford cited the cost at $730 for the modest building, which measured sixty feet by thirty-five feet and rose about eighteen feet to the eaves.

Those measurements suggest that floor space was approximately equal to a surface about two-thirds the size of a modern basketball floor. Blackford listed another $220 for equipment—again not at all an exorbitant cost. But for a school that had been closed during the war, had only twelve students in 1870, and was operating in the South during Reconstruction, the building was a creditable beginning (White 1989, 64, 76).

Perhaps the most complete freestanding gymnasium built on a boarding school campus arose at St. Paul's School in 1878, fifteen years after the Williston gym. Erected "on the site of the 'old bowling alley,' which was removed to the rear of the School for temporary purposes," the building focused on internal function rather than external style and beauty. The structure included apparatus, baths, and a straight-away track in the basement. On the first floor, the gymnasium meas-ured eighty-five feet long, forty feet wide and twenty-one feet high, not as large as a present-day basketball court, but significant in those times. It included an oval track. Thus, the gym floor included clear space, unencumbered by scattered lay-outs of apparatus, as older gymnasia in colleges and universities tended to do. The inclusion of a second-floor auditorium with a stage at one end represented a unique feature, allowing the entire student body to assemble for lectures and demonstrations. The earlier appeal in the school paper for a building "devoted to the physical culture and training of the boys" and with "ample accommodations . . . at all seasons of the year, and especially during the severe winters and springs" would seem to have been answered. The reality of comprehensive or "ample ac-commodations" seems especially true because a bowling alley and "racquet courts" were provided in separate buildings. The latter had been provided in a wooden building erected about 1878, when necessary funds had been acquired. Subsequently, four squash courts were added to the facility (*Horae* 12, no. 3: 48–49; *Record*, Apr. 1877; Shattuck 1891, 68–69).

At Exeter, after several years of agitation by students for an indoor facility, suf-ficient funds were finally accumulated to erect the first gymnasium building. From monies in an unrestricted gift, added to by a special student gymnasium fund, the school raised enough capital to begin the project. At a final cost of about $15,000 (plus perhaps another $1,500 for apparatus), the new facility was ready in the spring of 1886 for students to begin their gymnastic routines. In today's terms it was a small place, measuring only sixty by one hundred feet, scarcely larger than a modern bas-ketball court. The school paper, the *Exonian*, received full credit for bringing the project to fruition. At the end of the academic year, the new building became the site of the festive June Ball. No doubt a suitable ballroom floor emerged by pushing the gymnastic apparatus off into a corner (Crosbie 1924, 242–43).

In the meantime, at Andover, Principal Taylor had announced back in early 1867 the opening of the academy gymnasium, housed in the newly available "old Brick Academy." This tiny gym served as the center of physical activity, surprisingly including four bowling alleys. Even though Andover boys, through several decades, complained about conditions, the Brick Academy remained the only indoor space for physical activity. School leaders failed to provide much money for new apparatus, and the space proved more and more inadequate as the student body grew. In addition, no showering facilities existed in the building or in any building on the campus. Finally, the outcry about unsanitary conditions on the campus, and particularly in the gymnasium, prompted the school's board of trustees to start the process needed to build a gymnasium. In 1885 the school paper, the *Phillipian*, took action to initiate a gymnasium fund. Monies accumulated slowly because the account relied wholly upon students for contributions. Harrison notes it may have been "a blessing in disguise" when, on June 23, 1896, the old Brick Academy was "gutted by fire." Despite numerous setbacks, the board of trustees eventually managed to raise $50,000, including a $20,000 gift from an 1860 graduate, Matthew C. Borden. The board of trustees approved plans for a new facility. The new Borden Gymnasium opened March 22, 1902. After years of frustration, the athletes had an adequate place for physical training, recreation, and bathing (Harrison 1983, 120–21).

Clearly, the financial cost of building a gymnasium often proved a daunting venture. Hitherto, football and baseball had required only open space. If fields did not seem available, any plea by student leaders for space in which to play their games usually required minimal cost. At times, students themselves even did the work of making fields fit for play. Acceding to student appeals for a gymnasium was a different matter. Funds for such a project constituted an obstacle not so easily overcome. Essentially, it became a matter of finding a donor to defray most or all of the cost or of establishing a "gymnasium fund." For boys in private schools, such a task was not insurmountable. Many of the schools' graduates were successful, well-to-do, and philanthropically minded. While awaiting the moment when someone would come forward with a gift, students argued forcefully as to why constructing a gymnasium would be a good thing. Exeter school historian, Laurence Crosbie, points out that "Nearly every issue of the *Exonian* urged the need of a place for exercise during the winter months." The class day historian "gave full credit for the new building" to the *Exonian* (Crosbie 1924, 242–43).

In addition to those schools already mentioned, other boarding schools built gymnasia just before the end of the century or at the beginning of the twentieth century. The motivation for such building varied. As noted, student pleas or protests provided powerful incentives. Sometimes a donor would simply step forward. At Woodberry Forest School in Virginia, it was growth in enrollment that necessitated building a gymnasium of sorts in 1893, just four years after the school's opening (Norfleet 1997, 27). Among the most notable of the new facility openings by the end of the century was a well-equipped gym at St. Mark's School in 1893 (Benson 1925, 132, 142), plus buildings at Worcester Academy in 1890 and Wilbraham Academy in 1896. Exceptional in the gymnasium at Wilbraham was a basketball court for the then-recently invented game (Wood 1971, 82). While at Worcester, Principal Abercrombie's report to the trustees declared that the new building boasted "an admirable running track, constructed on the very best knowledge of the anatomy of the body" (Small 1968, 15). Groton School had a gym by 1902, and authorities at St. Paul's School, probably at the urging of students and alumni for bathing facilities, authorized the building of an addition to their gymnasium, paid for by a gift from A. R. Whitney. Opened in January 1902, the new portion of the gym contained dressing rooms, "shower baths," and for the crews a "rowing tank" (Pier 1934, 257). At Woodberry Forest, the school paper for June 1905 proudly announced that the school was to have a "new" gym (after earlier smaller spaces) that would provide ample room for basketball, track, and pitching practice (Oracle WFS, 1905, no. 8: 4). By the next November, the paper stated that the "new" gym measured ninety feet by forty feet and was fitted "with every modern athletic appliance." In the near future, a running track was to be added (Oracle WFS, 1905, no. 1: 6).

School authorities had learned that an indoor facility not only helped the boys exercise in the winter months but also provided space for practice and conditioning of spring sports teams in the off-seasons. It had become apparent to school leaders that, for a boarding school to attract students and to survive, a gymnasium erected on the campus, along with bathing facilities, was absolutely necessary.

Directors of Gymnasia

With the erection of separate buildings for gymnasia, another significant development in the evolution of schoolboy athletics occurred, namely the appointment, either full-time or part-time, of an overseer for the gymnasium. Williston in 1864, Phillips Andover in 1867, and St. Paul's in 1878 all moved in this direction. Initial appointments signified the beginning of formal attempts to legitimize physical training in the curriculum, the first such action since the employment of Beck at Round Hill School early in the century.

Williston's first appointee to superintend its new gymnasium was Henry

Goodell, a Williston graduate of 1858, later to become president of Massachusetts Agricultural College (now University of Massachusetts at Amherst). During his three years as director, he inaugurated a required daily gymnastics regimen, modeled after Hitchcock's new plan at Amherst College. Goodell had graduated from Amherst in 1862, certainly enough time at the school to have learned from Hitchcock. While at Williston, Goodell also served as an instructor in physiology and hygiene. After Goodell's resignation in 1867 to accept a professorship at the newly opened Massachusetts Agricultural College, several other directors held the post within the next two decades. Still, this parade of directors did not discourage the Williston headmasters. They adhered to their commitment to foster physical training and, aided by the example of Hitchcock's program at Amherst, evolved a more stable program by the turn of the century. The seminary leadership's commitment to place required physical training in its curriculum marks probably the first secondary school, either public or private, to do so (Sawyer 1917, 171–72; *Holyoke DT-T* 1941, 21).

Andover also appointed a "Teacher of Gymnastics." In 1867, three years after Goodell's engagement at Williston, Sereno D. Gammel from Boston came to the campus to teach gymnastics to anyone who ventured into the renovated "Old Brick" gymnasium. Perhaps because of the poor facilities, the Phillipians' zeal for exercise waned. Although a beginning had been made, little progress occurred in physical training at the school during the next forty years (Harrison 1983, 58).

Over time, the role of gymnasium director gained significance. In 1878, Lester Dole took charge of the newly erected gymnasium at St. Paul's and also acted as rowing coach, a fact which to the school historian marked the beginning of the modern phase of rowing at the school. Dole's appearance marked one of the first appointments of a faculty member at any secondary school whose responsibilities included the coaching of sports. According to Pier, Dole's personality and sense of responsibility made him a great favorite with the boys.

> Lester C. Dole, instructor in gymnastics, was one of the most hard-working and conscientious men in the school. Besides having entire charge of the Gymnasium, he assisted in the coaching of the younger boys in cricket and football; gave boxing lessons and fencing lessons; . . . coached all the crews, both on the rowing weights in the Gymnasium and in the boats on Long Pond; . . . supervised much of the swimming at the old swimming hole. . . . He was a great favorite with all the boys, because of the eager and merry disposition that he showed in the exercise of his duties. (Pier 1934, 155, 200)

Certainly Dole's role was somewhat reminiscent of the "games-master" in the English public schools. True, Dole would not likely fall into the heretofore traditional category of a master, for his duties as an instructor in gymnastics, among a myriad of other tasks, fell outside the realm of teacher or instructor in the classical sense. Nevertheless, he assumed an important position in the ever-widening life of schoolboy sports and exercise.

Remembering the absence of any association with exercise and athletics in his own background, Coit can be given credit for envisioning a role for the proper person to oversee exercising and some sporting activities of the St. Paul's lads. One former student credited Coit's "wise appreciation of manly sport" to the rector's native intuition and "long experience as an interested observer." The gymnasium perhaps hastened Coit's conclusion that indoor facilities, along with a year-round involvement in the physical domain by his ever-growing student body, called for tighter supervision. Coit may have acquiesced to student requests for someone to aid them in mastering rowing and cricket skills (Conover 1906, 84–88). It seems difficult to imagine that Coit brought Dole upon the scene without the urging of some students and possibly a master or two, who had interests in the sporting endeavors of students. For example, in April of 1877 there appeared in the daily record of the school a newspaper account of the proposed new gymnasium, noting that funds were being raised. The building was to be "devoted to the physical culture and training of the boys. . . . The experience of past years has shown the necessity of ample accomodations [sic] (e.g., bowling alley, apparatus, racquet court, etc.) of this kind at all seasons of the year, and especially during the severe winters and springs. Every academic institution in the country recognizes the importance of such facilities for developing health and strength" *(Record,* Apr. 15–19, 1877). Even Coit, the nonathlete, could not withstand this kind of pressure.

Dole's unique role in the tightly woven classical curriculum at St. Paul's does not seem to have prompted other boarding schools to follow suit. For example, at Williston with its succession of gymnasium directors, each serving only a few years, none appeared to have been involved to any degree with student sporting efforts. Moreover, many of the men lacked the qualifications to continue teaching physiology and hygiene as introduced by the first director, Goodell. The gymnasium simply represented a place for compulsory exercise. In the words of Sawyer, "These directors of physical education were not athletes as the term is now understood. But they had the elements of leadership." Some of Goodell's immediate successors had been officers in the war. Thus, Sawyer's assertion suggests that he thought the Williston boys learned discipline as well as gymnastics under the tutelage of such men. However, recollections and poetry written by former students indicate that many of the boys felt that gym work was a "grind." They labeled the building "The Terrible Gym." In the view of some, Captain David Hill, who had been wounded at Spottsylvania and subsequently entered Amherst, "was a great believer in set-up exercises and in drilling. He installed a sort of organ which ground out marches while he barked commands to the leg-weary pupils." Lines from a student poem that appeared in the school paper of October 1871 characterize the boys' attitude:

> Oh! The Gym, the terrible Gym!
> Racking the brain and wearing the limb!
> With clubs and wands and dumb-bells and things;
> With springboards and ladders and weights and rings;
> And worse than all the Captain brave,
> With ire aroused, and his countenance grave,
> And with many an order and stern reproof
> For the frequent stamp of studential "hoof";
> So what with our work and our terror of him,
> Our muscles sore and our oeulis dim,
> Its celestial bliss to "cut" the Gym.

Captain Hill stayed on the job five years and then left to enter law practice. The contrast with Dole is dramatic. The popular master Dole stayed at St. Paul's many years and coached in several sports as well as teaching gymnastics (*Holyoke DT-T* 1941, 21).

Thus, two divergent approaches describe the strategy of headmasters when they installed a director of the gymnasium. The Williston model appears to have been the more frequent plan, namely that the director headed a gymnastics program aimed at the development of the boys' physiques. The appointment of Dole at St. Paul's School fourteen years later represented the beginning of a trend toward employing a director of the gymnasium who could also assume coaching duties. With his selection of Dole, the wise rector met the rising tide of athleticism as well as the growing concern for physical development. Yet, it was not universally clear what this physical development encompassed.

Confusing nomenclature appeared in school papers regarding the relationship of muscular Christianity to exercise, gymnastics, and athletics. For example, this account appeared in the first issue of the *Exonian*, April 6, 1878, "Gymnastic exercises ought to be provided in such a way all students may reap the advantages of it. . . . We hope that our suggestion will in a short time bear fruit in the shape of a commodious building, in which the muscular Christianity of P.E.A. will find every appliance dear to the true born athlete" (Crosbie 1924, 241). It appears that the gymnasium, in the mind of the Phillips Exeter columnist, ought to be for every student to practice his "muscular Christianity." However, the "true born athlete," of which there probably were not too many, would find the gym to be quite a special place. A Willistonian had written in a similar vein a year earlier:

> The increased interest which has been taken in athletics during the present school year ('76–'77) is very gratifying, especially to those of us who believe in, and in our humble way try to follow, the precepts of 'muscular Christianity.' . . . Old Williston has long enjoyed the reputation of sending out her boys physically as well as mentally well-equipped, plucky and manly, and the way things have gone this year gives us good reason to believe that her record will be still brighter in the future. (*Oracle* WNS, 5, no. 3: 28–29)

Creeping into the accounts of school life appeared numerous reasons why the physicality of the energetic but often restless schoolboy ought to be attended to. However, it was not always clear whether this would be accomplished through physical training or through athletics. Words such as *plucky, manly, moral improvement,* and *muscular Christianity* appeared in inconsistent and sometimes confusing fashion. In general, exhortations hearkened back to similar language so frequently associated with British school athleticism. In the eyes of students, the need for a gymnasium became the rallying point for an argument about the good things that could happen to them through physical activity. The degree to which school authorities grew sympathetic to students' pleas for a place to train in the name of muscular Christianity cannot be determined. But most boarding schools had an allegiance to such precepts.

The Move Toward Directors of Athletics

Perhaps the most striking example of the expanded role assigned to the gymnasium director occurred at Exeter. Shortly after his arrival on the campus in 1895, Amen, the seventh principal, appointed Howard Ross as the director of the gymnasium and also of athletics, likely the first such position for any secondary school, either private or public (Crosbie 1924, 177; Williams 1957, 88). A graduate of Bowdoin College, Ross came from Manchester, New Hampshire, where he had been in charge of a gymnasium. Amen quickly had seen the need to restore order out of the chaotic condition of school athletics and neglect of an adequate physical training program. He asked his good friend and former roommate at Exeter and Harvard, Dr. William Hyde, president of Bowdoin, if he could recommend someone to be the director of the Exeter gymnasium. Without hesitation, Hyde recommended the twenty-three-year-old Ross, who became the first permanent faculty member as Director of Athletics (*Phillips Exeter Bulletin*, Jan. 5, 1935, 7).

Physical culture and athletics had been joined, to become in the future an uneasy alliance for many educational institutions. However, for Exeter, Ross proved to be the answer in bringing order out of a troublesome athletic program, punctuated mainly by the ugly behavior of students surrounding the Exeter-Andover rivalry. Amen's intent in the appointment of Ross centered on the need for someone to put into place an acceptable program that provided "proper outlets for physical energy" (Williams 1957, 88). Andover soon followed suit when, in 1897, Principal Bancroft made the popular Alfred Stearns its first director of athletics. A star athlete during his days as a Phillipian and also at Amherst College, Stearns ranks among the first to have experience in organized sport as part of his qualifications to assume a position as director of athletics. He also became head coach of the baseball team in 1898, the first full-time faculty member to coach a sport team in the history of Andover. Following Stearns's appointment, athletic relations between Andover and Exeter reached a friendly and amicable environment (Harrison 1983, 126–29). Thus, the two Phillips academies within a short span of time reorganized entirely the conduct of athletics and physical training. Without question, Andover and Exeter set the model for other schools to follow. An aggressive sport and exercise program became an important cog in the training of boarding school lads.

The gymnasium proved to be a focal point in the latter decades of the nineteenth century for the development of organized sport programs in the boarding schools. By its very appearance as one of the campus buildings, the gymnasium served as a daily reminder of the prominence that physical health and activity held for the developing schoolboy. But another reminder of exercise, sports, and school spirit had also made its appearance on boarding school campuses. Like the advent of gymnasia, the saga of the school paper occurred over several decades.

6

Scribes and Pundits

THE RISE AND ESTABLISHMENT of the school newspaper, starting with student writings, incidental items, and announcements and progressing to a fully developed tabloid, occurred during the three decades from the 1850s to the 1880s. One regular feature eventually concentrated on campus sports. It began with simple recording of contest results but gradually evolved into a description of games and, finally, a justification for school athletics. The progress from reporting to advocacy involved several issues that grew in importance as the scope from informal sport to organized athletics grew. Thus, school writers often focused on issues such as the need for a gymnasium, permission for school teams to play contests off-campus, permission to attend off-campus games, the need for more teams, values attained from sports, pleas for students to pay athletic association dues to cover team expenses, and competing for success but with honor. Playing a key role in keeping athletics in the forefront of campus affairs, the school newspaper's editorial writers offered a plethora of comments about what needed to be done for sports to be more successful.

Appearing either weekly or biweekly, school papers began to emerge on the scene by the mid-1870s, but initial efforts came much earlier. Not all such enterprises proved successful; some disappeared after two or three issues. Then, invariably, another student organization or group would launch a tabloid under a new name. Such fits and starts occurred especially at Phillips Andover and Williston. Evidence indicates that the first efforts aimed at publishing a campus periodical occurred at Andover in 1854. A literary organization, the Philomathean Society, founded the *Mirror of the Philomathean Society*, a publication that appeared under other titles during the remainder of the century. The magazine devoted itself to student essays and poems (Allis 1979, 207). What may have been the first reference to sport and exercise that ever appeared in a campus literary venture came out in the *Philo Mirror*, a shortened name for the publication, of March

1858. A campus pundit observed, "For sport and exercise, Old Winter has favored us to an unwonted degree, with excellent skating. The dignified professors, the thoughtful 'Theolog,' the fun-loving Academy boy and—last but not least—the gleeful damsels have, each, taken their share of the healthy and pleasing exercise." Winter, however, also brought snow and, of course, for young boys, the urge to hurl round white missiles. Thus, the same issue of the *Philo Mirror* carried a formal admonition: "Members of the school are particularly requested not to throw snowballs at the teachers of the Academy or the professors of the Theological Seminary" (Harrison 1983, 13).

Apparently, in an attempt to put before the Andoverians a publication that would focus more on campus humor, the first issue of the *Phillipian* appeared in 1857. However, that effort stumbled, with no further edition being issued until 1878. In the meantime, the *Philo Mirror* carried sport articles with considerable amounts of information. For example, the March 1867 issue listed all the campus baseball clubs along with the names of the president, secretary, treasurer, and captain of each team. No explanatory text, though, accompanied the listing on the five and one-half by eight-inch page *(Mirror* PAA, 1867, no. 2: 39). In another account, an editorial scribe wrote that he thought ball-playing had not been pursued with much vigor during the summer term, "owing to the scarcity of its lovers" *(Mirror* PAA, 1867, no. 3: 34). By the end of 1878 the *Phillipian* had emerged as the principal paper on the Andover campus.

Pioneering Journalism at Other Schools

In 1860, Coit wrote to one of his St. Paul's students that he (Coit) had concluded an "occasional paper" might be a good idea. The student had previously broached the idea in a letter to the headmaster. Coit even went so far as to suggest a name for the publication, *Horae Scholasticae* (School hours), a title that prevails to this day. The headmaster did not intend to supervise the overall production or editing of the newly founded enterprise; he hinted that interested students should take over that responsibility, which they did. "It was not difficult to seize upon material being produced in the course of things—compositions, translations from the classics, poems and orations delivered on school occasions. Besides, the school generated a certain amount of news" (Heckscher 1980, 37). In the first issue, June 1, the "certain amount of news" manifested itself in a recording of the cricket match between the recently formed Old Hundred and Isthmian cricket clubs. No mention of players, strategies, or records found its way into the new paper. The writer simply recorded that "the match commenced about two o'clock P.M. and took about

3 hours" *(Horae* 1860, no. 1). Although Coit may have meant for the *Horae Scholasticae* to be a literary endeavor in which students could practice their writing skills based on what they had learned in the classics, he apparently did not object to the newsworthy accounts that appeared even in the first issue.

At a school only four years in existence, the paper had established itself as a force on the campus. Editors saw coverage of sports as important assignments. The second issue, for example, carried a more lengthy account of the annual Old Hundred-Isthmian cricket match, which highlighted the July 4 campus celebration. However, the scribe reporting on the celebration spent more time commenting on the audience than on the game, observing that a tent had been set up for spectators. The match, again, lasted about three hours but could have gone on longer, thanks to the novel phenomenon of ladies in the audience voting for continuance. "It was quite a pleasant and exciting affair, and the ladies present seemed to be quite interested in it, as they voted for another inning at the close of the first" *(Horae* 1860, no. 2). The *Horae Scholasticae* holds a place in the history of sports as being the earliest continuous school paper to carry sporting accounts.[1]

The St. Paulites published a campus paper only on an intermittent basis during the next few years. But volume five for 1871 carried several sport stories. For example, in May of that year one writer complained that our "amusements have been very limited." Cricket had been the principal sport. Baseball had not been encouraged. If one were not a "cricketer," there had been "hardly anything to do." Therefore, adding boating, as had been proposed, would be beneficial to student life *(Horae* 1871, no. 1). In what may well have been an historic first, the initial page of the July 1871 issue carried a sport story as the main event of the Anniversary Day celebration. A description of that special day again featured the cricket match between the Old Hundred and Isthmian clubs. Several pages later, readers also found another full-page sport story, "The First Boat Race at Long Pond" *(Horae* 1871, no. 3). The initial football story to appear in the *Horae* reported that "a football convention was held and a code of rules laid down" in order to avoid the "endless disputes concerning the rules." The paper carried a list of the new rules for all the boys to digest *(Horae* 1871, no. 4). Thus, it became clear that the *Horae Scholasticae* had become a permanent organ of reporting and editorializing on events and issues affecting the daily life of St. Paul's boys.

Appeals for funds to support athletic endeavors appeared for the first time the next year. The expansion of the number of sports put pressure on purse strings.

1. The *Williston Sharpshooter* appeared in 1860 but ceased publication within a few years.

9. Henry Augustus Coit about 1870. Appointed the first headmaster of St. Paul's School in 1856, Coit served for almost four decades. Courtesy of St. Paul's School Archives.

The enterprising zealots for boating sent out pleas for monetary support. One realist urged, "Although a great deal of enthusiasm may arise now that the boats have arrived, in addition to enthusiasm we need money; and an appeal is made to those who have not already contributed, to come forward with their subscriptions." The appeal for funds to support school sports appeared as an ongoing saga on all the boarding school campuses. In the case of these St. Paul's boys, they were realistic about the various kinds of costs to be incurred, for example, paying for the boats, "freightage," maintenance of the boats, repair of the boat house, and "various other small matters" (*Horae* 1872, no. 1).

The *Horae Scholasticae* had reached a level of stability by the early 1870s. Editors conducted business in keeping with the Coit philosophy that there would be no crassness and no commercialism. One editor proudly proclaimed that pages in the *Horae* contained "no vulgar advertisements—no haberdashers, no importunate tailors, no sporting goods agencies. 'We have from cover to cover simply the *Horae*" (Heckscher 1980, 37).[2]

2. Despite the claims of Laurence Crosbie and Myron Williams that the *Exonian*, founded in February of 1878, represents the first newspaper published by students in an American secondary

Within a few years, boys at other boarding schools launched their own versions of a school newspaper. The age of experimentation over what constituted the core of a campus paper seemed to be over. Most of these later papers began publication without interruption, and many continue to this day. No evidence indicates that headmasters had a direct hand in the establishment of a paper, as did Coit at St. Paul's. But other headmasters helped to ensure a successful enterprise. For example, Perkins at Exeter, after agreeing to the start of a school paper, made sure the early editors followed traditions of "journalistic fairness and usefulness." In Crosbie's words, Perkins had "to curb and to encourage the youthful and fiery editors" (Crosbie 1924, 128).

Meantime, in New Jersey at Peddie School, founded in 1864, students published the *Chronicle* in 1871. Thus, Peddie holds the honor of being one of the earliest secondary schools to issue a campus publication that sustained itself over decades. A product of the school's literary societies, Academia and Kalomathia, the *Chronicle* began as an annual, became a quarterly in 1884, and subsequently was issued as a monthly publication (Geiger 1961, 109).

During 1877–78, papers were established at several schools, beginning with the founding of the *Vindex* at St. Mark's School in February of 1877. Benson, the early St. Mark's historian, called the years 1874–77 the "Golden Age" at the school for it marked the end of its infancy and the establishment of control and stability. The beginning of the *Vindex* capped this period of maturation. In the fall of 1877, the newspaper demonstrated leadership with an appeal for the organization of football. Up to this time St. Mark's lads had played only baseball on an organized basis. A *Vindex* writer editorialized that football was "the game of games." A short time later, interested students put three campus elevens in place. Benson does not say how many games were played but notes that on January 7, 1878, St. Markers engaged a "team of Harvard Freshmen," with three of them being alumni. *Vindex* writers felt compelled to do some "Monday morning quarterbacking," just like contemporary sports writers! When a code of rules for football was published for the school, one wonders if the *Vindex* was the instigator. Certainly within a year after its first issue, the *Vindex* had proved to be a significant force in the escalation of athletics on the St. Mark's campus (Benson 1925, 65, 70–72).

Boys at three older boarding schools also persuaded authorities to authorize a campus newspaper in 1878. In April, Exeter principal Perkins gave his permission to the founding of the *Exonian*. In May, Worcester Academy lads started the *Acad-*

---

school, the evidence seems clear that the *Horae Scholasticae* holds the honor (Crosbie 1924, 203; Williams 1957, 59).

emy Weekly. Then the *Phillipian* reappeared in the fall, following a lapse of twenty-one years after its one-year experiment in 1857. This start-up cluster of school papers cannot be explained fully. It may have been pure coincidence. However, the *Exonian* managers may have initiated the practice of sending copies of their paper to neighboring schools, a procedure that gained prominence in subsequent decades. An editorial comment in the *Exonian*, dated October 12, 1878, chided the Andoverians for their failure to produce a campus newspaper. It seemed strange that Andover had not begun one of its own, the editorialist commented. Some Andover boys envied what Exeter lads had accomplished. But the editorial then observed that steps had finally been taken for a bimonthly school paper. Crosbie noted this was the first reference to the new *Phillipian*, reborn in the fall of 1878 (Crosbie 1924, 204).

By February of 1881 the boys of Lawrenceville School produced their first school publication, the *Graduate*, a monthly journal. More literary in scope, the editors switched the publication the next October to a campus news format. Although still retaining its magazine page size and style but renamed the *Lawrenceville Record*, it carried baseball and football stories. At the time, the Lawrenceville paper featured sports as a regular section. An early account in October 1882 centered on an editorial in which the writer expressed the need for practice if the football team expected to succeed. "The important question is, what amounts of regular and earnest exercise and practice are we going to accomplish? . . . when you practice enter into it with vim and earnestness. . . . We get out of school at 4:30. Every player ought to be ready for play in fifteen minutes, and the game should be started by a quarter to five," reasoned the pundit. The first story of a contest against an off-campus team appeared in the November issue of the *Record* when the school writer sadly described the first defeat at the hands of the Pennington team (Mulford 1935, 76–79, 215). The *Record* continued to carry sports stories, serving as a reservoir of valuable historical information on Lawrenceville athletics until 1886, when the student editorial board ceased its publication. It was replaced by a weekly newspaper, the *Lawrence*. "The idea was borrowed from the papers published by some of the other schools such as Exeter and Andover. . . . (we) thought that a publication coming out once a week having more the newspaper type [*sic*] might be of more interest in recording school events," observed the managing editor of that time (Mulford 1935, 215).

Pleas for Money, Other Issues, and Chitchat

As sports evolved into an organized structure, the plea for money appeared frequently in papers. School administrators and boards of trustees still held to the notion that students would have to defray the costs of their fun and games activity. Student managers of various sport teams and athletic associations found themselves faced with a serious reality: the cost of operation. Equipment, especially uniforms, although primitive compared with today's elaborate athletic gear, caused a higher level of expense. When teams traveled off-campus, usually by train, that also added to the expense sheet. As a result, those in charge pleaded almost constantly for money to fund their school's growing sport undertakings.

The school paper became an important means for informing the student body of the needs of the football and baseball teams, and later, of other athletic aggregations. For example, in 1884, an editorial writer in Peddie School's *Chronicle* complained that too much money went to the diamond team and not enough to the football and lacrosse teams. Later, in the year's final issue, a story reported that football jackets had arrived so that the team could play "in earnest." The following October of 1885 the *Chronicle* put out another call for help—this time not for money but for in-kind help: a football field construction crew. "Now the campus is full of ridges and hollows, and some one is likely to be injured in playing. If the boys would turn out and help in the work, we would have it comparatively level. Then goals are needed at each end of the campus. This could also be done by the boys." The paper apparently succeeded in its exhortation; Peddie played its first interscholastic game the next fall (Geiger 1961, 126).

Earlier, a strong reminder had appeared on the front page of the *Phillipian* at Andover in 1879, asserting that barely one-half of Andoverians had contributed the requisite three dollars a year for athletics. The plea for monetary support occurred in an article discussing the role of the athletic association in relation to the school. After a detailed discussion of issues, the writer urged more lads to join the student athletic association and do "their part toward sustaining the school honor" (*Phillipian*, Mar. 8, 1879). Seven years before, St. Paulites had found their expanding crew enterprise to be costly. Students had read hard facts in the *Horae Scholasticae* of April, 1872, when they learned that their boating aspirations could not subsist on the $150 remaining in the treasuries of the school's two new clubs. Although the competition would "be confined strictly to ourselves," it would entail expenditures well beyond what the treasury then held (*Horae* 1872, no. 1).

Clearly, sport programs needed the school paper to report to the student body, not only the results of contests, but also the responsibility of each boy toward the preparation for and conduct of the program, especially the financial obligation entailed. Student-led athletics needed all the tools that could be mustered to survive, including various kinds of advocacy. In its final issue of the school year,

1880, the *Oracle* at Williston Seminary appealed to Willistonians for the new term: "We hope the members of the school will not only be willing to enter these sports but also to contribute pecuniary assistance both of which are needed to insure success" *(Oracle* WNS, 1880, no. 2). In April of 1891, the student body at Suffield School (then known as the Connecticut Literary Institution) found this hortatory comment in a story on the progress of athletics: "Although somewhat crippled in its actions, by a lack of funds, enough has been done to awaken confidence in the future of the Association, and to cause us to feel that its welfare should be of interest to every student" *(Senior* 1891, no. 2). Thus, student-run sports programs, universally, and for decades, had to appeal for funds both to initiate and to maintain their operations.

Despite the always pervasive need for money, school scribes also found other serious issues to advocate. For example, the front page of the *Senior* in its second year of existence at the Connecticut Literary Institution carried the account of its football game with Williston. Attention concentrated mainly on the use of outside players. Williston had won using the latter tactic, and the Suffield writer clearly felt the impropriety of losing to a team that had not used its "own men" exclusively *(Senior* 1891, no. 2). It had not taken long before pundits pointed to issues of fairness or cheating in their columns! Nowhere did the power of persistent advocacy by sport columnists over the years bear fruit as it did at Exeter and Andover. Constant print in the *Exonian* and the *Phillipian* for a gymnasium finally came to fruition. In the case of the *Exonian*, the class day historian publicly announced that the school paper had been responsible for the erection of a gymnasium (Crosbie 1924, 243). When Borden Gymnasium at Andover became a reality in 1902, it virtually ended any further newspaper advocacy in that direction.

Issues of moderate frequency, but of no less importance, also arose. At Andover, student fans were not to attend off-campus games. An irate pundit, outraged at the edict passed down from the principal, in this case the highly respected Bancroft, wrote in the *Phillipian* in 1878, "We are meek; we are humble; we have the most profound regard for the powers that be; . . . But now and then, when the spirit burns within and the lamentations of two hundred youths are heard . . . we do venture to express an opinion . . . that the action of the faculty in refusing permission to all except sixteen men to attend games played out of town is not for the best interests of the school—that is, the athletic interests" *(Phillipian* 1878, no. 2). Andoverians feared that their classmates on the field of battle would not receive their share of cheers, thus dampening the playing spirit of the school team. Apparently, the irate writer looked ahead to the 1879 Exeter clash. The initial football game between the two schools had just taken place, won easily by Andover, one goal and five touchdowns to zero. Nonetheless, Exeter's team had been cheered on by eighty boys who had come down on the 12:37 train. The *Phillipian* writer, following the summary of the game, could not help but hint that the Andover faculty and administration should reconsider their policy: "We were glad so many of the Exeter boys could witness the game on the 2nd inst. [*sic*] Would that the powers that be might be moved to give us Andoverians a like privilege." As if to clinch his case, the scribe declared that the athletic interests and intellectual interests of the school were "intimately connected." After all, faculties of "both American and foreign schools" have indicated that field sports "are highly conducive to mental vigor" (*Phillipian* 1878, nos. 2–3). Eventually school authorities relented. In a few years Exeter and Andover authorities permitted the student bodies to witness the annual football game en masse.

At Williston a few years earlier, irritated student writers had taken aim at a regulation that restrained its teams, in this case the baseball club, from playing games off campus. In November of 1872 a Williston pundit asserted, "we are still held under a very stringent, and to the students, extremely disagreeable regulation, prohibiting our going out of town to play match games, which rule, of course, is very detrimental to the full development of the science of base ball among Willistonians" (*Supplement to Mirror* WNS, 1872, no. 1). The following May the *Mirror*, a publication of the Gamma Sigma literary society, continued the assault upon the obnoxious regulation. In the column titled "Base Ball Items," a writer penned a proactive reasoning, "As every ball season comes round, it is with a feeling of regret that we call to mind the fact that the Williston nine is not allowed to leave town to compete with other clubs. It seems as if, were the restriction removed, our men would be more stimulated to practice" (*Mirror* WNS 1873, no. 3). The persistence of scribes in succeeding years brought results. In November of 1875, the *Oracle*, the Adelphia literary society magazine, reported that the faculty had permitted the Williston baseball team to play in a tournament at Northampton, five miles away (*Oracle* WNS, 5, no. 1). The change in policy "proved a success," even though the men lost. "Our fellows played excellent [*sic*]," but the game was played in September, barely two weeks into the term. The Williston nine had "barely organized."

School papers also became an important vehicle for printing critical information. An aspect especially important in the early decades of athletics centered on the publication of rules and on eligibility of student athletes. As schools established athletic relations with each other, it often became necessary to publish the conditions under which their games would be staged. Regulations of the ruling athletic bodies also appeared. Such occurred, for example, in the revisions made to the constitution of the athletic association at Andover in 1896. A full account appeared in the *Phillipian*. It included an outline of the role of officers, makeup of the athletic board, and the listing of subscribers (Harrison 1983, 114). Similarly, the *Grotonian* in 1903 devoted a considerable amount of space to "The Constitution of the Groton School Athletic Committee" *(Grotonian,* June 1903, 219–21).

In addition, the campus newspaper brought a new form of communication among students. They could now be heard in a continuing and more lasting form of dialogue. Probably no topic held more interest than the exploits of fellow classmates in school activities. Chitchat items appeared in columns under such titles as "School Items," "Phillipiana," "Here and There," or simply "Items." For example, "The new cricket ground is at present in a very flourishing condition. Several blades of grass have already appeared on the cricket field," observed a hopeful *Horae* scribe in May of 1871. A one-line item appeared in the October 1897 *Grotonian* lauding the exploits of alumnus Percy Haughton, who "led the batting average of the Harvard Varsity base-ball nine last spring." A downcast *Phillipian* scribe inserted a note in a "Phillipiana" column for November 21, 1885, "We were pleased to see so many of the old fellows (grads) at the Exeter game, and only wish that they could have seen us win." Exeter had won, thirty-three to eleven. Besides local sport items in the tidbit columns, an assorted array of one- or two-line announcements, scores of college games, and the humor of campus happenings appeared in print. To wit, a terse one-liner was printed after the 1885 disastrous Exeter game, "The goal posts are still standing" *(Horae* 1871, no. 1; *Grotonian,* Oct. 1897, 14; *Phillipian* 1885, no. 10).

The Sports Page and Ideology

When managers of school teams, especially the grid and diamond aggregations, went off-campus to play or to host games on campus with opponents from nearby schools, life on the campus could reach tolerable, even exciting levels. Attending games off-campus gave students a respite from the drudgery of Latin and Greek classes. The freedom to witness and cheer their comrades took on a new meaning, never experienced by boys of earlier times. Many lads equated success on the playing field by their school teams with the prestige of their school. Thus, winning assumed a new importance, and school papers exhibited the glow of victory with their stories. Those who saw an off-campus win enjoyed reading about the game they attended. A new form of reading had emerged—the sports page!

Reports about the athletic prowess of their peers brought attention to a new aspect of preparatory school education. Columnists took advantage of opportunities to write their thoughts about the values of athletics. One can marvel at the exhortation of an 1879 Worcester football enthusiast: "Half the pleasure and benefit arises from the zest in which we play; so don't stop to consider the probabilities of victory, but play for the exercise and fun" (Small 1968, 13). What literature provided undergirdings for the Worcester writer's opinions? Could he have read Tom Brown's *School Days* and absorbed the moralistic musings found therein? Certainly, this remains a possibility. Nevertheless, the Worcester scribe suggested a new aspect of writing—that of the sports columnist. Similarly, a *Phillipian* joyously wrote about the first contest with Exeter and postgame celebration. "Every Phillipian was jubilant over the well-earned victory of our eleven in the game with Exeter. They showed their appreciation of our men by coming out in a strong force and taking both elevens to the depot in good style, and then escorting the victors to the residences of the teachers, where enthusiastic speeches were made" (*Phillipian* 1878, no. 3). Not too long in the future schoolboys could find glorified stories (if their school won) in a special section. School editors tended to group sport stories into one part of the paper, reminding one of a modern-day sports page. For example, on a three-column page of one *Phillipian* the initial two columns were filled with sport material about the first Exeter football game. The remaining column carried ads. A start toward featuring one page of sports had taken place.

As organized team sports advanced in breadth, other sports came on the scene. At Worcester Academy, track and field, often called athletics at that time, took on an exalted position as a campus sport. A second-place finish by the track team in the annual Boston Amateur Association Indoor Interscholastic Meet evoked this enthusiastic reaction upon their return to Worcester. A jubilant writer described it in the *Academy* for March of 1893, "At their arrival at the Union Depot they were met by a large party of the fellows who had not been fortunate enough to attend the games, and then began the whoop of war! Horns to the number of 70 or 80 were brought into requisition, and as many healthy lungs began forcing volumes of air through them. The procession formed at Franklin Square, with Mr. Abercrombie [headmaster] chief marshall. . . . The column took its line of march up Front St. The sight was awe inspiring" (*Academy* 1893, no. 6).

The Worcester enthusiast's reporting points to the fact that school papers eventually carried an array of topics pertaining to sport. Besides describing games played, including lineups and a few statistics as to who scored and who stood out as "stars" of the game, writers touched on issues of health, benefits from sports participation, effect on school spirit, the impact of traditions, and appeals for team support. Writers felt free to act as sideline quarterbacks. An 1885 story from the *Phillipian* illustrates how several such themes merged into one account and concluded with the opinion and admonition of a columnist:

> To the team we would say that upon them devolves the honor of upholding the reputation of the school in athletics, and the measure of that honor will be according as they do their part well and faithfully; yet to do this will take steady and earnest practice, and strict attention to business while doing so, and, as in a former issue, we would urge them to learn more effectually [*sic*] the art of passing, the lack of which was a serious drawback on last year's team.
>
> In conclusion we would say that every fellow in school should feel that he has a share in whatever is the result of the games be it success, or failure, and that by his support or non support he may aid or deter the team from success (*Phillipian* 1885, no. 2).

By the 1880s, sport had become firmly entrenched amid an array of exalted values. As they observed and thought about the fledgling sporting enterprise on their respective campuses, chroniclers in school papers unknowingly propagated a sport ideology. Such terms as *manly, honor, toughen, physical prowess, pride, hard work, duty, plucky, noblest, perseverance,* and *cool-headedness* crept into the editorial columns, indicating the seriousness that schoolboy writers attached to sports. They put before their student bodies, as well as parents and alumni, a story of student life that had not existed in prewar days. Enthusiastic accounts added zest to campus life and contributed immensely to the growing popularity of school athletics. After a Worcester Academy victory over Exeter, proclaimed on the front page of the *Academy Weekly,* November 5, 1896, a writer exhorted, "Our football season is over; but the spirit of the final game ought to live on and influence the whole work of the year. This is the true purpose of football." The Worcester gridders had won "on their merits" and because they "showed more grit." Elsewhere in the same issue, an editorial writer, noting that athletics had received increased attention in the country during the past fifteen years, pontificated, "But better than this, physical training in a broader sense is commanding our attention more and more . . . it raises the standard of morals among men, and this will amply justify us in the giving of our time. . . . Good training develops patience, self-denial and continence—the best of virtues. The ancient Greeks realized the value of all these things and required their athletes to be men of unblemished characters, and train faithfully in a gymnasium for at least nine months" (*Academy* 1896, no. 8). Thus, the initial stage in the development of boarding school sports—student control—moved into its final years espousing a sport ideology.

The school paper had proved to be of inestimable value in undergirding the gradual acceptance of athletics as a justifiable school activity, carried on by the boys themselves. It brought sports to public attention in ways not possible through merely oral communication. The written page provided a permanence to records and opinions. Advocacy issues gathered strength when paper after paper hammered away on a particular viewpoint. Rules, policy, and philosophy in printed circulation reached wider audiences with greater accuracy than could oral reporting or hearsay commentary. Reinforcing the sports page ideology in the 1880s, adult leaders like Peabody began actively promoting athletics as a means for moral education. The rationale, that is, character development, gained widespread acceptance when voiced by leading headmasters.

7

Morality and Sport

Groton's Endicott Peabody

MUCH HAS BEEN WRITTEN about Endicott Peabody—about him as an exceptional school leader, his lengthy tenure, and the large number of Groton graduates who went into public service, the most notable being Franklin D. Roosevelt. But little has been mentioned about Peabody's ideas on athletics in the boarding school. Yet no history of schoolboy sport would be complete without considering his leadership regarding the educational value of athletics. For Peabody, this meant building moral character. He spoke on the topic to groups of educators. On behalf of the Church School Masters, he urged President Theodore Roosevelt to reform football so that honesty and fair play would reign. Such was Peabody's renown that educators from Virginia visited him for advice on how to run their school. In short, his reputation and influence extended well beyond the confines of his own Groton School.

Yet it was at the school that he implemented and honed his athletic philosophy and program. According to Peabody's philosophy, athletics reached far beyond being mere pastime. His ultimate goal of nurturing within his pupils a manly, Christian character embraced sports as an essential ingredient. Speaking more on the importance of athletics than had any previous or then-current headmaster, Peabody invariably focused his theme on the relationship of honorable sports-playing to one's gentlemanly, everyday conduct.

Despite the relatively late establishment of Groton, in 1884, compared with other well-known schools, such as the Phillips academies and St. Paul's School, Peabody's early reputation as a leading schoolmaster soon gained considerable acclaim. His initial renown stemmed from an upbringing amidst the well-entrenched and highly regarded Peabody family. Notables such as Phillips Brooks, a leading Boston churchman, and J. Pierpont Morgan, the famous New

York financier, took an active part in the early days of Groton, both serving on the first board of trustees (Ashburn 1967, 66–67). But Peabody's preparation for leading such a school began with his own training in an English public school, where he was known for his athletic skill and his sense of morality.

The Young Endicott Peabody

Born in 1857 to Samuel Endicott and Marianne Lee Peabody, the young Peabody spent his childhood in Salem, Massachusetts, where his father carried on a successful shipping business. In his thirteenth year "Cotty," as his friends knew him, moved with his family to London, a change that would set the course for his later life. It began with his enrollment in 1871 at Cheltenham School, located in the central regions of England, west of London. During his five years at this school, the gangly but muscular Peabody turned his energy toward cricket, rowing, and racquets. He excelled in sports-playing and throughout his life retained as a priority being in good physical condition. As for his classroom achievement at Cheltenham, not much is known, but one friend recalled later that Peabody "was fairly industrious." He went on to say that "what we boys noticed, was his resolute character." He was always concerned with "right and wrong" (Ashburn 1967, 20). This mix of love for athletics and maintaining a physically fit body, combined with strong moral precepts, later formed the cornerstone of Peabody's philosophy for Groton boys.

After Cheltenham, Peabody enrolled in Trinity College at Cambridge to study law. While there, he continued his athletic pursuits but also developed spiritually. He counted among his close English classmates a small cadre whose ties with the Anglican Church made an impact upon him. Raised as a Unitarian, young Peabody discovered a warmth and feeling in the Anglican Church that he had found wanting in his Unitarian surroundings. These Anglican influences played an important part in his decision to form Groton within the Episcopalian framework (Ashburn 1967, 33).

After three and one-half years at Trinity, the tall, physically striking Peabody returned to the United States to begin training in the family business at Boston. Despite the promise he displayed as a budding financier, he apparently experienced a serious void in his life. After counseling sessions with Phillips Brooks, himself a convert to the Episcopal Church from the Unitarian faith, Peabody received the kind of support he sought and entered the Episcopal Theological School in 1881. He interrupted his studies in January of 1882 to spend six months as an interim pastor in a small church in Tombstone, Arizona. Besides being the first to preach a sermon in the initial Episcopal church in Arizona, the twenty-five-year-old "Cotty" started baseball, created a more caring attitude among Tombstone citizens, and supervised the erection of a church building (Ashburn 1967, 43–44, 47). His six-month stay proved to be a rewarding experience and bolstered his desire to become an Episcopalian priest.

Peabody returned to Massachusetts in July 1882 to finish his theological studies. During his final year at the seminary, he traveled to Southborough to serve as an interim chaplain at St. Mark's School. So well did he carry out his tasks that the trustees considered calling him as the next permanent headmaster. For Peabody, such consideration buoyed his desire to pursue a role as a school chaplain. But a chance remark by an old friend, the Reverend Leighton Parks, rector of Emmanuel Church in Boston, spurred Peabody to think in different terms. Parks suggested that if Peabody did not receive the call to become the next St. Mark's headmaster, he should start his own school (Ashburn 1934, 13).

As Peabody mulled over this suggestion, he received further encouragement. Relatives residing in Groton, the James Lawrence family, with the aid of others among his folk, promised him a site if he would start a school. After inquiries among friends about financial assistance, all of which were affirmative, he decided to get on with the project. The Lawrence family then purchased a ninety-acre farm on the outskirts of Groton and made it a gift to Peabody. Fortunately, he had influential family members and friends to call upon as prospective members of his board of trustees. Those invited all accepted, with Brooks becoming the first chairman, at the initial meeting in Boston, February 23, 1884 (Ashburn 1934, 15–16; 1967, 65–67).

The School

What kind of a school should it be? Peabody had begun to face that question during the months in which he had pondered the feasibility of founding a school. While at the seminary, he made an ally in Sherrard Billings, who had formerly taught at Adams Academy but had answered a call to the ministry. They exchanged thoughts about the "pressing need for schools in which religious education and a Christian life should be stressed." Peabody remembered his days at Cheltenham and felt "the pull of a system which would allow for culture on one side of the scales and sportsmanship at the other" (Ashburn 1934, 14). Then, too, he was not far removed from the influence of famous English Victorian headmasters Thomas Arnold and Edward Thring, both of whom he quoted from time to time, especially in his numerous sermons (Ashburn 1967, 22–30). Peabody and

Billings concluded that a school could function in which boys and men lived, worked, and played together. Billings became Peabody's first master.

The board of trustees in its first meeting drafted a preface to the initial announcement of plans to open a school. It stated that Peabody "wished to make an attempt to found a boys' school in this country somewhat after the manner of the Public Schools in England." The announcement then provided the interested reader with the school's purpose: "Every endeavor will be made to cultivate manly, Christian character, having regard to moral and physical as well as intellectual development" (Ashburn 1967, 67; 1934, 17). The new Groton School would attempt to accomplish what most other American boarding schools intended to do, except Peabody would go one step further—he expressed outright concern for the physical development of the student. Peabody's training in England and his leadership at Groton over the next five decades would substantiate the initial emphasis on the physical being of students as integral to the total education of boys. Stating this concern in the objectives of the proposed school gained public attention. It was this announced emphasis on the development of the body as well as of the mind that few schools had attempted in the time prior to the founding of Groton School.[1]

The circumstances surrounding Peabody's undertaking worked favorably for him. Besides his English school training, he had spent much of his first years among Boston Brahmins, who virtually assured Peabody his school would survive. As James McLachlan points out, "It was the age of the investment banker; through his family Peabody was connected to two of the most powerful investment banking firms of the day—Lee, Higginson and Company, and the House of Morgan. The Higginsons and Morgans sent their sons to Groton, and others followed their example" (McLachlan 1970, 268). Furthermore, Peabody quickly rose in the ranks of headmasters as a budding school leader with a promising and influential future ahead of him. For example, as early as 1889, Columbia authorities inquired if he would be willing to be considered for the presidency of the university, an offer he declined (McLachlan 1970, 258). Peabody also gained fame for his

---

1. Notable exceptions had occurred. Williston Seminary had announced in its catalogue of 1864 that daily exercise would be a regular requirement to improve the physical, mental, and moral development of the student. Although Frederick Gunn in the 1850s had combined study and sports-playing, no record seems definitive as to the exact year that he instituted an organized or systematic program for physical development. St. Paul's hired Lester Dole in the late 1870s to direct the gymnasium and coach some sports. However, no firm evidence exists that regular exercise became a requirement immediately on campus.

10. The Reverend Endicott Peabody, founder and longtime headmaster of Groton School, about 1885, the year after the school opened in October 1884. Courtesy of Groton School Archives.

preaching. In addition to his role as pastor of Groton Chapel, he preached to students and faculty at Columbia University, Amherst College, Harvard University, Loomis Institute, and Wellesley College, as well as the U.S. Naval Reserve contingent at Newport, Rhode Island. He also appeared frequently before secular groups. For example, he addressed the public school teachers of Gardner, Massachusetts, and the Colony Club in New York on the education of boys; he also spoke before the National Collegiate Athletic Association on the American and English ideals of sport.[2]

Most importantly, Peabody's ideal of what a boys' school should be struck a responsive chord among many Victorian families in and around Boston and New York City. Before the Eastern Convention of his church in 1888, Peabody probably explained most fully why he saw the need for a boys' school. Because busy fathers had no time to help in forming good character in their sons and mothers spent most of their time tending to household duties, the sons were left unattended, out in the city on their own, and "with unhealthy notions of manliness."

2. Beginning in 1897, the *Groton School Log* lists Peabody's speaking and preaching engagements.

Thus, Peabody intended to create a school that provided boys with a home away from home in good surroundings (Peabody 1888). He argued that a school within the Christian tradition contained the elements to rescue a boy from any tendencies toward illicit behavior. Ashburn's words explain further, "Early Groton parents, like many of their contemporaries, were privately disgusted with the bringing up of well-to-do American boys of that period. They thought them spoiled ladies' men tied to women's apron strings, and heartily welcomed the chance to send their sons to a place where the boys had to stand on their own feet and play rough-and-tumble games." Peabody helped to counteract the trend toward effeminacy by building his school upon the theme that Groton was a family affair and he was the father. Mrs. Peabody played the important supporting role, especially for the younger boys. "In loco parentis" meant just that to Peabody, according to Ashburn. Parents, even though almost all of them knew little about English public schools, had read or heard of Thomas Arnold and strongly affirmed his concept of a school that focused on turning out boys ingrained with gentlemanly habits. Because Peabody filled that role, Groton had strong appeal (Ashburn 1967, 70–71). The family school idea distinguished it from many other boarding schools; the combination proved to be exceptional.

Peabody the Headmaster

Several schools such as St. Paul's (Coit), Phillips Andover, (Bancroft), Worcester Academy, (Abercrombie), Lawrenceville (Mackenzie), St. Mark's (Thayer), and Hill School (Meigs) gained stability and fame due to the strong leadership of long-serving headmasters. But none outlasted Peabody. His tenure of fifty-six years at the helm of Groton School will likely never be surpassed. He set in place an ideal and he never wavered from it. Every year for more than two decades, the school's catalog stated the prime objective: "to cultivate manly, Christian character." More than five decades later, Peabody stood firm in his belief. On May 25, 1940, he delivered a speech at St. Mark's in which he declared the purpose of a church school: "The work within the School is personal, intensely personal. It is not primarily a question of buildings or endowments, or even intellectual achievements. The Supreme task is the development of character" (Peabody 1940).

Along with Billings, who agreed to come to Groton and forego his ministerial career, and William Amory Gardner, fresh out of Harvard where he had graduated summa cum laude, Peabody himself completed the first faculty. They were known in Groton circles as the Great Triumvirate. Twenty-two boys enrolled the first year, and all resided and boarded in the newly constructed building called

"The School." When Phillips Brooks died in 1893, the building was renamed "Brooks House." To emphasize the familial atmosphere, Peabody and his wife, Fannie, after nightly prayers bade each boy a good night. Mrs. Peabody added to the personal attention given to the younger "Grotties" by conducting "parlors" three times a week, where she read selected passages from well-known literary pieces (Amory 1940, 16–17).

Peabody intended to keep school enrollment low in order to maintain the family atmosphere. He used his masters as assistants in attending to the needs of students. He wrote, "Masters are men who are united first of all by devotion to a common cause or loyalty to an institution and then become friends, one of the other, through their love for the school and its boys" (Peabody 1909a, 524). Peabody required much of his instructors as he intended that they throw themselves "fully into the lives of the boys in all their engagements and experiences. It means being present at lectures and other entertainments, at . . . matches, even practices for games" (Peabody 1932). In a subsequent letter to one of his trustees, Peabody outlined nine qualities requisite in a successful master. They included being "an athlete able to play with boys in some of their games and coach them in others. This will give him a good opportunity to know the boys and will also provide the sense of proportion in the relation of the School to athletics" (Peabody 1934a). In fact, the meshing of the masters and boys became one of the distinguishing features of Groton.

The headmaster was irritated that outsiders viewed Groton as a school for sons of the wealthy. Almost from the time of its founding, the school carried this reputation among some people. But others, especially Ellery Sedgwick,[3] did not believe all Grotonians came from comfortable means. "I found many boys as poor as I, and at the time my father was very poor. If the school was filled with snobs, I knew them not. . . . I am mistaken if term bills were not of major concern to at least half the parents" (Sedgwick 1946, 66–67). Peabody made sure that snobbishness did not pervade the campus. He established a spartan fare for day-by-day existence. Each boy when he started had only a twenty-five-cent weekly allowance—no boy could spread his wealth around even if he had it. Cubicles, small spaces of six by ten feet, made up the sleeping quarters. The washroom contained assigned tin basins for each lad with three nearby hooks. For study, boys

---

3. Sedgwick, who for thirty years edited the *Atlantic* (1908–38), graduated from Groton in 1890 and later served as a Groton master (1894–96). In 1909 he became a member of the school's board of trustees and served for most of three decades.

used assigned desks in the large schoolroom located in the "school house" (*Newsweek* 1944, 80).

Peabody expected his family to lead busy lives for he abhorred loafing. To curb any such tendency, he established a school day that contained few idle moments. However, boys had Wednesday and Sunday afternoons off to pursue their own recreational activities, such as countryside hikes, canoeing, or walks into the village of Groton in addition to sport practices. Always concerned about righteousness, Peabody kept in mind strategies for combating the inroads of evil thoughts in the minds of his charges: "For moral evil you have got to consider the care of the body, and the best thing for a boy is to work hard and then, after a short interval, to play hard, and then to work hard again and then to play hard again, and then, when the end of the day has come, to be so tired that he wants to go to bed and go to sleep" (Peabody 1899, 628).

The Groton boy enjoyed only two vacations during the school year: Christmas and Easter. Otherwise, he was campus-bound except for an occasional trip to Cambridge to watch Harvard play football or baseball, but such a trip would usually include only those on the school team. Later, when the St. Mark's football game took place at Southborough, the entire student body traveled to the game.

Throughout his career, Peabody always held fast to his overriding mission— to develop manly Christian gentlemen who would become citizens of the commonwealth of Christ. As McLachlan observed, "Peabody . . . was a moralist rather than an intellectual" (McLachlan 1970, 248). Doing the right thing proved to be the driving force guiding the rector as a headmaster. His goal was also to produce public servants who could do their duty for the country. Speaking before a group of clergy in 1901, Peabody declared, "What we want to do is to raise up a race of men . . . who see their duty ahead of them and are determined at any cost to achieve that duty. That is the great need in America today" (Peabody 1901). To that end, schools had to develop character in boys. The English public schools aimed at that, hence their stress on athletics. In 1909, Peabody declared to his fellow headmasters, "It is through such simplicity of living as athletic prowess requires that the temptations to evil can best be reduced to their lowest terms" (Peabody 1909b).

No better place existed for the lads to practice their morality than in their physical endeavors, especially in playing football, playing baseball, or rowing. In June of 1892, in his semiannual report to the trustees, Peabody wrote that the addition of two more boats had given new impetus to athletics. He declared the importance of offering a variety of sports so that all boys in the school "may be sufficiently interested" to participate. Further, he asserted that "Athletics, in due proportion, play a most important part, not only in developing muscle and vigor, but in assisting to keep up a healthy moral tone in the School."[4] Peabody held fast to a daily exercise regimen in between sport seasons, especially during the winter (Peabody, Headmaster's Reports, vol. 1). Not surprisingly, he even expressed concern about the moral welfare of his boys during their vacations. In December of 1903 the headmaster wrote to parents, asking that they "insist upon moderation in theatre-going" for their sons during the Christmas holidays. Moreover, he asked parents to monitor the content of plays before allowing their sons to attend. "If parents will send back their boys in a healthy state of mind, as well as of body, they will greatly assist us in the work which we are trying to do at Groton" (Peabody 1903). Throughout his years as headmaster, Peabody exemplified in his own person what he asked of the boys: a healthy mind in a healthy body.

It is not clear whether Peabody thought of himself as a muscular Christian. But residing in England for his formal schooling, he became exposed to the ideas of Charles Kingsley, Edward Thring, and Thomas Arnold. From Kingsley, the rector gained inspiration to be drawn toward the ministry. He yearned to be like Kingsley. From Thring, he learned that games could be an educational tool to lead a boy to take on gentlemanly ways. From Arnold,[5] he adopted notions about liberal education, about the prefect system, and about manliness and religion. Yet Peabody grasped the significance of muscular Christianity. During his stay at Trinity College, Cambridge, he read a biography of Kingsley upon which he reflected, "[it] introduced me to a man of vigorous, virile, enthusiastic character; a gentle, sympathetic, and unafraid example of muscular Christianity" (Ashburn 1967, 25–26, 29, 38, 106).

No other headmaster of his time demonstrated such allegiance to physical fitness as did the Groton schoolmaster. For many years he took part in the morning exercise routines, participated in by the entire school, plus his other physical activities such as bicycling, rowing, and playing "fives" (Amory 1940, 16, 17, 72).[6] One writer opined that he "elevated exercise almost to the status of a sacrament"

4. Groton master and archivist Doug Brown claims Peabody purposely downplayed sports in the winter term. He wanted boys to spend time reading but still insisted on regular exercises in the gymnasium.

5. Ashburn devotes a chapter to the influence of Arnold and Thring on Peabody's professional life. See Ashburn 1967, 22–30.

6. For a brief history of the English game of Fives, see Money 1997, 71–80.

(*Newsweek* 1940, 34). He played on school teams, especially football, until his late thirties. Speaking before the Eastern Convention of his church, Peabody made it clear how a healthy body contributed to the welfare of the society: "We need some systems which shall develop the whole of a boy's complex nature—physical, moral and spiritual, and not simply his mind, for we ought never to lose sight of the fact that we can never produce a nation of vigorous thinkers unless we have vigorous physiques as a basis" (Peabody 1888).

Peabody often saw athletics, as an extension of the physical, as part of his three-tier approach to education. For instance, he asserted before a group of Harvard undergraduates, "A man knows that in order to succeed in athletics he must lead a clean life, he must avoid softness of life, and keep himself in excellent physical condition. Thus, athletics ministers to the better life of young men" (Ashburn 1967, 126). Athletics and physical tone went hand-in-hand. Paul Wright, who served as a master under Peabody, remembered the rector saying, "there's no way in which you can use your mind and your spirit effectively if your body isn't well developed and well trained" (Wright 1981).

11. Groton's first football team in 1885 featured founder and headmaster Endicott Peabody, second from left in striped shirt. One of the first masters, Sherrard Billings, just behind Peabody, with mustache, served as captain. Courtesy of Groton School Archives.

Growth and Value of Athletics

Peabody incorporated character-building through sports as a fundamental precept in the foundation of his school. He stated his position clearly in the *School Review* in 1899 and reaffirmed the viewpoint two years later in a speech before the Clericus Society in 1901. "One has not the slightest hesitation in saying that to run a school on a high standard of morality without athletics would be a practical impossibility. Athletics are of the most immense importance in establishing righteousness in the school" (Peabody 1899, 628).

In particular, he favored football. The question of whether or not Peabody planned to require boys to participate in football remains unanswered. Available evidence does not indicate that he wrote down an official decree. However, Ashburn pointed out that, "Theoretically a boy does not have to play the game (football in this case), but moral suasion on the part of the faculty and students makes it almost impossible to avoid doing so." Only by serving as a manager, or being physically incapacitated, or definitely not being a player when in the upper school, could a boy escape participation (Ashburn 1934, 101). Because Peabody purposely kept his school size relatively small, he could carry out this policy of virtual, required sport participation. During the first three decades, graduating classes seldom numbered more than thirty-three and most remained less than thirty.[7] One can imagine the closeness of companionship among classmates. Not to be counted as a member of a team might have been unbearable. Yet, not all played; future president of the United States Franklin D. Roosevelt (class of 1900) served as manager of the baseball team.

From the start, masters, including Peabody, played on the football, baseball, and crew aggregations. This practice continued until the end of the century. It was Peabody's idea that such participation strengthened the relationship between masters and boys. In the words of the Reverend John Crocker, successor to Peabody (1940–65) and a Groton graduate in 1918, "One of the very important emphases the school always had was a close relationship between the faculty and the boys and if you did the same thing with a faculty member it just meant that you got to know him better and it became easier to have him as a friend and that was very important" (Crocker 1981). A young Grotonian without that special relationship with masters or with classmates would feel out of place indeed. Playing on a team proved a better alternative than being a solitary figure in the library! It remained a moot point, however, for no prospective young enrollee "would have

7. See Ashburn 1934, 185–93, for names in each graduating class of Groton's first fifty years.

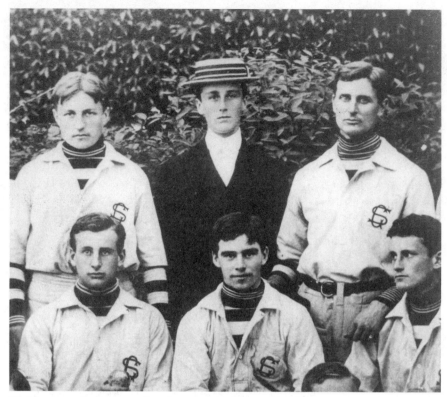

12. Not every Groton boy played on a team. A young Franklin D. Roosevelt, in suit and straw hat, served as manager of the baseball team in 1899. Courtesy of the Franklin D. Roosevelt Library, Hyde Park, New York.

gone to Groton if he were to ask for a special exemption from sports-playing" (Wright 1981).

One enrolled at Groton knowing full well that being involved in sports constituted part of his education. As Sedgwick saw it, "To make a school 'tick,' organized and compulsory athletics are regarded as a prime essential. Of course the normal boy . . . dotes upon them" (Sedgwick 1946, 70). As Groton grew during its first decade and a half, more boys reported for football than could be handled effectively through just a school team and two or three subordinate elevens. It became evident that a change needed to be made in order to satisfy all boys. In 1901 an editorialist complained in the *Grotonian*, a monthly journal, "Of late years sufficient interest has not been taken in the play of the lower elevens. The older boys have not coached; the younger boys have not played their hardest, so that this year the necessity of a change of system has been evident to everyone" (*Grotonian*, Oct. 1901). To ensure a place for everyone in games, Peabody, along with student sport leaders, formed a club system. Every boy became a member of a club, which then sponsored a sufficient number of teams to include all.

In 1901 two football clubs were formed, the Monadnock and the Wachusett, similar to the St. Paul's system. The names derived from two distant small mountains that loomed to the west and northwest of campus. Leaders of the school team, often referred to as the varsity, donated time as coaches. Three teams comprised the makeup per club. By matching the Monadnock first eleven against the Wachusett first team, the second teams against each other, and likewise the third elevens, each club amassed points for victories. By season's end, the club that attained the highest number of points gained the school championship (*Grotonian*, Oct. 1901). It appears that baseball did not originally incorporate such a system, apparently because baseball and crew both took place during the spring, thereby splitting the student body and reducing the number of aspirants for each sport. Later on, however, both sports did become part of the club system. Occasionally, enthusiasm among Grotonians for golf and tennis during the spring resulted in school tournaments. Stellar performers occupied a special place in the makeup of the compulsory sport system. They found their niche as members of the school team (varsity), whose schedule of games included those with other schools.

And so it was. Peabody had his school moving in the direction he envisioned; involvement of the entire student body in football gladdened the heart of the rector because he thought the game did the most in developing those traits associated with being "manly." To Peabody, football proved "a great power" in character development. "For when a boy is playing fairly, playing hard, keeping his temper whatever the score may be, and playing for his side he is getting lessons in honesty, courage, self-control and unselfishness, and these lessons may have as much power for good upon life as the teaching of the school room." Besides all of that, football served as an excellent conversation piece. The gridiron and its accompanying "heroes" provided preferable topics to meditate upon and to discuss, compared to other appealing but "less virile" subjects (Peabody, n.d., 10–11). Peabody had more faith in "a football player than a non-football player, just as the boys did" (Ashburn 1967, 100). It was no wonder that Peabody encouraged and almost mandated that the entire student body play football.

Peabody did not forget what lay at the heart of sports, namely fun, although he would not have likely used that term. Instead he described sport as being recreational. In a 1925 annual report to the trustees, concerned about overemphasis in athletics and the "exaggerated importance of winning," he pointed out that, "When games lose the element of recreation and enjoyment as they have done for some years now in the university, the time for reorganization seems to have arrived" (Peabody, Headmaster's Reports, vol. 2). His concern that sport remain a fun-filled activity reminded many of its true nature. But Peabody walked a tight line between the eager sport-loving boy and those who found games a depressing experience. Sedgwick experienced such a life at Groton. Yet Peabody liked him and trusted him, later bringing him back to Groton as a master and in time a long-serving member of the board of trustees (Sedgwick 1946, 68).

More than any previous headmaster with the exception of Frederick Gunn, the rector stayed in touch with athletics when his own playing days ended. He regularly either bicycled or rode his horse around the playing field to observe practices and games. The young aspirants, student coaches, and masters no doubt played enthusiastically when the headmaster watched their efforts and performances.

Gymnasia and Indoor Exercise

Peabody also realized that when the football season ended, suitable means needed to be undertaken to continue physical activity. Wintertime proved to be a challenge in maintaining a level of fitness as well as being entertained in fun-like activities among the Grotties. So Peabody had a gymnasium of sorts built. If he intended to hold to his promise that attention to the physical ranked high on his list of priorities, then a gymnasium was necessary. Unfortunately, the original barn-like building that had been used as a gymnasium burned down in March of 1886, in Groton's second year. Through the generosity of Augustus Hemenway, a new structure was also finished in 1886 (Ashburn 1967, 89). It housed not only daily calisthenic sessions but also daily chapel and Sunday church services. Groton had increased its student ranks to fifty, necessitating two separate classes to carry out the daily exercise regimen (Ashburn 1934, 26, 33).

When the enrollment climbed to more than 100 students, it became evident the school needed a new gymnasium to accommodate the burgeoning student body. Peabody noted in December of 1900 that the present facility was not only too small but also the ventilation so inadequate "that a great part of the benefit which should be derived from calisthenics is lost." Thus, at the December meeting of the board of trustees in 1901, Peabody's report introduced a plan for a new building at the "cost of about $50,000 plus $15,000 as a permanent fund for the maintenance of the plant" (Peabody, Headmaster's Reports, vol. 1). Again, through the help of Hemenway, the erection of a gymnasium took place in

1902–3. When completed and put into use, the rector reported to his trustees, "The new gymnasium proved thoroughly satisfactory" (Peabody, Headmaster's Reports, vol. 1). The wintertime hiatus from outdoor sports had been solved with the gymnasium. Eventually winter activity would include intramural basketball and hockey, as well as indoor track and "gym team" events (Ashburn 1934, 36).

But the task of finding a suitable director of the gymnasium proved to be a continuing ordeal. Several directors of the gymnasium programs came and went. Finally, Peabody found his man in Albert Cross. The rector reported to the trustees in early December of 1906,

> We have at last discovered a Physical Instructor who is thoroughly equipped in the science of his special work. The relief which Mr. Cross has brought to the Head Master in taking more complete oversight of the physical condition under which the boys live, and in organizing the calisthenics and gymnastics of the school is so great as to excite in the Head Master's heart a sense of lively gratitude to the gentleman, who by his handsome contribution, made it possible for us to engage this instructor.[8] (Peabody, Headmaster's Reports, vol. 1)

But after six years Cross left to be replaced by William Jacomb, who then stayed until 1933. That part of the curriculum that had worried Peabody for years prior to 1906 was adequately tended to by Cross and Jacomb over a period of twenty-seven years. With this phase of the curriculum safely in the hands of qualified masters, Peabody gained time to attend to athletics and its relationship to Groton ideals.

School Teams, Schedules, and Rules

In the beginning the varsity or school teams in football and baseball comprised the main ingredients of the sport program, although rowing and tennis soon appeared. Fives, a transplanted English game, emerged at a later date when courts became available. In keeping with Peabody's philosophy, sports began the same year the school opened; opponents were eagerly sought out, and faculty played side-by-side with the boys. Schedules with other schools expanded quickly.

Similar to the initial beginnings of sport at boarding schools of earlier times, the playing of football initially took place spontaneously. Gradually school teams evolved out of these mass games. Under the captaincy and leadership of George

---

8. Doug Brown, Groton master and archivist, believes the "gentleman" Peabody referred to was E. H. Harriman, railroad magnate and father of Groton student W. Averill Harriman, later a well-known government servant.

Rublee, Groton's first graduate, a baseball team emerged as the first sports aggregation. In the spring of 1885, just months after the school opened, Rublee's group played five games, three against Lawrence Academy, one against a pickup team from the village, and one against a pickup team from Harvard. Groton managed only one victory, against Lawrence. The following fall in the school's second year, Billings, the only master to captain a school team at Groton, organized the first football team. Only one game took place and that against Hopkinson School, located in Boston. The Grotonians began their long history of football with a defeat, apparently even with Peabody in the lineup.[9]

In baseball the following spring, the nine played only five games again, four against a pickup group from the Groton community and one against Cambridge Theological Seminary, Peabody's alma mater. The team broke even, winning two (including the seminary), losing two, and tying one. Not until the third year did the baseball team meet another boarding school on the diamond, that being St. Mark's. From there on, the Groton baseball managers, certainly with the approval of Peabody, gradually expanded the schedule, at first with a number of independent nines such as "The Gentlemen of Boston," "The Puritans," "Cuban Giants," picked teams from nearby Ayer and Groton Village, and various aggregations from Harvard and other private schools. By 1891 the Grotonians played ten games; from that time on the schedule hovered around nine to fifteen games per season, weather permitting.

In Groton's second football season Peabody permitted an expanded four-game schedule. As with Phillips Andover and Phillips Exeter, an opening game with the Harvard Freshmen was arranged. The series only continued for three years as the Crimson first-year men completely overwhelmed the Grotonians in each game. After the Harvard defeat in 1886, the Grotties won their first football game, defeating Roxbury Latin. The taste of victory inspired the eleven to wins over St. Mark's and Hopkinson.

The St. Mark's game marked the beginning of a long-standing rivalry between the two schools, which continues today. In the initial game, William Thayer, fresh out of theological training and a first-year Groton faculty member, scored the first touchdown and Peabody the second. A third master, Billings, also played as Groton went on to a victory. Historians of both schools described Thayer as "very lively" and Peabody, "very large" (Ashburn 1934, 102; Benson 1925, 97). In order to preserve neutrality, the game took place at Lancaster, a village located

---

9. For a complete list of athletic opponents and scores for Groton's first fifty years, see Ashburn 1934, 202–17.

about midway between Groton and Southborough. The victory proved to be an auspicious one for the Grotonians, because St. Mark's had fielded a football team for several years previously. But efforts to continue the game on an annual basis ran into a snag. St. Mark's football manager objected to the practice that Groton pursued — masters playing in school team contests.

St. Mark's had joined a newly established Interscholastic Athletic Association, the earliest of its kind among boarding schools, composed of Hopkinson, Roxbury Latin, and St. Mark's. Their rules forbade tutors playing on football and baseball teams. Because Groton refused to recognize the edict, according to Albert Benson (St. Mark's 1888), no Groton-St. Mark's game took place in 1887. The advantage Groton held with the niftiness and power of the Thayer-Peabody tandem rankled the St. Markers. As in the Andover-Exeter rivalry, dissension within the ranks of the opposing parties tainted the relationship between the two schools, something that distressed Peabody.[10] However, in 1888 the series resumed with masters playing, but under certain restrictions. No master from either team could play if he weighed more than 150 pounds! This ruled out Peabody. Moreover, only two masters could play and no varsity men could play. In baseball no master could pitch (Benson 1925, 98; Ashburn 1934, 102–3).

For some unknown reason Peabody insisted that all contests with other schools, except for the St. Mark's games, be played at Groton. Lancaster remained the site of annual St. Mark's-Groton games through 1890. After the 1891 cancellation, the teams began to alternate locations beginning in 1892 at Groton. Interestingly enough, Peabody served as an umpire or timekeeper at a majority of the games. Yet serving in such a role would not have seemed to pose a conflict of interest to Peabody. His sense of fairness and rules was such that, in the words of George Martin, a 1906 Groton graduate, "If he [Peabody] had been attacked by a thug he would have observed the Marquis of Queensberry rules" (Martin 1944, 162). Officials conducted the game without pay, and to do otherwise would have lent a sense of professionalism, an attitude Peabody abhorred. "He saw no reason why a member of our faculty couldn't officiate," said Wright (1981). Home-field advantage apparently mattered little to Peabody. For him there was no question but that visitors would be treated fair and square.

As the years passed, Groton carried out a varied schedule of games. Other

10. The Groton-St. Mark's football series experienced only two more interruptions. They occurred in 1891, because of the death of the daughter of St. Mark's headmaster, William Peck, and in 1918, due to World War I. Thus, along with the Andover-Exeter rivalry, the Groton-St. Mark's series ranks as one of the longest in secondary school football history.

boarding schools dominated the list of opponents, but private day schools were also included. A long string of games with Boston Latin and Boston English high schools took place regularly over the first fifty years. Also, games with the Harvard Freshmen occurred on a regular basis. Many times school football teams, in the company of Peabody and other masters, traveled to watch Harvard and Yale teams, especially the Harvard-Yale game. Invariably, they went to watch ex-Grotonians play.

The school crew, beginning in 1905 with its first race against an off-campus opponent, the Harvard Freshmen, did not race against an opponent away from Groton's home base on the Nashua River until 1923. Few nearby boarding schools sponsored rowing "eights," forcing the crew managers to schedule races against such opponents as Union Boat Club, Harvard Freshmen, Harvard Second Freshmen, M.I.T. Freshmen, and "Gentlemen of New England." Most years the Grotonians included two outside opponents per season and once staged three races (1908). Because all races took place at Groton, the only explanation for the paucity of matches with outside crews might be the cost of transportation and the somewhat difficult means of transporting a shell to Groton.

One sport that never reached acceptable status despite the longtime agitation for its adoption was hockey. According to Ashburn, Peabody never thought it a good idea for interschool athletics to be "unduly emphasized in all three terms" (Ashburn 1934, 121). Wright affirmed the rector's position about overemphasis on sports. "Athletics must never be allowed to become the tail which wagged the dog!" he wrote. "His list of priorities was clear. The spirit, the mind, and the body—all exceedingly important—but important in that order" (Wright 1982). Thus, hockey remained dormant during Peabody's years, except for "pickup" games on the ice of nearby ponds whenever suitable weather prevailed.[11]

By the turn of the century, Groton football and baseball teams played full schedules. The Constitution of the Groton School Athletic Committee, adopted in 1903, placed the sports program on an organized plane. Significantly, despite Peabody's aggressive role in the earlier years, he had now stepped aside in order for the boys themselves to take more control in the management of their teams. The constitution required the membership on a team of a master, as an adviser, but ap-

11. The next headmaster held the same belief as Peabody. Doug Brown, Groton master and archivist, said that in his student days, he had heard then-Headmaster John Crocker say, on more than one occasion, that making hockey and basketball major sports would place undue emphasis on athletics.

parently not necessarily Peabody. Members included the football captain, the baseball captain, the boats captain, the captain of the gymnasium, the secretary and treasurer (who also acted as chairman), and the advisory member (*Grotonian* 1903, 219–20). This change does not imply that the rector abdicated the attention that he had devoted to athletics throughout the school's formative years. But he now had an enlarged school and additional responsibilities.

Peabody and Coaching

Not only did Peabody think one could not run a school for boys without athletics, he also thought you could not survive without loyal and dedicated masters. In order to carry out the objectives of the school he needed a united front, men who not only upheld scholarship and morality but who also liked to intermingle with the lads on the playing field as coaches. They were the *triple threats*, a term Fred Harrison used in describing Andover masters, beginning in the twentieth century (Harrison 1983, 226). Speaking to the Harvard Teacher's Association in 1906, Peabody clarified, "If it is important that there should be honesty in the class-room it is equally necessary that there should be honesty on the playground and the masters of schools are responsible for the athletic tone of their schools just as much as they are for the ethical tone, or for what we call in a narrow way the moral tone" (Peabody 1906, 4). As late as 1934, Peabody reaffirmed publicly what he thought about hired professionals. At the opening of the school year, he told the faculty, "We cannot emphasize too strongly the value of our boys being instructed by the masters rather than by professionals" (Peabody 1934b, 5). Finally, in 1935, Peabody reiterated the importance of the masters versus the professional coach, on the occasion of being awarded an honorary doctor of humane letters. Address-ing the annual convocation and the Board of Regents of the University of the State of New York, he asserted, "The quality of an intelligent amateur in games will come to the rescue when we are threatened, as we often are, by the standards and techniques of professional coaches" (Peabody 1935, 13). It would be a large order for any headmaster to find a cadre of men who could fill these qualifications. Yet Peabody managed to gather about him a faculty that remained faithful through long periods of time.

Peabody encountered one of his first differences with another headmaster over the conduct of athletics, centering on the use of professional coaches. Of all people, the conflict occurred with Thayer, the former Groton master who took over the headmastership of St. Mark's in 1894. After five consecutive defeats at the hands of Groton, Thayer, apparently from his vantage point as a former, successful football player, perceived that St. Markers needed more expert coaching. So he wrote the rector early in the fall of 1906 that he planned to employ a professional coach. In his December report to the trustees about the controversy, Peabody noted that the game with St. Mark's that fall had been played "under somewhat peculiar circumstances":

> Although this was a departure from the agreement which had existed between the two schools, we decided to allow the match to take place. We realized that the St. Mark's boys had been constantly defeated, and that it seemed to them important that they should make a fresh start under new conditions created by the changed rules governing the game. Before the match was played I proposed to Mr. Thayer that hereafter if either school should decide to have a professional teacher in athletics it should withdraw from the competition with the other school, and this is now the condition under which future contests will be carried on.
>
> The result of the match indicated that professional instruction is not always effective in bringing out a winning team. (Peabody, Headmaster's Reports, vol. 1)

Even with a professional coach at the helm, St. Mark's went down to defeat again in 1906 at Groton. However, the St. Markers had learned a great deal about playing football; at least Peabody thought so. He further reported to the trustees that the Southborough masters and boys had upgraded their skills and knowledge about football as a result of the experiment and that from then on they would not rely on a professional coach (Peabody, Headmaster's Reports, vol. 1). Whether Peabody's position and logic regarding his reliance upon in-house coaching influenced other headmasters cannot be substantiated.

To what extent Peabody's precepts affected other school leaders does not unfold easily. One vehicle that offered opportunities for the expression of ideas opened up with the formation of the Headmasters' Association in April 1893. Leaders from both private and public schools in New England and the mid-Atlantic region convened in Boston for the initial gathering. Peabody wrote to his lifelong friend, Julius W. Atwood, that it "is calculated to have a good deal of effect upon secondary education" (Ashburn 1967, 110). The association was also another venue by which Peabody became known. As his reputation as a school leader grew, other headmasters, some from beyond New England, sought his advice.

Schoolmasters from Virginia Visit Peabody

In 1897 tiny Woodberry Forest School, near Orange, Virginia, was facing a crisis of continuance. The founder, Captain Bob Walker, sought counsel from Dr.

Launcelot Blackford, then a longtime headmaster at nearby Episcopal High School in Alexandria, Virginia. Blackford advised Walker to travel north and visit with Peabody at Groton School. Captain Bob took his son, J. Carter Walker, newly graduated from the University of Virginia, and traveled to Groton. What he and Peabody discussed is not known. But Peabody would certainly have talked about his philosophy for educating Groton boys. After their meeting, Captain Bob and his son returned to Virginia and launched, in effect, the second beginning of the school, with J. Carter Walker at the helm for the next fifty years. The Virginia school, which may owe its continuance, in part, to Peabody's advice and encouragement, deserves a brief recounting here, because it originated in similar fashion to and in the same decade as Groton.

Woodberry Forest began as a family affair, much like Peabody's school. Located in the Piedmont section of Virginia, a residence built decades before by the brother of James Madison, the fourth president of the United States, became home to Captain Bob in 1872. Two years later he married. In the next decade, the couple produced six sons. By the time the oldest son, J. Carter, reached school age, Captain Bob faced the problem of educating his brood. "The question of their schooling was one which eventually turned a simple family history into the fascinating saga of a great educational institution" (Norfleet 1955, 4–7).

September of 1889, when Jay Thompson Brown came to Woodberry Forest, marked the official beginning of the school. As the small enterprise entered the final decade of the nineteenth century, Captain Bob felt the growing pains the school had experienced. In 1892–93 twenty-four students were enrolled. Captain Bob's six sons were adequately educated, with the oldest, J. Carter, attending the University of Virginia. By 1896, three teachers and fifty-three students comprised the school, and the first catalogue named it Woodberry Forest High School (Norfleet 1997, 21; 1955, 10–11).

Little athletic activity had taken place heretofore because of the small enrollment. In addition, and unlike Peabody, Captain Bob had no English public school background in sports. However, the boys themselves had found place and time for baseball, in accord with the spirit of the time and their energy. In the academic year of 1890–91, the school sponsored its first baseball team. With the help of students and others, a baseball diamond was raked into place. Bats for the team were homemade out of hickory grown near the campus. Locust Dale Academy, only five miles or so from Woodberry, provided the opposition. The Woodberry team won one of the three games played. From this seemingly inauspicious beginning, baseball picked up the following year and continued. Before long, the school was playing annual games with the University of Virginia, although the university's team considered them practice games. As well, Woodberry Forest also played baseball against Episcopal High School in Alexandria, Virginia, a school fifty years older and seventy miles to the north, a much further distance than the thirty-mile trip to the university at Charlottesville (Norfleet 1997, 17, 26). To find competition, thus, the Woodberry Forest boys had to travel much further than did boys from Groton or most of the New England boarding schools.

The second and third baseball games with Episcopal, played on April 23 and May 28, 1898, go down as notable ones. Much like Peabody playing football for Groton, playing first base for Woodberry Forest was J. Carter. Playing third base for Episcopal was teacher-coach Archibald "Flick" Hoxton (WFA Baseball Archives, File 37).[12] But nontraditional students also played. An "old boy" from Woodberry Forest recollected that, in the later 1890s, games with Locust Dale were "made up of masters and a few 'ringers'—possibly taking spelling only" (Dandridge, n.d.)!

Football also appeared on the scene about the same time. A field, laid out in a nearby area, became the site of future games. The first football game played by Woodberry likely occurred in 1891 with Bethel Military Academy as the opponent.[13] Thus, when Captain Bob sought the counsel of Peabody in 1897, inclusion of baseball and football at Woodberry Forest provided common points of interest.

At the time of their meeting, Captain Bob had lost his main teacher and had to decide whether or not to go ahead and expand the school or forget the enterprise. He eventually resolved the situation by having his son, J. Carter, take over as headmaster. Their visit with Peabody had proved helpful. In January of 1898, Captain Bob wrote to Peabody, thanking him for the visit and requesting the recommendation of a Groton graduate to teach at Woodberry Forest and also a copy of Peabody's rules for Groton. In succeeding years, Woodberry Forest expanded and succeeded as a result of its "second beginning" in 1897; J. Carter developed a professional kinship with Peabody that lasted the remainder of their lives and brought Walker into the Headmasters' Association (Norfleet 1997, 32–35; 1955, 17–18). The imprint of J. Carter Walker on Woodberry Forest was noted at the

12. Hoxton eventually succeeded to a thirty-four-year career as headmaster of Episcopal High School, following Launcelot Blackford. J. Carter Walker served more than fifty years as headmaster at Woodberry Forest.

13. In 1901, Woodberry Forest and Episcopal High School met on the gridiron for the first time. A century of *continuous* football competition between the two schools was celebrated in 2001.

time of his retirement in 1948 by the *Richmond Times Dispatch*: "Arnold of Rugby never stamped his personality on the boys of that famous school any more indelibly than J. Carter Walker has stamped his upon those at Woodberry Forest" (Norfleet 1955, 31).

The Subject of Sexual Evils: Peabody and Walker

The rector deftly exercised a balancing act between the spirit, mind, and body in leading Groton. His idea of a small family school with himself as the reigning father gave credibility to the words *in loco parentis*. A good father would be concerned about his son's health, his character development, his sense of morality, and his purity of mind. But Peabody had an advantage over real fathers. He could strengthen all of these traits through athletics. In a small school he could implement a program of compulsory athletics that would succeed, for he had his students on campus twenty-four hours a day.

Furthermore, his use of athletics as an educational tool rested on his belief that games-playing maintained a wholesome mood on the campus. As in the English public school, the threat of sexual misconduct, usually masturbation, occupied the minds of Victorian headmasters. The countermeasure to this unwanted behavior focused on providing a full schedule of daily school activities, culminating in athletics for two to three hours prior to suppertime. At the end of a hard day, Grotonians were ready for bed. As Sedgwick observed, "Two hours of football practice will take the starch out of the highest spirits. It may dull a boy's intellectual capacities, but it makes him docile as a sheep. Exhausted boys are good boys; that is no secret in any dormitory" (Sedgwick 1946, 70–71).

Whether or not Peabody preached this view to J. Carter Walker is unknown. But Walker espoused similar views. Speaking to a conference of school principals at the University of Virginia in June 1908, Walker titled his talk, "The Fight for Purity in the School." [14] Walker's opening indicates that he held views almost identical with those of Peabody on the importance of morality:

14. That Walker was far from unique in his view can be verified by Peter Stearns's concise assertion, "Victorian culture severely proscribed male masturbation." In Stearns's description, "Social democrats in Germany, cereal manufacturers in the Midwest, and the whole medical establishment raged against the evil consequences of masturbation, which was said to cause diseases ranging from blindness to insanity to acne. The belief . . . was more widely and intensely expressed than ever before" (Stearns 1979, 92). For a summary analysis of the conflicting sexual messages encountered by young boys and men, see Rotundo 1993, 119–28. Although Rotundo's evidence comes from middle-

Gentlemen, our subject this afternoon is our responsibility as teachers for the moral instruction of the boys in our schools. I shall not dwell, in the few minutes allotted to me, upon the vital importance of personal purity as the basis of character. We all know that out of the heart are the issues of life. But I doubt if many of us realize how gigantic is the fight to which we are called. On this point let me say at least this: my study of this question and my experience with boys have both led me to the conviction that almost no boy escapes entirely the sin of self-abuse. (Walker 1908, 1)

For Walker, as for Peabody, one way to combat such moral evil was through athletic participation. Walker places athletics under the larger heading of building school spirit:

The development of a pride in the school, of what we call school spirit, is natural, and under favorable conditions may become intense. In a boarding school this sense of the corporate life of the school is the chief agency of moral instruction, a force greater than the influence of the head master or of any group of masters who would attempt to work independently of it. Such development is, I suppose, not possible in a day school. But it has been proved in the English day schools that the corporate life of the school community can become a powerful instrument of moral education. The development of a strong school spirit fuses the individuals of the community into one compact, corporate whole, with common opinions and common feelings. Individual standards give way to the common standards, and the school comes to have a moral atmosphere of its own. (Walker 1908, 8–9)

Among the agencies for developing school spirit was athletics. Competition with other schools, in Walker's opinion, could be made "to stimulate a generous rivalry" that would, in turn, strengthen the spirit of the competing schools (Walker 1908, 8–9).

Despite such an idealistic notion of how athletic rivalry could be developed, Walker would find within two years that he, along with Hoxton of Episcopal High School, had to combat the evil of gambling within the ranks of their respective students. Of course, the purity of college football had been a matter of national, as well as local, concern a few years earlier.

---

class men, it seems highly likely that boarding school boys would have come into contact with these prevalent beliefs.

The Subject of Football Evils: Peabody and Roosevelt

By the early twentieth century, the status of college football had bothered Peabody for some time. It dismayed him to witness Harvard and Yale football games and see all lifelong moral lessons vanish as cheating and brutality prevailed. Peabody's experience at Groton had proved to him that carefully supervised play and enforced regulations could bring out the best in boys playing football. He explained his policies to his board of trustees in a report dated December 13, 1905:

> In view of the controversy concerning Foot-ball which is being waged so vigorously at the present time it may be interesting to place on record a brief account of our experience with the game at Groton. *It has been the most important sport in the eyes of the boys ever since the school was founded.* The number of serious accidents which have occurred has been exceedingly small. *There has never been a boy ruled off the field for foul play.* [Sentences in italics underscored by Peabody.] Schools which in the early days were inclined to take advantage of us, and to play an ungentlemanly game, now send teams to meet our boys in a spirit of friendly rivalry. While there have been many instances of the work of individuals being interfered with by foot-ball[,] the requirement that a boy shall attain a certain average in his studies during the foot-ball season has incited the majority of the boys to unusual effort, and the life of the school, both intellectual and moral, is generally a little finer during the foot-ball season than at other times. (Peabody, Headmaster's Reports, vol. 1)

Yet other school leaders were also upset at the football evils they saw. As a result, in the fall of 1905, Peabody penned a directive to President Theodore Roosevelt at the request of the Church School Masters.[15] Peabody knew the president well because the Roosevelt boys attended Groton, and the president had spoken at Groton's twentieth-anniversary Prize Day celebration in May of 1904. Apparently appointed as a committee of one, the association's motion asked that Peabody "take such steps as he deemed feasible toward bringing about reform in foot-ball." So he did. In the same December 1905 report to the trustees, he wrote, "In accordance with this vote I suggested to the President of the United States that he should call a meeting of the coaches of Harvard, Yale and Princeton Universities to discuss the whole question with them. At this conference Mr. Roosevelt laid es-

---

15. The masters of church schools in New England and the middle states met at Groton for the first time in 1904. They came at the invitation of and as guests of Peabody and Groton School. See Peabody's 1904 report to the trustees (Peabody, Headmaster's Reports, vol. 1).

13. President Theodore Roosevelt spoke at Groton's twentieth anniversary in May 1904. Peabody, in bowler hat, is driving the carriage. Courtesy of Groton School Archives.

pecial [*sic*] stress upon the necessity of honest coaching, and there is reason to hope that this is the first step in a thorough-going reform in our athletics" (Peabody, Headmaster's Reports, vol. 1).

Peabody had hoped for too much, of course. It may have been a first step, but it was only a halting one. According to sport historian Ronald A. Smith, the overriding desire for victory prevented any progress toward fair play. The mild statement sent by Peabody in behalf of the Church School Masters' Association failed to change attitudes and carried little clout.[16]

The rector may have been naive in thinking that Roosevelt had the power to exercise change in the growing competitiveness of university athletics. He also may have believed that coaches could uphold honest play just as his own football

16. Norfleet asserts that Virginia's General Assembly seriously considered outlawing football toward the end of the 1890s. They were concerned, as were many in the country, with the brutality and injuries in the game at that time. Norfleet writes that testimonials by Joe Walker, brother of J. Carter Walker, and others dissuaded the General Assembly from taking action. She gives no account of Joe Walker's testimony (Norfleet 1997, 27). For a more detailed account of the college football coaches conference, see Smith 1988, 193–94; Rader 1983, 140–42; and Lewis 1969, 720.

coach, Guy Ayrault, did. In the words of Peabody before his board, "The standard of fair play which I believe to characterize our boys is due to the teaching of Mr. Ayrault, who has coached our Eleven for many years. *If the same honesty had been insisted upon by the coaches in our Universities the story of foot-ball in the colleges would be a very different thing from what it is today.*" [Sentence in italics underscored by Peabody.][17] He went on to say that the root cause of the unsavory environment surrounding athletics stemmed from the deceitful instruction of coaches. Where teaching occurred at a high level of integrity, then games became the "greatest possible value to the education of our youth" (Peabody, Headmaster's Reports, vol. 1).

As a frequent spokesman for the headmasters, Peabody had a stake in the growing debate over the deceitfulness associated with college football. Writing to Yale coach Walter Camp in November of 1909, Peabody affirmed, "In my work at Groton I am convinced that football is of profound importance for the moral even more than for the physical development of the boys" (Ashburn 1967, 195). Peabody went on to say that football contained the element critical to making soldiers, and thus was necessary for the country. However, he acknowledged that the game had to be made more safe, as well as honest. To this end he carried on correspondence with Camp about rules and even about regulating cheering so that the opposing team could hear signals. Conscience, not winning, was key. "If the cheerleaders could be instructed to lead the cheering at the proper times—that is, during the intermissions and when a good play on their side has been made, or when their side needed encouragement,—and to avoid interference with the signals of the other side, I am sure that we should all feel clearer in our consciences" (Peabody 1911; Camp 1909). Peabody and other headmasters were concerned because their schoolboys tended to emulate the questionable play of Harvard, Yale, Princeton, and other college teams. Peabody, they thought, could do something about the scandalous conditions surrounding the university and college game. He could not, of course. However, his intervention set in motion a series of meetings involving Roosevelt, Camp, and leading football rules-makers of the day, plus Harvard and Princeton coaches and representatives. Eventually, the debate over rules led to the subsequent formation of the National Collegiate Athletic Association (Smith 1988, 202–8).

17. Ayrault became Groton's first permanent coach of varsity football in 1896 and remained in that role until 1923. Ashburn says that under Ayrault "a great game became a classroom wherein values were taught of high worth" (Ashburn 1934, 60, 105, 109).

But Roosevelt had reminded listeners at Harvard in 1907 of the model that boarding schools had put forth in the conduct of schoolboy football. "The preparatory schools are able to keep football clean," he declared, "and to develop the right spirit in the players" (Moore 1967, 61). Perhaps in the long run Peabody had won his point. He had convinced his friend that football could be played honestly, an act that all headmasters applauded.

Influence of Endicott Peabody

No headmaster up to or during his time had espoused so much about athletics as did Peabody. The fact is not surprising, for no other headmaster combined the personal athletic background, the English public school training, and the physical fitness and muscular Christianity practice that Peabody brought to Groton. How much influence did he carry beyond the Groton campus? Some headmasters took note of the all-embracing characteristic of Groton athletics. In 1899, Randall Spaulding, principal at Montclair High School, wrote to the secretary of the Headmasters' Association, "In the matter of athletics, the question was raised what to do with the large number of boys who are mere lookers-on at the games. We should aim to induce all to participate. The Groton school was cited as a fine example of athletic organization, a visitor having found eleven football teams practising [sic] at one time" (Spaulding 1899). Wright had no doubt about the influence that his headmaster held in educational circles. He claimed, "If there were fifty people in a room and he walked in you would know that someone of unusual stature, not simply physical, someone with an unusual stature had arrived. He had that kind of presence. Now if he attended any kind of gathering of educators, be they teachers, headmasters, public school superintendents or principals, when Dr. Peabody spoke, people listened" (Wright 1981). Wright's viewpoint was reinforced by the president of the Headmasters' Association at the time of Peabody's death. In a letter to the membership in May of 1945, President Perry Dunlap Smith wrote, "Let us hope that with the loss of such a stalwart leader as Endicott Peabody, our sole remaining Charter Member, we may be spared further grievous losses in the years ahead. . . . There were giants in those days indeed" (Smith 1945).

These testimonies suggest that Peabody's messages about the conduct of sport had reached the ears of numerous schoolmen; certainly many educational leaders had had the opportunity of listening to him. For example, Peabody received a thank-you letter from Teachers College Columbia University in February 1908: "It means a great deal to these teachers gathered here from all parts of the world and from all walks in life to hear the men who are successfully solving the large problems in education and setting standards for us to follow" (Stevens 1908). Frequently, he had addressed such groups at Columbia, Harvard, and Dartmouth. New York City and Boston teachers' groups scheduled him as a speaker. Local teachers' societies in Massachusetts such as those at Gardner, Springfield, and Worcester invited him to talk. He also appeared before the National Collegiate Athletic Association in 1913, speaking on the American and English ideals of sport.[18] This array of public appearances extended into his latter years in the 1930s.

Especially before groups of teachers, Peabody reminded them of their obligation to uphold character-building. At a conference on elementary and secondary schools held at Dartmouth in 1905, he spoke on developing character in the school and the responsibility of teachers in carrying out this mandate. At the Harvard Teachers' Association, he addressed the group on the bad aspects but also the benefits of football. At an Episcopal church gathering in 1907, he asserted that Groton's organized games constituted an "integral part" of school life and the school would do poorly without them. Before the Headmasters' Association, he recounted his experiences at Cheltenham, where games "educated the judgment and will" and created a desire for fair play. Before teachers' groups and college conclaves, it would not be unusual for Peabody to speak of the rampant dishonesty that coursed through college football. What educationists in other audiences heard was that sport enhanced morality and the "moral tone" of the school.[19]

There can be no doubt that if sport indeed could aid in the development of character, Peabody came closest to carrying out this mission. In his memorial eulogy for the Headmasters' Association, Exeter's Lewis Perry asserted, "The three fundamental principles for which Groton has stood in the past fifty years are practice of religion, training in character, and sound scholarship. All these stem from Mr. Peabody himself. He represented all three" (Perry 1945). Leaders at boarding schools that emerged during Peabody's early Groton years and at other existing boarding schools typically espoused the same precept as Peabody did—namely character development through athletics. But the Groton headmaster led the way.

18. The address was subsequently printed in the *American Physical Education Review*. See Peabody 1914.

19. Examples taken from Peabody's sermons and speeches in Groton School Archives.

8

Ringers and Other Skulduggery

UP THROUGH THE CIVIL WAR, the issue of fair play in schoolboy sports had not emerged as a problem. Boys competed among themselves, hammering out rules as they played. Nor did they concern themselves with legalities about who got to play the games and who did not. Especially with the introduction of the club system as occurred at St. Paul's, the program flourished because almost every boy had membership in one of the sport clubs. This in-house type of competition had no need to focus on eligibility of players. Nor were audiences an issue. Neither numbers nor intensity of fans caused problems. Little was at stake compared with what would develop when school rivalries flourished.

With the contesting of sports between two schools, the picture changed dramatically. A school team meant that the best players from one school competed against the best of another school. When these contests became regular occurrences, rules had to be clear, fair, and detailed. These were not just rules of how the game was played, but rules about who could compete and who could coach. The stakes grew as rivalries flourished. The honor of the school was on the line, especially when contests became a part of rivalry, such as the Andover-Exeter annual clashes or the Groton-St. Mark's contests. Audiences also increased, escalating the stakes. Groton, for example, would charter a train to take all the boys to the St. Mark's game. Several thousand might watch the Phillips schools do battle. The importance of athletics in the culture at large and at colleges and universities also increased audience interest. Not surprisingly, in such a context, some students eventually figured out how expert players, not enrolled as regular students, could be injected into the lineup. Rules of eligibility now became necessary to the conduct of sport.

Although schoolboy newspapers, as well as headmasters, voiced the virtues of sport in moral terms, it should not be surprising that illegalities surfaced. Human vicissitudes could account for some abridgement of rules and generally accepted

140

moral standards. In addition, not all schools operated under the stern and consistent moral leadership of an Endicott Peabody at Groton. Moreover, teenage boys, as a part of their maturation, would inevitably challenge rules to some degree. The available evidence from the boarding schools researched indicates that the following examples of efforts to win at all costs were far from rampant. But the rivalry between Exeter and Andover serves as an early illustration of how winning, at times, became the overriding goal of competition.

Andover-Exeter Rivalry

When sports competition between the two sister institutions began in 1878, what started out as friendly annual games in football and baseball between the two academies turned into a series of ugly episodes. Accusations of chicanery and cheating flew back and forth for a number of years and almost canceled the rivalry. How leaders at the two schools managed the problems interested other headmasters. Had winning become that important? It had.

Student leaders, in their zeal to vanquish, devised means to win that went beyond the implicit rules and objectives of the academies. Fred Harrison, longtime coach and athletic director at Andover, portrays the events and circumstances leading up to serious confrontations, especially in the use of "ringers."[1] An intensity surrounded these annual clashes that reached an importance never before witnessed in schoolboy sports. Local papers, as well as Boston and New York sports writers, covered the contests. The annual Andover-Exeter game in football reached an average attendance as high as 5,000 to 6,000 spectators by the mid- to late 1880s. Baseball games averaged 2,000 spectators. Harrison writes, "It is impossible to overestimate the importance attached to the football and baseball fortunes of the school in those early days. The morale of the academy rose or fell with the successes and failures of those two varsity teams" (Harrison 1983, 77, 90). The same emotion existed on the Exeter campus. The honor of the school was at stake. An editorial writer in the *Phillipian* for October 3, 1885, put the responsibility squarely upon the team. "To the team we would say that upon them devolves the

1. The term *ringer* derives from horse racing. A horse entered fraudulently in a race was called a *ringer*. That is, he resembled another known horse, but the little known "ringer" was of superior ability. By extension, the term has come to mean any athlete with superior talent who is fraudulently competing at a lower level. The men competing as "ringers" for the boarding schools were older, better, and more experienced athletes who were enrolled briefly in school or for only one course. In other words, they were not normal students in age or in curriculum studied (Morris and Morris 1977; Barnhart 1988).

honor of upholding the reputation of the school in athletics, and the measure of that honor will be according as they do their part well and faithfully" *(Phillipian* 1885, no. 2). The heavy emphasis placed upon the fortunes of the football and baseball teams inevitably led to excesses.

Perhaps a harbinger of negative events to come began with alleged improprieties revealed by the *Phillipian.* The student baseball committee in the spring of 1885 attempted to hire a non-Andoverian to pitch for the school team. Students objected to this action, not on the grounds that it was cheating, but on the premise that it would deprive an Andoverian of the opportunity to play on the team! After reconsideration, the committee dropped the idea (Harrison 1983, 85). The next November, another minor scandal struck the Andover campus. The funds of the Athletic Association, under the control of student officers, were depleted. The *Phillipian* broke the news that the Athletic Association had lost two to three hundred dollars, calling it a "dishonor to the school." However, a new Athletic Association soon replaced the derelict one, and eventually monies were replaced. One solution to chronically short treasuries was to charge admission to games, a strategy implemented by the Baseball Association (Harrison 1983, 74; *Phillipian* 1885, no. 8). Honor meant a great deal in the hearts of most prep schoolers at a time when the Victorian ideal of morality and gentlemanly conduct pervaded a large segment of American society.

The lesson to be learned over these events did nothing to deter the intensity that surrounded the rivalry. It became apparent that winning the traditional game, whether it be in football, baseball, or any other sport, symbolized a successful season in the sport at hand. But winning without right principles seemed abhorrent to most athletes. One Andover pundit wrote on the subject in the fall of 1886: "The proper object of school and college athletics should be, not professionalism but education. Professionalism is inconsistent with the line of work in which we are engaged, both in its principles and in its methods, . . .it also tolerates an unscrupulous practice of resorting to trickery in order to more surely accomplish its ends" (Harrison 1983, 79).

What precipitated this outburst resulted from the lack of respect for the rules that the Exeter team had exhibited in the annual football clash that fall. According to the provoked Andover editorialist, the Red (Exeter) team played sixteen men at times instead of eleven, an example of the "unscrupulous Trickery" to which Exeter had resorted. Other tactics also went against the "open, manly dealing," which the Andoverians "ought to expect" from their arch rival. For Exeter also kicked and showered "abuse" on the Blue (Andover) whenever a play went out-of-bounds. As well, the Red team applied trickery to a rule that allowed a team to retain the ball if it lost ten yards. Apparently, the Red quarterback deliberately ran backwards more than ten yards whenever his team failed to advance the required five yards in three downs. According to an 1882 rule, a team had to give up the ball if, after three downs, it had not advanced the ball five yards or given up ten yards (Harrison 1983, 79–80).

Bad feelings between the two schools began to reach ominous levels. The *Exonian* and the *Phillipian* cast barbs and accusations back and forth. The unruly student life at Exeter did not help matters. Beset by a change of administrative heads after Albert Perkins resigned in 1883, the school during the late 1880s and early 1890s was led by a series of men who failed to take charge of disciplining students. Exeter student sport leaders carried on much as they pleased. Finally, in the spring of 1889, the emotionalism surrounding the baseball game at Exeter burst at the seams. The year before, an Andover student, J. H. White, had transferred to Exeter, because Andover "management refused to make him concessions" (Harrison 1983, 86–87). Whether the fact that journeyman White pitched a three-to-two victory over his former teammates caused resentment, or whether the mockery displayed by the Exonians at the Andover team as the latter waited for the homeward-bound train to arrive at the Exeter station precipitated anger is not known. But a melee erupted. In the ensuing skirmish, someone struck a blow to the head of E. G. Coy, the acting Andover principal. Another assailant knocked an Andover boy unconscious. Andover faculty members present managed to disperse the fighting factions. Apparently, no Exeter instructors could be found to help in quelling the riot. Shortly after the Andover party returned home, the faculty informed Exeter authorities that athletic games between the schools had come to an end (Fuess 1917, 456–60).

In the fall of 1889, Andover and Exeter did not play each other in football; it was the first break in their athletic relations since the beginning in 1878. The Andover faculty had put its stamp of disapproval on the Exeter students' behavior in no uncertain terms. Hereafter, faculty intervention in the athletic affairs of Andover teams became a permanent reality. In the future, no important steps in the conduct of Andover athletics would take place without faculty approval.

The fracas culminated in several years of bickering between the two schools, mainly through negative editorials in both school papers. As Claude Fuess pointed out, "The two schools had not learned as yet 'to love the game beyond the prize" (Fuess 1917, 459). The need for adult leadership to set objectives aright was apparent. But in contrast to the steady and continuing leadership of Cecil Bancroft at Andover, Exeter had not enjoyed such stability at its helm after the retirement of Gideon Soule in 1873. Three principals in the following twenty years, against some built-in odds, steered a rudderless ship. As a result, lax manners and morals pervaded the student body. "Exeter had begun to slide," concluded Myron Williams, school historian (Williams 1957, 66).

Seeking someone to put Exeter back on track, the board chose Dr. Walter Q. Scott, a former cavalryman in the Civil War, who, it was thought, would put his military training to work in establishing discipline. Unfortunately, Scott did otherwise. Whenever brawling or rioting occurred, the principal called upon policemen from the town of Exeter to intervene. Friends and alumni of the academy, aghast, saw this as anathema to the tradition of Exeter. For more than 100 years the academy had relied upon the gentlemanly behavior of its students in maintaining its own discipline. In Scott's last days at the academy, however, just prior to his resignation, the riot at the railroad station took place.

During the following months, students from both schools attempted to patch up their differences. From Andover a special committee of three student sport leaders, including Alfred Stearns, who would become Bancroft's successor in 1903, met with a like committee from Exeter. Representatives drafted a proposal, the essence of which stated that both sides would behave themselves and "the students of the home academy, except the members and managers of the athletic team, will not under any circumstances go to the station or follow, or in any way whatsoever molest any of the members of the visiting academy" (Harrison 1983, 93–94). Committee members then presented the proposal to their respective student bodies, who approved. To further illustrate the growing power of the faculty, the proposal then went on to the faculty of each school, who in turn affirmed the document. Thus, in January of 1890, differences appeared to have been settled between the schools. Alas—further complications arose.

A report in a weekly sport tabloid in early 1890 carried the news that Captain White may have manipulated the Exeter admission process; a star baseball catcher who had played professionally had enrolled. Both school newspapers "exchanged the usual insults based on mutual distrust" (Harrison 1983, 95). It was characteristic of the constant bickering and cheating that had overshadowed the Andover-Exeter rivalry the preceding ten years. This latest incident proved to be the last straw. Somehow, the faculties of both academies, probably through appointed committees, assembled and drafted an extensive set of rules to govern the rivalry.

The early accounts of accusations over eligibility centered on certification of players as bona fide students, entitled to membership on school teams. Eligibility acted as the chief vehicle to guarantee fair and equal chances of winning. Steps taken by students to bolster their team's chances of winning through illicit use of athletes who did not attend the school, or who accepted money supplied by student athletic boosters to enroll at Exeter or Andover, raised the ire of faculty members. To enlist ill-prepared but athletically gifted boys to represent the school prompted the joint committee to take action.

In May 1890 the committee released a document, "Rules for the Government of Athletic Contests." Both faculties adopted it, thereby signifying a milestone toward faculty control of athletics. This far-reaching document inaugurated the codification of rules that served to guide the conduct of athletics between the two institutions. It also provided a model for other secondary schools to follow, with detailed emphasis on what characterized a bona fide member of a school team.[2] Fuess explains the motive for the changing attitude in the Andover faculty. "The growing complexity and importance of athletics, and especially the difficulties which arose in connection with the breach between Andover and Exeter in 1889, convinced the Faculty that a somewhat tighter rein was needed" (Fuess 1917, 500).

Despite this affirmation of rules of conduct, incidents and accusations of skulduggery continued to plague the harmony of athletic relations. Peaceful relations existed in 1890–91, but they did not last. Following the annual football game in 1892, new allegations came from the Andover camp, appearing first in the *Andover Townsman*. After two consecutive defeats, Exeter attempted to tip the balance in its favor by enticing four young stalwarts to the New Hampshire school as postgraduates. They proved to be excellent gridders and played significant roles in the 1892 win over Andover, twenty-eight to eighteen. Outraged *Phillipian* writers

2. Regarding eligibility, the document stated: "3. No one shall be allowed to take part in the contests between the two schools: (a) who is not a bona fide member of the school he represents; (b) who has ever received money for playing or teaching any sport or game or who has ever engaged in any sports as a means of livelihood; (c) who receives compensation for his services in athletic games in addition to the expenses necessarily incurred by him in representing his organization in any athletic contest, except that he may have his board paid at a special training table; (d) who has left the school and become a member of any university, college, scientific school or professional school. 4. No one shall be allowed to play in the annual base-ball game *(sic)* who enters either school after the first week of the winter term. 5. The direction of these contests and responsibility for their character shall lie with the two faculties, and all games shall be played under rules approved by the standing committee of the two faculties" (Harrison 1983, 95–97).

accused Exeter of professionalism, declaring that Exeter had brought the four into their academy to play football. They based their case on the fact that three of the four had already left school following the game and the other intended to leave at Christmas time. Stung by these charges, the *Exonian* fought back with accounts that denied any wrongdoing, asserting that all four did exceptional work in the classroom and that the return of graduates for further study did not represent an exception to the rules. All four had exercised a right to participate in the school's activities. A loophole in the 1890 codification of rules had been unearthed. No rule prevented "post graduate" boys from joining sport teams. They were bona fide students! Both faculties then passed revisions to remove the oversight. The revised version of the 1890 document appeared in the school papers for all students to read. The revisions represented the first time that representatives of both faculties quickly acted to exert their power in response to a circumvention of regulations pertaining to athletics (Harrison 1983, 97–99).

Improbable as it may seem, in May of 1893, the *Boston Globe* carried a story that Exeter had a paid player on its baseball team; he had been a member of the "Northampton Pros" team the preceding summer. Andover authorities immediately declared him ineligible to play in the annual game that spring. If Exeter did not remove him from its roster, Andover would refuse to meet the Red on the diamond. The Exeter faculty denied that "Mr. Powers" was guilty and refused to drop him from the team. As a result, Andover canceled the game. Instead, the Blue played the Yale varsity in two games, a first time against Yale, losing both but by respectable scores. To partially atone for the cancellation of the big game with Exeter, the Andover faculty also staged a baseball game for the benefit of the student body. The "marrieds" overcame the "singles" in a slugfest, twenty-four to eighteen. The game gave notice to the students that the faculty, after all, had their best interest at heart by displaying an affirming attitude toward athletics.

At Exeter, the students displayed their anger at the turn of events by conducting a mock funeral service for the canceled baseball game. In a slow funeral march carrying a crude wooden coffin that contained the ball and bat to be used in the game, the players and fellow classmates paraded to an empty lot near the campus where, in a solemn graveside ceremony, they buried the baseball equipment. The battery of the Exeter pitcher and the accused Powers served as pallbearers. The ceremony reenacted the 1865 mock funeral, held when Principal Soule turned down the plea of his students for a game with Andover. Still, it would not be the end of the differences between the Red and the Blue (Harrison 1983, 100–101).

Shortly after the rival football game in the fall of 1893, won by Exeter, the Andover town paper carried a reprint of a story in the *Boston Herald*, headlined, "Exeter Star a Professional." William F. "Pooch" Donovan enrolled at Exeter at the age of twenty-four following his participation in professional races as a sprinter and hurdler. He had been a member of the performing Barnum circus troupe, the story pointed out. The *Herald* reporter who investigated Donovan's career further wrote, "Mr. Donovan is eminently well-qualified to make a successful half-back, but it is hardly in the interest of amateur sport for Exeter Academy to allow a recognized professional athlete to play on her eleven. It is certain that the principal of the school would not countenance any such unsportsmanlike action." Shock waves swept across the Andover campus. The student body met the following Monday morning and heard a negative report by the football manager outlining the growing professionalism at Exeter. He went on to relate how he could not trust the words of his counterpart at the rival school regarding the "legal status of his [Exeter] players." With that the Andover manager introduced a resolution, "That we, the students of Phillips Academy, Andover, indefinitely postpone all further contacts with the Exeter school" (Harrison 1983, 102–3). The students voted unanimously in favor of the motion, apparently with the approval of Principal Bancroft. It would not be surprising if Bancroft thought it fruitless to expect any apology from Principal Fish, despite the optimism of the *Boston Herald* reporter. Andover and Exeter did not meet on the playing field in any sport for the next three years, the second interruption in the series. In April 1895, Fish resigned, effective at the end of the school year (Williams 1957, 73).

Student-led athletics had run amok at Exeter. Doubtlessly, the scandal over White and Donovan embarrassed both institutions, but especially Exeter. Moreover, embarrassment to Exeter faculty and alumni was not contained. Readers of *Harper's Weekly* heard about the scandal from the rising young New Yorker, Theodore Roosevelt. In an article titled, "Value of an Athletic Training," Roosevelt lauded the benefits of athletics for building character. Conversely, when rules were broken, swift penalties should follow. Without crediting his source of information, Roosevelt declared that, if Exeter had professionals on its teams, the academy should be cut off from any competition with other schools and any games won with illegal players should be forfeited (Roosevelt 1893, 1236). Clearly, Exeter needed a strong adult leader to steer athletics on an even keel. The harried trustees finally found their man—Harlan Page Amen, an Exeter graduate. Amen took over in the fall of 1895 and faced many problems. Enrollment had dwindled; faculty morale had reached its lowest point; and the constituency had doubts about the school. President William Hyde of Bowdoin College said later, "No man ever faced a harder task than the Phillips Exeter Academy in 1895." But Amen, an idealist, organizer, and builder, moved in with confidence. "To Mr. Amen, who had only grateful memories of the Exeter of his day, the return was very much of a homecoming" (Williams 1957, 74–75). Within a year the wounds with Andover were healed. Amen and Bancroft saw to that.

Ringers as "Emergency Men"

One of the most frequent transgressions associated with professionalism focused on the illicit enrollment of boys or men with false academic credentials and no legitimate connection with the school. "Pooch" Donovan was a case in point. Overzealous sport leaders enticed off-campus, local boys with athletic ability to enroll, with expenses underwritten by student supporters. The sole purpose centered on ensuring success for either the football or the baseball team. Such maneuvering prompted a Worcester Academy editorial writer in late May of 1897 to castigate the evildoers. He wrote, "Within the week the fact has become known to the faculty that one of our baseball players, who joined the school early this term, was induced to come primarily to play ball, and that his term bill was paid by subscriptions from certain of the students. This matter was treated in a way which leaves no doubt as to the position of Worcester Academy in regard to professionalism. That it will not be given the least encouragement here but will be promptly suppressed, has been clearly shown." No doubt, this incident served as a source of embarrassment to Principal D. W. Abercrombie, who had appointed himself as president of the school's athletic association in 1885. However, it seems that the faculty acted promptly. The editorialist continued, "We feel that every fair-minded fellow must stand by the faculty in the action taken regarding all the offenders" (*Academy Weekly* 4, no. 30; Small 1979, 62, 80).

Some writers labeled "ringers" as "emergency men." A Suffield School (formerly Connecticut Literary Institution) writer observed in October of 1891 as to how these illegal substitutes were used: "It is customary among many preparatory schools, when about to play a game of foot-ball with a team from a similar school to secure the services of outside players, sometimes of those among the alumni who are on college teams, and when these are not to be had, of those who have no connection whatever with the school. In this way the question of victory depends not on which school has the better team, but on which can secure the services of the more and better players, and the real strength of the school is not tested." In a slight variation of this strategy, the writer continued, a school with "a rather strong team of its own" might secure the "services" of an "emergency man." If a team reached a stage in the game when it might be defeated, the "emergency man" entered the game, "a man whose playing is far superior to that of any of the team players, and who is used only when there is a posibilibly [*sic*] of the school team being defeated" *(Senior* 1891, no. 2). The Suffield writer's use of the word *customary* suggests that the practice of using nontraditional students was common. Perhaps the schools lacked sufficient numbers for a team or perhaps the masters wanted to play, as was the case at Groton in the late 1880s. However, it seems that the clear desire to win resulted in the employment of ringers or "emergency men."

School historians, with the exception of Harrison, fail to mention these misdeeds in the conduct of school sport. It is possible they had insufficient information to mention particular situations or, at the time of writing, thought them not worth recording. The experience by the Suffield School scribe occurred in a game against Williston on October 10, 1891. When the "emergency man was produced," Williston increased its score from fourteen to fifty points, thereby clobbering the Suffield gridders fifty to six. Joseph Sawyer in his history of Williston neglects to report this kind of irregularity. However, the *Willistonian* for October 17, 1891 reports the game. A left halfback named Bond scored five touchdowns and played in no other game. He was not enrolled as a Williston student. Archivist Rick Teller verified that Mr. Bond's first name was unknown and that he was not a Williston alumnus *(Willistonian* 32, no. 5, 1; telephone conversation with Rick Teller, archivist, Williston Northampton School, Jan. 11, 2005). Someone who read only the Williston paper would not have known from the newspaper account that Bond was an "emergency man." In another example, Roland Mulford, the Lawrenceville historian, chose not to render the reasons why the Larries broke off athletic relations with the Hill School in 1905, not to be resumed until 1917. It must be noted that Sawyer and Mulford wrote general histories of their schools. Attention to athletics was only one aspect of student and school life. By contrast, Harrison's history of Andover focused solely on athletics.

From today's vantage point, the use of "ringers," however rare or widespread, can be seen as part of the maturing of interscholastic athletics and refining of eligibility rules that developed at the end of the nineteenth century. When it was common for masters to play on teams, the use of outside "ringers" like "Pooch" Donovan may not have seemed so illegal to 1890s schoolboys as it does to the twenty-first-century reader. Sometimes the issue for the boys was, not legality, but school pride. The Suffield editorialist, for example, wrote that Connecticut Liter-

14. The Lawrenceville School's 1894 football team, posed on the field as though ready to snap the ball, a more realistic shot than a studio pose. Courtesy of The Lawrenceville School Archives.

ary Institution hoped to meet Williston again on the gridiron. He assured the readers that when that happened, despite the outcome, "we will play as formerly with *our own men.*" Ultimately, the practice pointed up the need for tightening eligibility rules so that competition could be as fair and honest as possible.

Gambling

Gambling in sport can be traced at least as far back as the 1700s, where cricket matches became the focus of gamblers. When cricket emerged as a favorite pastime of landowners in England, it became an activity for betting. Eventually, horse racing became another sporting activity for those who wagered. Sometimes, betting became the principal reason for staging horse races. But exactly when gambling entered the ranks of collegiate sport in this country in the later nineteenth century cannot be ascertained. If judged by school histories, it seems largely unknown in the boarding schools of that time.

Thus, it likely shocked J. Carter Walker, headmaster of Woodberry Forest School, when in May of 1910 he learned that a group of his boys had bet on the outcome of games with rival Episcopal High School. He immediately typed a missive to Archie Hoxton, associate principal at Episcopal, in which he said, "I have just received a letter from Dr. Massey [of the Theological Seminary, Fairfax County] about a subject with which I have been in correspondence with him: namely gambling between the boys of Woodberry Forest and Episcopal High School on games of baseball and football." Walker attributed the reasons for betting, to some degree, to the boys' notions that betting on their teammates showed school spirit. Further, he thought boys held the idea that the school's "chief business" was to win games. Walker also informed Hoxton that the report of betting had been laid before the entire student body, his faculty, and the board of prefects, claiming that gambling was evil and had to be ended immediately. Further, he asked Hoxton for cooperation to solve the problem: "I should value very highly a statement of your opinion of the extent of the evil, and your opinion also of the value of 'cooperation' between Woodberry Forest and the Episcopal High School, to stop or at least check it. If you or I acted independently of each other in forbidding the game between the schools, the one so acting would place his boys in an awkward position, and would subject them to taunts that would, I feel, be trying." For a solution, Walker asked if Hoxton would join him in requiring all the boys to sign a statement of no betting on the next game, as an alternative to canceling the next game, scheduled for May 21 of 1910 (Walker 1910). Immediately, Hoxton replied, saying, "you may count upon me to help in every way I can to put a stop to this discreditable practice. It is a problem that has been worrying me for some time past and I realize that this school's reputation has suffered." Hoxton reported that he obtained pledges from the entire student body that no boy would bet on the upcoming baseball game. During the next year, the two men continued to work on a permanent solution (Hoxton 1910; 1911). The competitive rivalry between the two schools continued. No letters in the Woodberry Forest archives reveal any further discussion of the matter between the two headmasters.

The introduction of cheating and the continual shakiness of the financial structure of student-led athletics had taken its toll. To solve the problems of professionalism and gambling, headmasters and masters had to intervene with clarity and decisiveness so that schoolboy competition could be conducted fairly, honestly, and on an amateur level. The next step in the evolution of schoolboy athletics was for the faculty to totally control the program. But the shift from student to faculty control had been occurring in different ways and over decades at the several schools. A look at leadership styles of headmasters can illumine this transition from student to faculty control of athletics.

9

Faculty Leadership

From Permissive Observer to Vocal Advocate

IN THE LATER NINETEENTH CENTURY, no athletic conference existed to pull schools together in seeking common goals and laying down rules. No board of trustees decreed that faculty should control the sports program. Moreover, no single pattern characterized the gradual authority assumed by faculty over athletics. Rather than a universal takeover, the shift to adult authority became more of a weaning process whereby boys learned to let go of their own athletic destiny and headmasters assumed responsibility for athletics. Several factors in the school and societal environment augmented this shift in control. First, the popularity of sport in American society was growing rapidly. Second, more athletic contests between schools, entailing travel and other costs, meant increased expenses. Third, more was now at stake, with the increased interscholastic competition and the use of occasional ringers. School newspapers heightened the interest in contests, encouraging more onlookers and school spirit. Fourth, the hiring of nonacademic coaches had been frowned upon by faculties. When headmasters and masters came upon the scene who themselves had experienced sports-playing in their own student days, control of athletics was in knowledgeable and experienced hands. Thus, this collision of more extensive and intense competition, coaching, larger crowds, and the need to control costs as well as set boundaries for the continued fair and equitable existence of athletics, meant that faculty supervision would become inevitable. But the shift to faculty control varied among schools, and it occurred over several years, depending largely upon the style and assertiveness of headmasters as well as their length of tenure.

The Headmaster as Permissive Observer

The type of headmaster who exerted the least authority over athletics developed in the earlier decades, though some, like Gideon Soule of Exeter, lasted in their posts until the latter third of the nineteenth century. Soule, a professor of ancient languages, led Phillips Exeter from 1838 to 1873. Thus, his tenure as headmaster began in an era when boys played spontaneously and extended into the time when interscholastic competition had caught on in the prep schools. Soule's pattern of authority encouraged self-assurance and manliness in his young charges. Students played games without interference during breaks in their rigorous schooldays. Yet, respect for each other, boys on the one hand and school authorities on the other, permeated campus life. Soule, for example, would doff his hat, in true Victorian courtesy, as he passed his boys in the street. In 1895, one alumnus from the 1840s said that, as students, "we were thrown upon our honor as gentlemen." Thus, in some respects, Soule's style was laissez-faire. "The Academy has no rules—until they are broken," he would declare in his annual talk on the conduct expected of the boys. But he would end with what school historian Myron Williams called his "anti-climax." There was one rule Soule held inviolable. "Whoever crosses the threshold of a billiard saloon, crosses the threshold of the Academy for the last time." Other than that, apparently, the ideal of the gentleman held that certain rules of conduct were implicit (Williams 1957, 43, 50–51; *Phillips Exeter Literary Monthly* 1895, 11).

A variation in the style of the permissive observer occurred with Matthew Meigs, founder of the Hill School in 1851 in Pottstown, Pennsylvania. Though a nonathlete himself, Meigs provided space and means for sports and recreational games soon after starting his school. Meigs may have been the first nonathletic headmaster to display an acute awareness that the play spirit of boys was central to their needs (Chancellor 1976, 239–40). Other headmasters of the era, like Samuel Hamill of Lawrenceville, typically considered such needs to be satisfied by a long run through the countryside.

Henry Coit of St. Paul's School displayed the same style of permissiveness, though he did exert authority with respect to the particular sports to be played. He had no time for baseball but approved rowing and cricket, the sports with English traditions and a history of gentlemanly behavior surrounding them. Coit saw American football and baseball as being fraught with shouting, fighting, and cheating. However, Coit's long tenure as headmaster meant that he lasted into the later decades when more boys sought more sports. His own style changed somewhat with the times.

The Headmaster Who Delegated Authority

A more active though still somewhat laissez-faire style of leadership emerged when headmasters allowed, or brought in, young masters with sports experience. In some instances these new masters were given a specific charge with respect to athletics; in other instances their own interests led to fostering sports. Whether his own son's affinity for rowing helped to change Coit's mind can only be surmised. But he moved beyond his permissive observer role when he hired Lester Dole in 1878 to supervise the newly constructed gymnasium and become the rowing coach (Pier 1934, 155). Subsequently, other masters were hired who participated with the boys and thereby fostered sports as well as camaraderie between students and masters. The same thing happened at Lawrenceville.

Nearing the end of his tenure in office, Hamill hired young Jotham Potter as a master in 1877. Shortly after his arrival, Potter introduced rugby with the constituted rules adopted by Ivy League colleges in the fall of 1876. As a student at Princeton, Potter had attended the historic rule-making conclave at Springfield, Massachusetts, serving as "clerk of the convention." Thus, in a sense, the "ruggers" at Lawrenceville played football with the first set of Americanized rugby rules (Mulford 1935, 75–76).

By the late nineteenth century, the practice of having masters play with the boys became common. Harrison, in fact, refers to "triple-threat" men, that is masters who could teach, play, and coach, as well as supervise the dormitory. Hiring this type of master became possible because intercollegiate sports had developed to such a degree that young masters came to the boarding schools with competitive athletic experience in their own backgrounds. A variation in that role occurred at St. Paul's, where interscholastic competition came late to the campus. For example, master John Hargate certainly did not institute athletic policy, although he served as the elected president of the Isthmian Cricket Club for several years, while another playing master, James Knox, won reelection over several years as president of the Old Hundred Cricket Club. School historian Arthur Pier records that masters played on the "club and school cricket elevens" as long as St. Paul's sponsored the game. Coit did not object to these masters being so involved, for it assured him that the games were carried on in a gentlemanly fashion (Pier 1934, 160, 174; Coit 1891, 68).

Perhaps at no school did the impact of playing masters assert itself more than at St. Mark's, beginning with the arrival of James Soley at the end of the 1860s. Soon after his arrival, he encouraged the establishment of crew and helped by rowing stroke on a four-man team in St. Mark's first contest against an off-campus aggregation, a Framingham, Massachusetts, amateur crew. The race probably took place before 1872 (Benson 1925, 39, 42–44). As a school that virtually started with interscholastic competition, St. Mark's ushered in the "teacher-coach" concept. Some of the masters brought notable athletic reputations to the school. For example, when William Peck came to St. Mark's in 1871 as a teacher of classics and literature, he brought with him the reputation of being "the best straight-arm pitcher in Massachusetts." Those talents contributed to the St. Mark's nine. Both Peck, who later became headmaster in 1883, and fellow master D. W. Abercrombie also played on the first football team fielded by the school in 1877 (Benson 1925, 55, 69, 71, 84). By the time Peck left St. Mark's in 1894, he had also spearheaded the move for construction of a new gym, later named after him (Benson 1925, 121, 125, 142).

The appointment of the Reverend William G. Thayer to succeed Peck as headmaster emphasized the trend, then beginning, of masters moving from one prep school to another and bringing their athletic experience with them. Thayer came from Groton, where he had been a beloved master for six years and had played on the school's early football teams. In fact, in the first game of the long-standing football series between the two schools, Thayer scored the first touchdown (Ashburn 1934, 61, 102).

In addition to appointing masters who played with the boys, the headmaster who delegated authority also appointed men to new posts, namely as director of the gymnasium and later director of athletics. As noted in chapter 5, by delegating authority in this way a headmaster made critical decisions about the direction in which school programs would expand. At the end of the century, when Harlan Page Amen appointed Howard Ross at Exeter and Alfred Stearns tapped Pierson Page for Andover, the headmasters displayed visionary leadership through delegating — not just existing duties — but also opportunities for expansion and initiative.

At no place did the transition to faculty control prove more startling than at Worcester Academy. When Abercrombie was appointed principal in 1882, he set in motion the adoption of new procedures to bolster the ailing school. One innovation he enacted in 1884–85 centered on the establishment of an athletic association with himself as the president. The new association included another faculty member and several student leaders, plus the captains of the football and baseball teams (Small 1979, 62–63). It seems likely that Abercrombie's one-year experience at St. Mark's as a playing master spawned ideas as to how best conduct the sports program. With Abercrombie's active involvement, Worcester athletics soared. "Athletic sports are encouraged and generously sustained by the Faculty and pupils." So did Cloyd Small use this quotation in describing the resurgence of sport under young Abercrombie's second year as principal (Small 1968, 13). Although Small does not say, it seems likely that the quote was taken from the school catalogue for 1884–85. In 1888–89, Abercrombie stepped up his control over athletics by appointing Joseph E. Raycroft, "under the supervision of the Boston YMCA," as a physical instructor. He was "at the same time a pupil in the full classical course." Small also lists Raycroft as the first director of athletics, serving 1888–92. Thus, Raycroft must have served as instructor and student simultaneously. Whether or not he was older than the typical student is not clear (Small 1968, 14).

In similar style of hiring for new positions, James Mackenzie at Lawrenceville made news. Succeeding the venerable Hamill as headmaster in September of 1883, Mackenzie soon appointed men to coach and to administer an athletic program that would involve nearly all the students. To that end, he hired Charles H. Raymond in 1889 to supervise "athletic exercises." He also brought in William J. George, a standout Princeton and All-American football center, to coach the Larries. This latter appointment ranks as one of the first instances where a headmaster filled a faculty position with someone specified to coach a particular sport (Mulford 1935, 81, 113).

When Roger Swetland assumed the role of principal at Peddie School in 1898, he deliberated for some time before making a decision as to the future of Peddie athletics. Long under the auspices of students, athletics relied on masters to lend a hand with coaching. But the new principal eventually decided to establish the post of athletic director, following in the footsteps of Amen and Stearns. In 1906, Swetland appointed his recent graduate, John Plant, as his first athletic director and his first appointed coach. Though he had played professional basketball, Plant had been well-schooled in the Peddie spirit under Swetland. Plant would inject that spirit into young, future athletes. During the twenty-year span he held the job, Plant left his mark by stabilizing athletics and emphasizing good sportsmanship (Geiger 1961, 50, 117–21).

The Headmaster as Vigorous Participant/Leader

A still different style of control exerted by headmasters was exemplified by those who chose to play the vigorous, athletic role themselves. One of the earliest of such men was, of course, Frederick Gunn. No headmaster of his time exhibited a more enlightened attitude toward schoolboy sport than he did. Gunn took charge in his new school from the beginning and decided how campus sports and games should develop at his small Gunnery school. He conducted the program mainly by example and through his spirited personality. A former pupil remembered that, "The master [Gunn] encouraged and almost compelled every kind of rational exercise as part of his character-building. He lent to sports not merely the stimulus of his personal example, but the keener spur of personal enthusiasm" (Deming 1887, 81). A muscular Christian before his time, in his days at Yale, Gunn shaped a concept of manliness in the 1830s through his own development of "muscle, health, imagination, taste [and] intellect." For Gunn, sports developed "a muscular character as surely as a muscular body." His sporting experiences at Yale preceded organized forms of athletics. According to Gunn's biographer, "Had he been in college twenty years later he would have been first in the University boat crew, the athlete of his class" (Rossiter 1887, 24, 25, 102).

As chronicled in chapter 7, the other early headmaster who played with his boys in interscholastic games was Endicott Peabody. From the founding of his school in 1884, Peabody played on the Groton eleven for several years. After his playing days, he served as referee and timekeeper for many games and generally used his active presence to exert his authority over the entire athletic program. By the 1890s, however, other schools were also gaining leaders experienced in sport.

At Woodberry Forest School, J. Carter Walker, who became headmaster in 1897, played on the baseball team, as did his brother, Joe, who served as business manager of the school. At Governor Dummer Academy at about the same time, the new headmaster, Perley Horne, appointed in 1896, proved to be that school's first leader who was also a sport enthusiast. Horne lent support to the football team by playing left tackle. Throughout Horne's regime, "it was customary" for masters to play on Dummer teams. The custom apparently ended when it led to "unpleasant relations" with some opponents (Ragle 1963, 84, 88).

When William Mann Irvine took charge of Mercersburg in 1893, a new academy located in south-central Pennsylvania, he had been, not just a player, but also a football coach. Fresh out of the theological seminary at Franklin and Marshall College, he came with eight years of experience playing football under rather lax eligibility rules, first at Princeton (five years) and then at Franklin and Marshall (three years), where he not only started football but also went on to play and coach for the next three years. As a player, Irvine proved powerful and fast at both tackle and guard positions. Moreover, "he was practically immune from injury." One can only speculate that he immediately introduced the game in his first fall at the new school. Mercersburg boys soon also displayed talents for running, jumping, and throwing, at the urging of Irvine, no doubt. In 1897,[1] the track team captured pennants for their laurels at the renowned Penn Relays in Philadelphia (*Mercersburg* 16, no. 2, 20, 16).

A few years later, in 1902, when twenty-two-year-old Frank Boyden became the new headmaster at the nearly defunct Deerfield Academy, he gave new meaning to the label of "vigorous participant/leader." At five feet four inches tall, he was outsized by his young charges. But he was fearless in competition! Boyden played because there were too few boys to make up a football team. Biographer John McPhee tells what happened. "He was the first quarterback Deerfield ever had. He broke his nose and broke it again. Taking the ball in one game, he started around right end, but the other team's defensive halfback forced him toward the side-line, picked him up, and—this was years before the forward motion rule—carried him all the way back to the Deerfield end zone and dumped him on the ground." Boyden also played first base on the school baseball team, despite his short stature. He was a good hitter and made headlines in local papers with his achievements. According to McPhee, "In sports, he captured and held his school." In the small program, Boyden not only coached football, basketball, and baseball but he did so until he was nearly eighty years old. Throughout that period, he was known for his emphasis on sportsmanship and courtesy. "Remember, it's better to lose in a sportsmanlike way than to win and gloat over it" (McPhee 1966, 5, 16, 28–31).

In dramatic contrast, it was the lack of sports-mindedness in a decade (1876–86) of Williston principals, including one interregnum, that postponed any permanent adult leadership in athletics at that school. However, in 1890, Dr. William Gallagher, who became principal in 1886, secured the services of Amos Alonzo Stagg to come up from Springfield College one day a week in the fall of 1890 to coach football.[2] Finally in 1907, school authorities reorganized the conduct of Williston sports, heretofore run by the students, and created an athletic ad-

---

1. A product of the Mercersburg growing track and field program, Walter Drumkeller, a graduate of 1897, participated in the second modern Olympics held in Paris in 1900. On display in the Mercersburg gymnasium are many pennants representing victories in football and track and field from the school's early years.

2. A famous athlete at Yale, Stagg was a graduate student at Springfield College in 1890. He was paid for this job and was Williston's "first non-playing coach," continuing through 1891 (Teller 2000; *Willistonian* 29, no. 2, 14).

visory board, which included teachers, undergraduates, and, surprisingly, alumni. School historian Joseph Sawyer pointed out that school heads could not ignore or be indifferent to the significant role that games filled in the life of schoolboys. "Without direction and control the sports will run away with a portion of the school, and hinder the legitimate work of other portions," he warned. Perhaps the 1891 incident in which the Suffield football captain accused Williston of using "ringers" was one of many incidents that eventually led to the 1907 plan (Sawyer 1917, 310).

The Headmaster and Master as Vocal Advocates

Some headmasters who participated also spoke out as vocal advocates for athletics, while others wrote extended pieces in public journals about the value of athletics. Endicott Peabody exhorted continually and fearlessly in favor of athletics as

15. Williston Seminary's 1890 football team, posed as if in a scrimmage, in a studio shot taken well before technology permitted live action shots. This team was the first of two Williston squads coached by the famous Amos Alonzo Stagg, although he is not shown here. Courtesy of The Williston Northampton School Archives.

a character-building aspect of schoolboy life. For example, in a paper on the English public schools presented at the Headmasters' Association in 1909, he declared that the English "recognize the valuable qualities which are generated by cricket and football and rowing and the minor sports. They believe that these games educate the judgment and the will—that they develop a desire for fair play and an ability to endure pain and disappointment. . . . they know full well that it is through simplicity of living as athletic prowess requires that the temptations to evil can best be reduced to their lowest terms" (Peabody 1909b). Yet, always, Peabody's advocacy assumed a sports program that was well-regulated by headmasters and masters. He wanted boys to play hard and to win, but not at any cost. Honesty, fair play, and sportsmanship, that is, the moral code of the participant, always formed the basis for his advocacy of athletics.

Like Peabody at Groton, when Amen took over at Exeter in the fall of 1895, he did not waste any time in informing the community how he felt about the Exeter tradition of character. Courtesy, honor, and dignity were demanded of all the students. A spirit of "loyalty, helpfulness and manliness in all the intercourse between instructors and students" was expected. Exeter boys, as young gentlemen, were to learn the "eternal worth of character" (Amen 1895, 13). In the same issue of *The Phillips Exeter Literary Monthly*, an article titled "The Gentlemanly Side of Athletics" appeared. Though without attribution of author, the article could have been written by Amen, meshing as it did with his writing on "The Exeter Spirit." In the words of the anonymous author, "When sport is seen as a phase in education, when body lends its assistance to soul and ascetic principles are entirely discarded, we may look for an athletic contest, in which, under deepest excitement, only feelings of perfect squareness will have a place in men's minds." In this view, "self-control and manliness" constituted the "alpha and omega of true gentlemanliness." No better school for developing these qualities could be found than on the football field. Yet the game could be less than ideal. When football was played by "ruffians," it was an entirely different game than that played by gentlemen. Football at Exeter would be played by gentlemen if Amen had his way (Amen 1895, 24–25).

Advocating the club system rather than interscholastic competition, Malcolm K. Gordon, a sports-minded master at St. Paul's School, also spoke out vigorously in favor of sports participation. Probably influenced by his own experience as a St. Paul's student, Gordon became a master in 1892. In that role he designed a medal to be awarded to the best all-round St. Paul's athlete of the year (Pier 1934, 216). For Gordon, the club system represented the best means for including all would-be players. Speaking to the prestigious National Education Association in 1908, he declared, "The club system, where many teachers mingle with many teams, is here at its best, for not twenty or thirty boys but practically a whole school is taught the true value of the game and is developed in all other wholesome ways, and by the intimate relations between teachers and boys, the game, boys and teachers are helped and the school is doing its duty by its boys" (Gordon 1908, 619). Gordon went on to challenge educational circles with the admonition that leaders should look closely at the role of athletics in the schools. True play, as practiced in the club system, was to be sought. Team games in particular were to be encouraged, "for in team games a boy's character shows up in a truer way than in any other phase of school life." But Gordon deplored the evil influences surrounding intense interscholastic contests, for example, "idle associates, betting, rowdyism in various forms, and financial extravagance." Like Peabody and Amen, he stressed the moral, educational value of athletics. With an all-inclusive athletic program the school had the opportunity to emphasize attributes such as sportsmanship, unselfishness, and the training of character in general (Gordon 1910, 470–71). By his appearance at the NEA convention and with a subsequent article in the *Century Magazine* in 1910, Gordon presented early arguments in public forums that would have reached beyond the community of boarding schools and their faculties.

Similarly, in 1914, Stearns, then Phillips Andover headmaster, wrote a powerful apology for athletics in *The Atlantic Monthly*. His key point emphasized well-run athletics as critical to "developing character and toughening moral fibre":

> In these days of increasing luxury, ease, and softness, the influence of wholesome athletics in developing character and toughening the moral fibre must not be ignored. Many a weakling is made strong through the lessons he masters on the football field. Here are taught and developed self-control and self-surrender, alertness of mind and body, courage, and the ability to think and act quickly for one's self. The meaning of democracy in its best sense is driven home with compelling force. Self-restraint is in the very air, and self denial for the benefit of all is a daily necessity. (Stearns 1914, 148)

Quite aware of the problems then obvious in school and college athletics, he targeted the coach, who, in Stearns's view, was often "vulgar and profane," indeed, sometimes "brutal." Rarely, Stearns declared, did the coach "exhibit, on the football field at least, those qualities which are demanded of a gentleman." Nonethe-

16. Alfred Stearns about 1903, when he became headmaster. An alumnus of Phillips Andover Academy, Stearns later served as baseball coach and athletic director before leading the school. Courtesy of Phillips Andover Academy Archive.

less, he argued that a good coach could be the leader in a wholesome program of athletics. His power might even exceed that of a preacher in the pulpit. In Stearns's words, "a clean and high-minded coach may exert on our boys a more uplifting and permanent influence than that perhaps of preachers and lecturers combined." The key figure who could make the difference between a wholesome program or a vulgar program was the headmaster. He and he alone carried the responsibility for turning athletics into the positive character-building program that it was meant to be. Stearns's authority for such assertions hearkened back to the founders of Phillips Andover and other early "institutions of learning." Those founders recognized that human beings were created not with mind alone. "To them character was the paramount issue. To them character, combining in just proportion mental and moral strength, was the surest foundation of true citizenship" (Stearns 1914, 150–52).

Here, then, was the nobility of sport that the nineteenth-century English master had declared to Tom Brown regarding cricket. The individual player learns both self-control and self-reliance, balanced with self-restraint or self-denial for the good of the larger group. In addition, for Stearns, a vibrant democracy demanded such qualities of its citizenry. Thus, he clearly connected the lessons of the playing field to molding the individual gentleman and beyond to the good of the country as a whole. Though the other headmasters might not have spoken so eloquently, they would have agreed with Stearns. This change in headmasters' attitudes, from permissive observer to vocal advocate, meant that school sponsorship of sport had become firmly established. It remained for headmasters and their faculties to figure out administrative responsibilities, clarify objectives, and implement programs so that the best educational opportunities existed for all boys, not just for a select few on school teams.

10

Finally, Athletics for All

BY THE TURN OF THE TWENTIETH CENTURY, most of the boarding schools were moving toward a philosophy of sport and physical activity that eventually developed into the concept of "athletics for all."[1] With faculty in control, adult philosophy tended to initiate the programs. When the boys had been in charge, sports had evolved depending on student interest and initiative. But the boys' joy in pure play shifted to some degree over time, as athletics became more highly organized and intense, involved only the best players for interscholastic competition, and became virtually required under the new philosophy of "athletics for all." Moreover, implementing such an egalitarian philosophy proved challenging for headmasters and athletic directors at the older schools, as well as at the new schools being started where location, enrollment, and budget added to the challenges faced by faculty. Although both boys and masters were now together in fostering sports, a brief retrospective will sharpen the differing motives between the two groups.

The Boy Attitude: Fun and Joy

The simple quest for fun and enjoyment marked the fundamental good that boys pursued when they organized sport for themselves. Most lads saw games as a substitute for exercise because it was more fun than doing a monotonous regimen of calisthenics. The perceptive Gunnery School headmaster, Frederick Gunn, early on grasped the true meaning of what attracted boys to sports. Speaking before a convention of teachers in Hartford, Connecticut, in 1877, he implored:

---

1. Exeter historian Myron Williams claims that Athletic Director Howard Ross first sounded the "athletics for all" philosophy. Williams does not clarify whether he means this attribution to apply only to Exeter faculty or to faculty from all boarding schools. Ross was appointed to Exeter in 1895 and served for thirty-nine years (Williams 1957, 88–89).

Our Declaration of Independence enumerates among the inalienable rights of man, life, liberty and the pursuit of happiness. But boys, with their scanty vocabulary, sum up all their desired rights in one expressive word. Strange that one small word should convey so much of meaning to the boy-heart! Fun! Boys have an inalienable right to their fun. Our Puritan forefathers thought all fun was devil worship, and they put it under the ban—they drove it from the family; they bolted it out of the school-house. . . . I would not admit any amusement that has the least taint of vice; but I do charge you, young teachers, let the boys have their *fun*. . . . protect it from dissipation—prevent only the excess; but do not bar the thing itself, rather share it with them.

Gunn went on to say that the boys' fun activities also provided opportunities for their overseer to encourage and discipline student minds and bodies and direct enjoyment prudently without lowering moral standards. "Good order, virtuous conduct, moral habits, a pure heart, and a clean tongue—these are essential to the life of any school." Thus, Gunn clearly adhered to a policy that fun needed to be a part of schoolboy life—but controlled (Korpalski 1977, 41).

Pleasuring activities engaged in by schoolboys had often raised the ire of headmasters in earlier decades. Instead of sharing with their boys, as Gunn advocated, they had banned play. Yet, the determination of schoolboy leaders to seek acceptable avenues for play persisted. The credo "sport for sports' sake" perhaps best describes the attitude that surrounded a schoolboy's yen for games-playing. An excerpt from a poem that appeared in the *Philo Mirror* in the fall of 1862 gives some insight into what Andoverians thought about their free time. Titled "Football—Fall 1862," it opens:

It is five o'clock, and after; and the day's work is all done,
And the boys are left at liberty to study, or have fun;
Some are going to the club rooms, some are going to their books,
Some are walking—to see others, and exhibit their own looks;
But the greatest crowd of fellows can be seen on the ball ground,
That fine place where fun, in plenty, is at all times to be found. (Quinby 1920, 14)

The gradual trend toward organization of football and baseball resulted from the joy and challenge that came in contesting against others, whether it be fellow students or those from other campuses. The latter provided special exhilaration when victory over an off-campus school team resulted. But as interscholastic games and the honor of the school became more intense, practice became critical, as some early school papers noted. Practice was not always fun!

Moreover, losing also became a part of the context. Boys had to learn that athletics contained an element of sadness and despair. Losing is never fun. As the intensity of competition increased the desire for and joy in winning, the despair when losing increased as well. Still, the thrill received from vying and striving for victory, always with courage (heart), came to the forefront and remained the core of the fun element for those who engaged in sport.

But fun and games also faced other drawbacks. Boys discovered they had to spend time making arrangements. They had to collect money and make fields ready. They found that vying against others from a different school heightened their enjoyment, but was the necessary practice and preparation worth the candle? One pundit from Andover, in later years, clearly saw the dangers in the direction school athletics had taken: "At present," he proclaimed, "we are in grave danger of making our school games seem too much like work. . . . When sport ceases to be fun, it is no longer sport" (*Phillips Bulletin*, Apr. 5, 1916). His insight reveals an unusual degree of astuteness rarely displayed by student writers at the turn of the century. Nevertheless, the games went on, even as the boys struggled with other elements of the competitive process.

To enhance the chances for upholding the school's honor and for attaining victory, a school had to place its best team on the field. Thus, the selection of players for the varsity or school team took on an aura of seriousness; often the student body entered the selection process through a committee chosen by students. Such a process raised questions. There would be those who did not think the committee selected the best players. In defense of "the football committee," one Andover scribe pointed out that the committee members had watched the men practice for three weeks. Readers had to "remember that it is a very difficult duty . . . to pick out a team and though the committee may err, yet they are not near as likely to . . . on account of their experience with the game and because they have taken especial pains to watch the men" (*Phillipian*, Oct. 3, 1885).

Then there were those who were not chosen. The joy of sport ceased to be available to all would-be players. Spontaneous mass play, as described by the Andoverian of 1862, diminished as athletics expanded to interscholastic schedules and sport emerged as an organized activity for a few. The issue then arose of how to serve the relatively small group of skilled performers, yet at the same time provide for those short on ability but still holding a desire to play. It was a challenge facing the masters as they edged toward a program of athletics for all.

Masters' Attitude: Health and Manliness

Although faculty defined their rationales for athletics differently in the various schools, some spoke in specific and comprehensive terms. For example, at Lawrenceville in 1885, the school annual, *Olla Podrida*, carried a story proclaiming the new reigning view of athletics under headmaster James Mackenzie:

> The *General Aims* that are held in view [in athletics] are easily stated. On the one hand, the extreme to which Athletism [*sic*] is carried in the English Schools is sought to be avoided, and on the other hand, manly, vigorous sport is encouraged and promoted. . . . Two results are sought: *First, that every boy should take an active part in that exercise he naturally chooses, and which seems best fitted to his health and constitution; secondly, that the school should have self-organized and efficient athletic associations and clubs, which should represent the School with honor in its contests on the baseball, football and lacrosse fields.* (Mulford 1935, 113)

The Lawrenceville philosophy clearly spelled out that every boy ought to be physically active in a "manly, vigorous sport." Yet, excessive involvement and the full-blown English ideology was to be eschewed. Boys at Lawrenceville were to have a choice in what sport(s) they wanted to play. Though not stated, the implication seems clear that some kind of sport participation was required. But a required sports program necessitated a logical rationale. Athletics, after all, did not fall into the same category as intellectual study, part of the raison d'être for a boarding school's existence. The area of physical health, however, seemed part of a necessary rationale for games-playing. Since the mid-nineteenth century, astute observers of young American males had recognized the need for exercise. Headmasters like Peabody were firmly convinced that we could not have a nation of vigorous thinkers without vigorous physiques. And college leaders were developing scientifically based programs of physical training. Justification of athletics for all on health/fitness grounds seemed unassailable.

The Lawrenceville statement spelled out that each boy should choose an activity "best fitted to his health and constitution." Thus, sports participation was understood to aid in physical development, that is, the sound body to accompany the sound mind. Combining fitness and character development via "manly, vigorous sport" did not seem incompatible to the headmasters and athletic directors who implemented athletics-for-all programs. Like many others, Michael Sweeney, hired by John Meigs in 1896 as director of the gymnasium at the Hill School, set in motion a program for both physical fitness and character growth. He used innovative ideas to make "gym work more varied and attractive." He also developed a "fitness-for-all" program (Chancellor 1976, 240–41).

Part of the emphasis on health and physical fitness was augmented by early leaders who combined work in sports with gymnastics and exercise. Many of these men also held the MD degree. Page at Andover was one of them. But the movement had started earlier with the work of Edward Hitchcock, Williston graduate and master there for seven years, before he began pioneering efforts in physical training at Amherst College in 1861. Interestingly, this emphasis on physical well-being was reflected in the Williston school paper as early as 1877. The student writer described, in his view, a balanced approach to athletics:

> Old Williston has long enjoyed the reputation of sending out her boys physically as well as mentally well-equipped, plucky and manly, and the way things have gone this year gives us good reason to believe that her record will be still brighter in the future. Not that we want her to turn into a seminary of prize-fighters, professional ball-players and oarsmen, far from it; but may she ever encourage within her walls every manly and healthful sport, and while "grinding in" the requisite amount of the languages and sciences, let her ever keep her kind maternal eyes open to the physical welfare of her numerous brood. (*Oracle* WNS, Apr. 1877, 29)

In addition to Hitchcock, another early and well-known leader in health and fitness was Dr. Dudley Allen Sargent. He founded the Department of Physical Training at Yale and completed his medical degree there in 1878. The next year Harvard appointed him to the post of director and assistant professor of physical training at its Hemenway Gymnasium (Weston 1962, 113). Both of these men would have been well known to headmasters and masters who prepared boys for college and university, as the following school paper excerpt demonstrates.

At Suffield School, then known as Connecticut Literary Institution, the first school paper, dated March of 1891, carried a lengthy article by Irving W. Larimore, "Teacher of Physical Culture." He pointed out the important benefits and aims "of this new movement in physical education." Stressing that the goal was more than simply gymnastic exercises or increase of muscle girth, Larimore quoted Sargent and summarized the new movement as "education of the physique with reference to the ultimate purposes of the whole man, body, mind and soul." Referencing Sargent, Larimore stressed the education of the "will" in pursuing a regular program of intelligent exercise and healthy lifestyle choices. Thus, in Larimore's understanding, and presumably in the understanding of boarding school leaders, the relationship between physical fitness and character development remained critical to the education of boys. A will that regularly worked the body toward health and strength, in turn, developed character and, as proved by the followers of Jahn in Germany, patriotism (*Senior*, Mar. 1891, 3–5).

Not all schools wrote in the comprehensive language that Lawrenceville used. But schoolmen typically employed the term *manly* to refer to playing in a vigorous but gentlemanly manner. Writing to the board of trustees of Governor Dummer in 1898, Headmaster Perley Horne declared, "We have taken up many lines of athletic sport and have our full share of success. The competition has been sharp, but manly. The teams that have represented the school have established a reputation for pure athletics. We intend to work daily toward our ideals in all our work and play" (Ragle 1963, 89). Horne expected competition according to understood rules of fairness and honesty. No cheating was to be tolerated. It seems clear that Horne saw athletics in the same light as did others like Peabody, Amen, and Walker, all of whom brooked no dishonesty.

Although *manly* or *manliness* became the ubiquitous terms used to describe sports and character development, other language hinted at the same ideals. John Plant at Peddie, for example, known for his sportsmanship, emphasized fair play. "Win if you can, but play fair" (Geiger 1961, 121). At St. George's School in Newport, Rhode Island, founder and headmaster Reverend John B. Diman followed the precepts of muscular Christianity. In the words of school historian Gilbert Taverner, " 'Muscular Christianity' . . . developing strong bodies through athletics and equally strong minds and spirits by a response to Christianity were widely sought as an ideal. There is ample evidence that Diman clung to close approximations of that ideal throughout his forty years as a Headmaster." The strong mind or the sound mind, as in the famous Latin dictum, included a mind fully developed with character traits such as duty, courage, purity, order, decency, and piety. To Diman, "hard play and hard work" represented the essence of life for a St. George's boy. Schoolwork first and "gentlemanliness" in sports was for Diman an "unarguable tenet" (Taverner 1987, 11).

Headmasters like Diman and Peabody, both ministers, surely had their ideals of character development uppermost in their firmly held beliefs about Christianity and education of boys. Frank Boyden of Deerfield Academy probably also held the same order of belief. But he displayed a pragmatic and realistic point of view when he commented about his boys, "We may wish they were interested in other things, . . .but we must meet existing conditions, and since they will have athletic sports anyway, let us control them and make them a moral force." To that end, Boyden used athletics to teach practical lessons. "No matter how able a Deerfield player was or how close a game had become, if he showed anger he was benched

If a basketball player said anything the least bit antagonistic to the man he was guarding . . . a substitute would go into the game" (McPhee 1966, 28–29).

Thus, when athletics-for-all swept over the boarding schools in the early years of the twentieth century, the explicitly stated or implicitly understood rationale included character development of the boys who played. One of the most lofty, yet precise, expressions of the relationship between games and character comes from an article titled "The Gentlemanly Side of Athletics." Printed in an *Exeter Literary Monthly* for 1895, the article's anonymous author declared that:

> It is not the physical benefit derived from athletic life which should cause it to appeal to one,—though this is great, but it is the closely connected mental and moral development.
>
> . . . The game does not make the gentleman but the gentleman the game. Foot-ball played by ruffians is ruffianly, by gentlemen, it has a power to ennoble, yes, truly ennoble. Because most men lose sight of the essential part, develop only a desire of victory at any cost, at any sacrifice of manliness and fair treatment, the game stands not uncondemned. *(Phillips Exeter Literary Monthly,* Oct. 1895, 24)

Demonstrating that the twin goals of health and character development proved de rigueur for schools of the era, the statement of objectives for Woodberry Forest High School, which appeared in the catalogue for 1897–98, provides a good example: "The object of the School is to supply a liberal education, including thorough intellectual training, careful moral instruction, and healthy physical development. . . . Every endeavor is made to elevate the taste and refine the manners. A cultivated mind, a healthy body, a manly, Christian character, make up the ideal" (Norfleet 1997, 63).

Such goals, however, did not originate with boarding schools. Providing a larger societal context consonant with the goals of health and character development was the outpouring of schoolboy literature that featured character training and athletics. Most notable were the Horatio Alger novels. Close at hand came the narratives of Burt Standish, creator of fictional hero Frank Merriwell, stellar athlete at "Fardale Academy" and then at Yale, and ever the ideal in sportsmanship and manliness. After the turn of the century came novels from Ralph Henry Barbour, with such stirring titles as, *The Halfback,* which would pique the interest of any young football enthusiast. The *St. Nicholas,* a magazine for children, featured articles emphasizing that "athletics and training built strength and character."[2]

---

2. For more on Alger and Standish, see Dubbert 1979, 36–39, 166.

Further emphasis on character development came from the Boy Scouts, the YMCA, and their antecedents. As David Macleod spells out, an emphasis on developing character in American middle-class, white, Protestant teenage boys permeated these social-service agencies between 1870 and 1920. Just as the boarding schools emphasized athletics as a means to building manly qualities, so these social-service agencies used recreation as a tool. Macleod comments on the pervasiveness of sport in American society at the start of the twentieth century, calling it "notorious . . . how seriously . . . Americans took team sports" (Macleod 1983, 3, 18).[3]

The degree to which the Civil War and its aftermath contributed to an emphasis on the value of team sports cannot be measured. But there is no question that some war veterans who became prominent public servants in the late nineteenth century valued team sports in the schools as the "moral equivalent of war." In his book *The Inner Civil War*, George M. Fredrickson discusses the concerns of Oliver Wendell Holmes Jr. and Henry Lee Higginson, among others—concerns about American society and young manhood during the Gilded Age. Both argued that strenuous and dangerous sport could develop courage and useful citizens. In addition, General Francis A. Walker[4] echoed themes of British athleticism in his Phi Beta Kappa address to Harvard men in 1893, when he declared that playing fields developed "something akin to patriotism and public spirit." These veterans had no love of war. Their concern was that young men could learn the hard lessons of war and develop tough moral character through a battle on the playing field without the actual bloodshed and death of armed conflict (Fredrickson 1965, 218–25). Indeed, the comparison of context and contest had not been lost on the young Andover poet of 1862 who described the mass of boys playing at football, fighting "as for a victory" and kicking "as though their life depended largely on the blow." At the end of the game, we see through the young scribe's eyes:

3. See also Peter N. Stearns's summary of the importance of sports to the middle-class concept of manhood (Stearns 1979, 101–3).

4. Oliver Wendell Holmes Jr. (1841–1935) had served with distinction in the Civil War. He went on to become a famous jurist, serving on the United States Supreme Court between 1902 and 1932. He married Fanny Dixwell, daughter of Epes Sargent Dixwell, headmaster of the Dixwell School in Boston. Henry Lee Higginson (1834–1919), also a Union solider, was devoted to music although he made his money in the Boston banking firm of Lee, Higginson & Co., a firm to which Endicott Peabody also had a family connection. Henry Lee Higginson founded the Boston Symphony Orchestra in 1881 and served as its solo underwriter until 1918. Frances Amasa Walker (1840–97) rose to the rank of brigadier general in the Civil War. He taught classics at Williston Seminary for three years after the war. Later he taught political economy and history at Yale for eight years and served as president of MIT between 1881 and 1897 *(Dictionary of American Biography)*.

> Now the men come off the playground, loth to
> leave their favorite game,
> But ah, see! for some are tattered, others
> bruised; still others lame;
> And, instead of decent students, from
> a field of active sport,
> They resemble worn-out veterans, from
> a field of different sort. (Quinby 1920, 15)

Theodore Roosevelt, who called citizens to strive for the active life, was perhaps the crowning proponent for the strenuous life, good character, health, and team sports. Before he served in national office, Roosevelt spoke and wrote repeatedly about the values of athletics and of character development. For example, in *Harper's Weekly* for December 23, 1893, he referred to General Walker's Harvard address and then went on to declare his own views: "Far above bodily strength, far above mere learning, comes character. No soundness of body and limb, no excellence of mental training . . . can atone for the lack of what . . . would be called the virtues: for the lack of courage, of honesty, of self-control, of temperance, of steadfast resolution, of readiness to stand up for one's rights, and carefulness not to infringe on the rights of others" (Roosevelt 1893, 1236). More than three decades later, Roosevelt still extolled the same traits of character. He wrote in his reflections on "The American Boy" that he should exhibit characteristics of being "fine, straightforward, clean, brave and manly." A boy needed "both physical and moral courage." In short, Roosevelt urged that, "in life, as in a football game, the principle to follow is: Hit the line hard; don't foul and don't shirk, but hit the line hard" (Roosevelt 1926, 404, 406–7).

Of all the sports, team sports and especially football held first rank in Roosevelt's view and in the minds of many headmasters. Roosevelt spelled out his reasoning: they called "for the greatest exercise of fine moral qualities, such as resolution, courage, endurance, and capacity to hold one's own, and to stand up under punishment. For this reason out-of-door sports are better than gymnastics and calisthenics." Further, the sports particularly valuable in developing "a vigorous and manly nation" were those that incorporated "a certain slight element of risk." They held greater potential for developing character (Roosevelt 1893, 1236). Like Peabody, Roosevelt stressed character as the bottom line.[5] In his Prize

---

5. Roosevelt's sons all went to Groton. In his 1904 Prize Day speech on Groton's twentieth anniversary, he declared, "I feel that Groton School is one of those institutions which preeminently stand for the development of precisely those qualities among the boys whom it sends forth to be the Ameri-

17. Caricature of President Theodore Roosevelt lecturing to boys at Groton School. From the *Cleveland Plain Dealer*, May 5, 1904. Courtesy of Groton School Archives.

Day speech at Groton in May of 1904, Roosevelt, then twenty-sixth president of the United States, declared that "a sound body is good; a sound mind is better; but a strong and clean character is better than either" (*Grotonian* 1904, 214).

Challenges with Athletics for All

When the boys had run their own sports program, those who were talented and interested could be assured of a chance to play. The less talented, ideally, provided

can men, American citizens, to do honor to themselves and their school by honoring the commonwealth to which we all belong" (*Grotonian* 1904, 218).

cheering from the sidelines, as early school paper accounts often exhorted. But sometimes the less gifted and the less interested became mischievous boys rather than a cheering audience. Andover sports historian Fred Harrison observed that the unathletic "warmed the bleachers or roamed the countryside seeking opportunity to get into trouble" (Harrison 1983, 153). Thus, headmasters came to view athletics, in part, as a practical means to an important end—social control. Free time and loafing led to trouble. A daily regimen of hard work sent exhausted boys to bed and to sleep each night. Of course this reasoning would not have been well received if publicly espoused. Yet the topic was addressed among schoolmen themselves, as when Woodberry Forest's J. Carter Walker spoke to his fellow principals on "The Fight for Purity in the Schools." Similarly, St. Paul's headmaster, Henry Ferguson, in the same decade is quoted as saying that athletics proved "useful servants but bad masters." Sports not only developed character but also were useful in Ferguson's words for "hygiene and morals." In other words, exhausted boys did not focus on sex. However, the publicly proclaimed, noble and laudable goals motivating an athletics-for-all philosophy were health and character development (Peabody 1899, 628; Heckscher 1980, 149).

When school leaders moved to this philosophy, they had to develop programs that enabled all boys to play and benefit from "manly" sports. This move toward a required or comprehensive sports program raised new questions. If character development and health were the goals and if sports participation achieved these goals, how should sports programs be organized? Obviously, not all boys could play in interscholastic competition. Further, not all boys liked sports competition. What about Johnny, who could not catch a ball but who liked to write? Or Freddy, who absolutely hated getting knocked down in football but who declaimed with brilliance in oratorical events? In this vein, young Charles Stowe, student at the Gunnery and son of Harriet Beecher Stowe, wrote his father in February of 1862 and complained about the "misserribal" game of football in which he was forced to participate. He had been knocked to the frozen ground by a fellow almost as big as his father and, subsequently, suffered severe pain and stiffness in his knee. Young Stowe concluded it was "useless" for him to kick a football (Korpalski 1977, 5). With similar distaste for sports, former Groton student Ellery Sedgwick described himself in this category of the unathletic: "I hankered for the individual life. I hated organized sports and—heresy of heresies—utterly disbelieved in their beneficial effect upon character. . . . I was certainly not a 'healthy-minded' boy nor an interesting one, and certainly I was secure from the temptations which come from being too attractive" (Sedgwick 1946, 68). For the boy like Sedgwick, who loved the life of literature and the world of imagination but who felt physically insignificant, required sport must have felt like punishment—certainly not fun!

How could headmasters help boys like Sedgwick and Stowe to benefit from manly sports? Moreover, were all sports equally beneficial? If a boy liked tennis or track and field, but not football, would the same goals of health and character be developed? Further, would required participation in sports result in character development, as well as or better than, voluntary participation? The answers did not come easily, and it is unclear whether or not headmasters discussed such questions among themselves. It seems more likely that decisions about the scope and content of athletics for all were made on pragmatic grounds, for example, the available budget, faculty, and facilities. Such criteria pointed to obvious decisions about the extent of an athletic program. But school enrollment also proved to be a challenge.

When headmasters had to decide if they could afford to give the boys a choice of sports, as the Lawrenceville statement specified, or if they could only provide one sport per season, a school with a small enrollment struggled. Dividing boys into teams of relatively equal weight and height proved difficult, if not impossible. Frank Boyden, for example, began his career in 1902 at Deerfield Academy with just seven boys, four of whom held reputations as renegades! When he announced that they were going to play football, the diminutive headmaster, physically overwhelmed by boys a head taller and thirty pounds heavier, survived through sheer force of his personality and resoluteness. His success can be attested to by the fact that his career lasted sixty years; Boyden played with the varsity teams until he reached the age of thirty-five years and served as head coach until he was nearly eighty. The school's enrollment eventually climbed to 500 boys (McPhee 1966, 14–15, 27, 29).

Of course, not all boys proved to be tough and sturdy. Headmasters also had to face the difficulties of finding a place for the boys who may have had some type of handicap. Soon after his appointment at Lawrenceville in 1882, Mackenzie's leadership resulted in new policies. By the mid 1880s, one-half of the boy's recreation time would be spent under a master "whose duty it is to see that all the boys not physically incapacitated shall take a fair share in the sports of their fellows" (Mulford 1935, 112–13). Just what Mackenzie provided for those boys who were "physically incapacitated" is not clear from Mulford's history. But, if a sports program were compulsory, then a place had to be provided for all boys, regardless of size, ability, and interest.

In addition, when implementing a two-tier sports program, such as the Lawrenceville statement stipulated, the interscholastic phase of the plan raised additional problems. Numbers of coaches, size and number of fields and gyms, and travel costs all increased as the number of teams playing other schools expanded. Opponents for school teams had to be scheduled. Costs of trips and uniforms had to be accounted for. Selection of the best players was crucial when teams played other schools. With a myriad of such decisions confronting them, headmasters at the larger schools in the 1890s appointed athletic directors to create appropriate plans for implementing the new philosophy. The expansion of sports, which came with the new century, helped such implementation at the larger schools.

Expansion of Sports

By 1900 playing fields graced the surrounding greenery of campuses, and gymnasia became commonplace. During the last decade of the nineteenth century, there was rapid expansion in the adoption of individual sports such as boxing and cross-country racing, although they had been introduced early in the century, along with wrestling, at Round Hill School (Bennett 1965, 60). At the turn of the century, competitive gymnastics, swimming, and wrestling found their way into an already growing variety of sports. Added to this were tennis and golf as well as track and field. Team sports such as football, baseball, cricket, and crew no longer held the sole attention of sport aspirants. Ice hockey and the newly created sport of basketball[6] took their place alongside the traditional games. With the arrival of a stable set of rules for American football, after many turbulent years association football (soccer) also emerged as a distinct and separate game, divorced from its relationship with the running game that characterized rugby and later American football. In several boarding schools, by the end of the first decade of the twentieth century, soccer had found a place alongside basketball and ice hockey. This proliferation of sports meant that, gradually, more and more boys donned athletic uniforms. In the words of Harrison, "Now every boy would have his chance, like it or not" (Harrison 1983, 153). Nowhere did this evolution take place more graphically than at Phillips Andover Academy. The expansion there serves as an example of the new sports that emerged.

6. In reality, ice hockey had been on the scene at St. Paul's in 1884. Pier asserts that the "first ice hockey in the United States was played at St. Paul's School" (Pier 1934, 141). Basketball was invented at Springfield College by James Naismith in the winter of 1891–92.

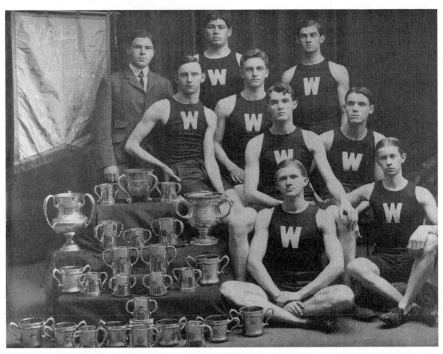

18. Worcester Academy track team poses proudly after Yale Games in 1902. Courtesy of Worcester Academy Archives.

By 1913 the Andover boys had inaugurated the following sports: boxing, track and field, tennis, lacrosse, fencing, ice hockey, golf, basketball, wrestling, competitive gymnastics, soccer, and swimming. Attempts were also made to establish crew and cycling, but both experiments failed mainly because logistical requirements proved insurmountable. Finding suitable places to hold matches and to find close-by opponents also proved troublesome. Analysis of Harrison's early history reveals that, with the aid of some masters, boys instigated these sports over three decades.

The erection of Borden Gymnasium in 1902 provided the much-needed indoor space allowing boxing, fencing, wrestling, gymnastics, and basketball to flourish—mainly as intramural activities with the exception of basketball. By the end of the century, Andover and Exeter competed annually in four sports—baseball, football, spring track, and tennis. By 1903 golf became the fifth sport in the rivalry. Hockey and gymnastics were added by 1914 (Harrison 1983, 448). As time went by, other sports took their place in the annual series.

Andover cannot take credit for being the first secondary school to introduce each sport mentioned above. For example, St. Paul's had introduced crew as early as 1856. Williston held intramural gymnastic meets as early as 1875. However, the extensiveness of sport offerings was a notable achievement at Andover. The academy boys can take most of the credit for being the first to provide an array of sports, which gave the Phillipians ample opportunity to play their favorite game. The Exeter series provided the means by which both schools could extend their sport offerings. Where sports required indoor space or a special place (e.g., a hockey rink or a swimming pool), then progress slowed because both schools needed better facilities in order to accommodate a home-and-home arrangement. Also, because not all boarding schools expanded their sports program as did Exeter and Andover, the two sister schools were forced to rely on nearby town aggregations and some public high schools to provide opponents in some of the less traditional sports. Finding appropriate opponents and facilities were only two of the many challenges that faced school athletic directors.

Athletic Directors at Large Schools

Andover and Exeter, the large schools,[7] launched new systems for the conduct of athletics, mainly through the efforts of two men—Stearns and Amen. For Exeter's new headmaster in 1895, a need for order became imperative in the wake of years of chaos surrounding school sports. Amen's first appointment was a full-time faculty member, Howard Ross, whose main duty was to straighten out the athletic program and place it on a respectable level (Williams 1957, 88).

For the next thirty-nine years, Ross guided a program of athletics and physical education that became the model for many headmasters. With the full support of Amen, Ross threaded his way toward an athletics-for-all blueprint for Exonians. He based his philosophy on the belief that physical education constituted a discipline as an academic study with its own set of values. Also, he believed that athletics presented opportunities for inculcating traits associated with character development. Following Ross's arrival on the Exeter campus in 1895, almost every Exonian from then on played in one or more of the growing number of sports, to "let off steam" and to reinforce values. Sport became an instrument to harness the antics of the boys. While Ross adopted the ideal of character development as an important objective of sport participation, Amen had also seen the practical value of social control (Williams 1957, 88–89).

---

7. By the turn of the twentieth century, Andover had grown to more than 500 boys (Harrison 1983, 136). When Amen assumed the reins at Exeter in 1895, he faced a student body of 191. When he died in 1913, the enrollment had grown to 572 boys (Crosbie 1924, 173, 182).

Meanwhile, Andover and its athletic director, Stearns, struggled to find a solution to the problem of fielding school teams in a growing list of sports while also providing opportunities for those not selected to play on varsity aggregations. Faculty control had halted the mismanagement of funds and the runaway schedule of games, but it had not provided an answer as to what to do with the nonathletes. Stearns struggled with the problem of justifying a system of athletics for a few while the rest of the student body remained neglected in terms of their physical welfare. The absence of a system for learning the fundamentals of personal hygiene and physical conditioning also bothered Stearns. As well, the haphazard conduct of games between classes and "street teams" proved wanting. The inconsistency that Stearns wrestled with would plague other headmasters in future years as enrollments grew (Harrison 1983, 136, 138).

Additional facilities helped to resolve Stearns's concern. Buffered by the completion of Borden Gymnasium in 1902, and a year later the opening of Brothers Field, Andover had the best athletic facilities in its history. When Stearns became interim principal in 1902, he brought in Pierson Page as the director of Andover athletics and physical education. Now Stearns had in place a man and facilities that could answer the ethical obligation Stearns felt in caring for the physical welfare of his charges. If the academy represented in loco parentis, then it also needed to teach and conduct practice in the rudiments of hygienic living and conditioning, he further reasoned. Upon his arrival, Page made physical training compulsory. When outdoor sports no longer could be held because of cold weather, a gymnasium program of wrestling, gymnastics, fencing, and boxing became the winter menu (Harrison 1983, 136, 138–39).

In his new plan, the well-trained Page required each student to sign up for a physical examination, which he then used to assign boys to teams based on height, weight, and strength. Those who had thought themselves unfit for such activities no longer could plead this excuse. A place had been created for everyone. A special physical-training program, administered by Page, sought to correct physical defects detected through a series of tests of physical inefficiency, known as the dreadful "PI" tests. The tests measured strength, agility, and stamina. Not all students treated the new compulsory program with enthusiasm. A group of detractors banded together for a year, protesting that their own traditions and customs had been compromised. Nevertheless, the Page program held on, and within a year many students came to realize its beneficial effects (Harrison 1983, 139–44). Harrison concluded that the period marked by the appointments of Stearns and Page inaugurated a program of athletics and physical education extraordinary in secondary education. "Thus in the short span of eight years—roughly from 1897 to

1905 — the Phillips Academy athletic and physical education program had been thoroughly revitalized. . . . In the coming decade these two [Stearns and Page] would introduce a program of athletics and physical education that was, when it was first mounted, unique among American secondary schools" (Harrison 1983, 152).

The uniqueness centered on the policy of compulsory physical education, which also included participation in a growing variety of sports. Every boy chose a sport. Depending on the season, by 1906, choices included football, baseball, basketball, hockey, track, tennis, golf, boxing, wrestling, fencing, cross-country, and gymnastics. An elite group played on the varsity teams; others played on selected class teams (seniors, juniors, etc.). The remainder of the student body could elect to learn the rudiments of several sports or take a "gymnasium class." If Page, through the routine physical examination, discovered a boy to have a physical disability, he then prescribed a physical-activity regimen for him to follow. In turn, the boy submitted a periodic progress report.

In 1905, Page revised the class team system, which had proven to lack parity. The upper two classes had completely dominated the games. Instead, he divided the entire student body into four groups, the Greeks, Gauls, Romans, and Saxons. Each boy, when entering Andover, elected which club he wished to be associated with during his Andover career, a plan that looked suspiciously similar to the system at St. Paul's. Perhaps, in the end, the large enrollment at Andover of 500 or more boys placed increased responsibility upon authorities for the care of students (Harrison 1983, 153–55). Interestingly enough, Page and Stearns remained open to other ideas that might further improve the system. Thus, the Lillard scheme came into being.

The "Andover Plan"

In 1907, Stearns appointed W. Huston Lillard as head football coach and English instructor. Although Stearns had begun coaching the baseball team in 1898, when he also served as athletic director, Lillard was the first teaching faculty member to hold the position of head coach. The practice of having paid professional coaches was ended. Lillard came from Dartmouth, where he had excelled in football, attaining All-American honors as an end. Following his graduation, he stayed at Dartmouth for graduate study. He then came to Andover in 1906 as an assistant under head coach Dr. John C. O'Connor, a physician from nearby Haverhill. When O'Connor resigned after two successful seasons, Lillard succeeded him with the overwhelming support of the faculty, Page, and Stearns. More significantly, Lillard's appointment put an end to criticism that had been aimed at professional coaches as being responsible for "illegal recruiting, and the commercialism which had crept into college athletics, particularly football." The precedent had been set, first with Stearns as baseball coach and now Lillard as football coach. The practice became a policy eventually adopted by almost all boarding schools, viz., placing faculty members in all coaching positions (Harrison 1983, 137, 155–56; *Phillips Bulletin*, Apr. 1907, 10).

After leading the school in two successful seasons, including wins over Exeter, Lillard took a sabbatical leave to study at Oxford in England. While there, he became quite taken with its intramural sports program. Upon his return in 1910 he proposed to Stearns and Page a new method of selecting the members of the varsity football team. Both of them approved his new approach. Instead of inviting candidates out for the varsity team and then proceeding through the unenviable task of selecting team members, Lillard proposed that varsity players would emerge from intramural teams coached by the faculty.

As had been the plan inaugurated by Page earlier, every Andoverian selected a sport. For those who elected football to meet their requirement, Lillard divided them into four groups, aiming for equal numbers. In the fall of 1911, more than 200 boys elected the gridiron sport, more than one-third of the student body. The management of this contingent of football enthusiasts presented a challenge. Lillard's idea called for the voluntary enlistment of faculty members; eight responded, including even Stearns, the principal, to aid in controlling and coaching the squads. During the month of September no games were played with other schools. Instead, students got rigorous training in fundamentals and in "field judgment." Coaches then selected those players who demonstrated the greatest prowess in the intramural games to be varsity team members. The selected varsity players began practice in mid-October.

The sensitive Lillard did his utmost to dispel any notions that the football program would be weakened by his plan. Football had emerged as the principal sport on campus and the fortunes of the team concerned the Andoverians in no small measure. Would it spoil the chances of defeating Exeter? In his explanatory essay in the *Mirror* for October 1911, he acknowledged this concern. He admitted that some young alumnus, after reading about his plan, queried, "That's all right about the step forward. But can you lick Exeter?" Lillard explained to the Andover community that his system would enhance "more wholesome conditions of sport," but it would not sacrifice the enjoyment and fun of playing. He would field a team "which knows the game and, more important still, a team which embodies the traditional fighting spirit of Andover." Lillard forecast correctly that first year, including a decisive win over Exeter (Lillard 1911, 1–3; Harrison 1983, 156–58).

19. Technological changes in photography permitted this action shot of the 1911 football game between Andover and Exeter, showing Andover's "flying fullback" Eddie Mahan breaking loose. Courtesy of Phillips Andover Academy Archive.

The Lillard plan signified that not only had compulsory sport-for-all reached wide acceptance among the boarding schools, but also that lessons could be learned by all the boys participating. His plan received national newspaper and magazine publicity as the "Andover Plan" and as a genuine amateur sport plan.[8] Curiously, Lillard refrained from mentioning the socialization benefits garnered from his plan. He may have had character-building in mind as an objective, but he talked about football and how to develop better players. Despite its much-heralded initiation, the plan eventually met with criticism. Boston newspapers objected because they got no news on Andover's football until well into the fall season. Some alumni were just disgruntled, according to Harrison. But Andover did win games! The plan devised by Lillard remained in operation until the mid-twentieth century (Harrison 1983, 157–60).

Smaller Schools and Club Systems

The club system, begun at the outset at St. Paul's, still held sway at the turn of the century. In the *Horae Scholasticae* for February 4, 1901, in an article titled "Bits of

8. The *Phillips Bulletin* for October 1911 features excerpts from *Collier's Weekly* on the new plan (*Phillips Bulletin* 6, no. 1, 9). The same monthly for January 1912 includes paragraphs about the Andover "system" from the *Philadelphia North American*, the *Boston Journal*, and the *St. Paul Dispatch* (*Phillips Bulletin* 6, no. 2).

20. An action shot of what is believed to be the 1911 Andover-Exeter football game, played on Exeter's field. Note that only a few players are wearing helmets, which were not required until later in the twentieth century. Courtesy of Phillips Exeter Academy Archives.

School History," a student writer pointed out, "These clubs [the Isthmian and the Old Hundred] became great rivals in cricket, and every boy in the School, was a loyal member of one or the other. Cricket was the chief game in the early days of the School and as the number of boys grew each club supported as many as four regularly organized elevens, and as late as 1884 a boy considered it about the highest honour to represent his club on a first eleven" (*Horae* 1901, 121).

The club arrangement had become well-entrenched by 1875, when an "Athletic Club" was advocated by the school paper in March of that year. Rival clubs for rowing and cricket already vied for campus supremacy. The new athletic club was "open to all who have arms and legs, and who will take a little pains to improve them." The term here referred to track; the scribe pointed out that "one can practice running and jumping at odd moments, in the intermissions and in his daily walks." Thus, if a fellow felt he could not devote the time required for football or crew practice, he could "easily be able to give [his] attention to the little preparation needed for these athletic games" and still entertain hope of success. St. Paul's did not regularly engage in interschool competition. Thus, the rigor of training could be downplayed (*Horae* 8, no. 5). But the club system reigned as a prime example of sports for all, a plan that lasted at St. Paul's until the beginning of the sixth decade of the twentieth century.

The words of Malcolm Gordon, the longtime and revered sports-loving mas-

21. Halcyon and Shattuck boat crews on Long Pond about 1896. Courtesy of St. Paul's School Archives.

ter, summarized the club system's tone and philosophy. In the *Century Magazine* for January 1910, Gordon advocated the values received from the all-encompassing sports program: "A diversified system of games the year round must be presented, so as to attract all boys naturally. The boy thus gets his exercise; but, coupled with the development of the body, are other requirements which be supplied, such as sportsmanship, healthy rivalry, unselfishness, and the training of character in general. These are developed in the multitude by local club competition, where every boy from oldest to youngest plays with his equals" (Gordon 1910, 470).

Gordon's moralism squared with Henry Coit's legacy. The late headmaster had early on accepted the importance of sports as an educational tool. By the time Coit wrote in the *Forum* for September 1891, his views had matured from an early, more limited view of sport and physical activity. He declared,

> Our boys are the men of the future. They must have bodily health and vigor to begin with, and all their physical powers unimpaired and in good working order. For men should be manly, and while a puny, delicate man may have the truest manliness and a burly, self-indulgent animal of the same genus have little or none, a sound, healthy body in a boy goes far to insure his manliness and freedom from the tendency to abnormal precocious vice. Great care will be taken, therefore to encourage and cultivate such exercises as are instrumental in producing a sound body. The playing fields, ball courts, tennis grounds, and gymnasium will receive the same attention and oversight as the school-room.

That "attention and oversight" to the playing fields and gym included emphasis on true amateur sport. No professional elements or incitement to betting would be tolerated. Cheating and "loud coarseness" would be discouraged. In Coit's view it was "a great gain for any boy to learn early to bear defeat gracefully, and to scorn an advantage, won by the sacrifice of truth, courtesy, and honor" (Coit 1891, 3–4). For Gordon, as for Coit, all this could be better achieved via the club system than with an interscholastic schedule. Gordon remained a strong advocate of intramural athletics during his long career at St. Paul's.

Several schools, including newer ones founded in the 1880s and the 1890s, used a variation on the St. Paul's system, sometimes with and sometimes without an interscholastic program in addition. For example, Lawrenceville began a unique program of its own under Mackenzie. He installed the house system, whereby students were quartered in homes built especially for a dozen or more boys (Mulford 1935, 103ff.). A schoolmaster, usually a department head, had charge of a residence. Similar to the system used in England, each house fielded its own teams. When the school grew to about 200 boys, the house system served well in providing Laurentians with quarters in a familial atmosphere centered on close ties with other housemates and a master. Although Lawrenceville also fielded varsity teams, not all schools did so.

Mount Hermon School, by edict of the headmaster and after several years of contests with other teams, eliminated interscholastic contests on philosophical grounds. Founded in 1880 by Dwight Lyman Moody, the famous evangelist, Mount Hermon ostensibly came into being as a place to provide an introductory education for those who wished to enter Christian service. Located near North-field, in north-central Massachusetts, the school grew rapidly, reaching 300 students by 1897. Thus it approached the size of Phillips Exeter. Accompanying its growth, Mount Hermon had a burgeoning athletic program that was more or less student-led. Unlike Exeter and Andover, neither Moody nor its headmasters had yet appointed an athletic director. As a consequence, school authorities witnessed athletics getting out of control. Athletes skipped morning classes in order to prepare for their afternoon games. For off-campus contests, players tended to absent themselves from campus for a longer time than was necessary. Team managers excused players from their required work obligations. Eventually, faculty and friends of the school raised questions as to whether sports had preempted the religious tone of the school. In the spring of 1897, despite the fact that the school had fielded an undefeated football team the previous fall, publicity turned into a crisis that rocked the school. Moody called for a formal discussion of the issues. He had serious misgivings, believing that intramural competition conferred all the benefits of physical exercise and carried none of the disadvantages of off-campus contests. Although there were other ways to regulate the undesirable behavior, Moody decided to ban any further interscholastic contests. He wanted all students involved in physical activity instead of just developing a few stellar performers. The ban on interscholastic play held for thirty-five years (Carter 1976, 232, 91–92).

Similarly, when Horace Taft, brother of William Howard Taft, twenty-seventh president of the United States, founded the school named after him in 1890, he established a philosophy like that of Moody. According to Taft, "The main thing is to see that an opportunity is given to the ordinary boy which is equal to that given to the members of the school teams." He accomplished this by organizing class teams or clubs that included all the boys and where good-natured rivalry could thrive. In the beginning, Taft seems to have copied the St. Paul's system. Playing other schools in scheduled games came later (Taft 1942, 269–70).

As at the larger Phillips academies, Peddie School relied on one man to carry out the physical education and athletic program. John Plant began his teaching at Peddie in 1906 and stayed there the rest of his career. As the first director of athletics, Plant initiated a program that included a schedule for the elite performers and also "A Peddie sport for every boy." When Plant was eulogized at a dinner in his honor later in his career, one graduate declared, "How many boys benefitted by the attention he spent on them and on the development of their bodies! He inspired us to play, or play at, all sports. I was never good enough really to excel at Peddie, but when I got to college I found I could play almost any sport creditably and, what is just as important, with real enjoyment. This was all thanks to John Plant and his inspiring character" (Geiger 1961, 118).

Schools with Enrollment and Location Challenges

As new schools were founded, it was not surprising that they followed the lead of established institutions, given that masters sometimes moved from one school to another. For example, E. G. Coy, the first headmaster of Hotchkiss School (1892), assumed that post after twenty-two years teaching at Phillips Andover. He had, in fact, been the master who had sustained a blow to the head at the Exeter railroad station melee three years previously, following the annual baseball game between the two rival schools. That year, in the absence of Cecil Bancroft, Coy had served as the acting Andover principal. Thus he brought experience as a headmaster and with athletics when he moved to the young school tucked away in the northwest corner of Connecticut. Isolated, and with distance exacerbated by minimal train travel, Coy authorized an aggressive campus sport program. For competing campus teams, Coy pushed for two clubs, the Olympians and the Pythians. All boys belonged to either club, including the medically excused who probably served as managers and sideline helpers. The creed, "the greatest good for the greatest number—not glory," guided the boys, who were divided into two "athletic societies" designed to compete against each other. Even the boys given medical excuses were included in these clubs (Wertenbaker and Basserman 1966, 9–10).

But Coy did not stop with this plan, which emulated the St. Paul's system. In 1896, Otto F. "Monnie" Monahan arrived on campus and stayed for the next forty-two years as director of athletics. He had the reputation for being able to "turn the puniest boy into an acceptable player at something." He believed in every boy "competing to the limit of his ability, in playing to win, and in fair play." He also believed firmly that "healthy bodies make healthy minds" (Wertenbaker and Basserman 1966, 14–15, 26). Even before Monahan came, Hotchkiss teams had organized and met other teams. Surprisingly, tennis became a focal point. In the spring of 1896, the netters entered a tournament at New Haven and came home champions. The win motivated a huge celebration by the entire school with masters giving speeches and congratulations, accompanied by food and a march through the streets of Lakeville (Wertenbaker and Basserman 1966, 13–14).

Some schools, of course, faced the problem of very small enrollments. Governor Dummer, for instance, could not find suitable opponents. Andover, located just a few miles westward, would have overwhelmed the Dummer boys in competition. Consequently, Governor Dummer conducted a limited schedule in football and baseball. Although the school had been founded in 1763, 121 years passed before Dummer fielded its first football team in the fall of 1884. Not until Perley Horne came to Dummer in the fall of 1896 as headmaster did athletics attain proportions that permitted the involvement of most of the boys. Never reaching an enrollment of more than about fifty-plus boys, Dummer would have been hard pressed to field more than one sport team per season. It was customary during Horne's tenure for him and other masters to play on the school teams with the boys. But it would be some time before the Dummer lads had a choice of participation from among two or more sports in a season. Though the school struggled for funds, the academy ultimately managed to maintain and further an athletic tradition that aimed for character development via athletics for all (Ragle 1963, 81, 84–85, 87–88, 132–33).

The same issue of small enrollment also faced Connecticut schools. The

22. What may be Governor Dummer Academy's first football team poses proudly for the camera. School historian John Ragle says the first team played in 1884. Archivist Kate Pinkham says that this picture is labeled the first team; the football in the picture is dated 1885. Courtesy of Governor Dummer Academy Archive.

Gunnery had been unable to field a football team until 1892, more than four decades after the school started. Writing about the American game of football, one scribe noted that the school's first team had "met with fair success, although it has been hard for the regular team to get practice, as there are not enough players in the school to make up a club eleven" (Korpalski 1977, 50). Four years later, Choate School, founded in 1896 at Wallingford, Connecticut, a few miles north of New Haven, started with only four boys. The school expanded to fifty-one students and five masters by 1908. Because several of the boys could bring their own canoes to school, canoeing on the nearby Quinnipiac River became the main sporting activity during the early years (St. John 1959, 5, 7, 16, 23–24, 60–61). When George St. John came as headmaster, he faced the reality that an equitable program of athletics for all with such a small student body proved impossible: "In that first year (1908) what worried us most about our athletics was that we couldn't have intramural teams in which boys of all sizes could get into games in which they were equally matched with their fellows. We wanted every boy—for fun and health and mood—to play games in which he was fairly matched. And there were nowhere nearly enough boys to make up teams to fit everybody. In our small school we were robbing boys of that" (St. John 1959, 26).

Facilities, of course, determined athletics as much as size of student body. A benefactor had given the school a wooden gymnasium in 1904 and also an athletic field. This gym, unlike earlier ones in other schools set up primarily for exercise, provided clear playing space. Because a small enrollment did not handicap a school in fielding a basketball team, as it did with football or baseball, Choate goes down as one of the first schools to seriously take up the new winter team sport. In 1908–9, they captured the state championship, coached by the same master who also taught the classics (St. John 1959, 9, 25).

Also begun in 1896, St. George's School in Newport, Rhode Island, started with eight more students than did Choate. Its founder and headmaster, the Reverend Diman, held credentials similar to those of Peabody, that is, university and seminary training, parish pastor service, and a trip to Europe in his past. In fact, Diman might have heard Peabody speak when Diman attended Cambridge (Episcopal) Theological School in the later 1880s, for at that time Peabody was already a popular speaker and preacher in the area (Taverner 1987, 2, 5). As might be expected with the waters of Newport near by, crew became an important sport. Yet, Diman, the muscular Christian, moved soon to provide play space for his boys in other sports. Unlike Peabody, he was no athlete himself, although he looked like one and believed in sports for his boys. By 1901 he had overseen the grading of tennis courts; pastures became playing fields; and in 1903 the construction of a gymnasium occurred with open floor space for basketball. Diman had earlier hired a young master, Alan Wheeler, to take charge of physical education. Although all boys belonged to one of two clubs, the school also played off-campus contests. Some were with nearby high schools, but an "extensive athletic program" involved "over-night train rides and sometimes hotel accommodations." Like the relative geographical isolation faced by Hotchkiss, St. George's could not command an easy or extended sports schedule with other boarding academies. Thus, cost of travel and time away from studies proved obstacles to off-campus competition. When the cost of railroad travel and hotel accommodations improved, and when Diman felt the boys were not neglecting study, they expanded their slate of games (Taverner 1987, 23–24, 26, 33–34).

This sampling of boarding schools makes clear that the difficulties in implementing athletics-for-all, along with an interscholastic program, proved daunting but by no means overwhelming. So ingrained had sports become in the life of these schoolboys, that headmasters could not and would not think of eliminating sports. They would regulate and implement according to their size, location, budget, facilities, faculty, and coaches. Not all schools could have extensive sports opportunities for every boy as well as a full-blown interscholastic schedule. Yet they all had sports programs to fit their means.

The End of an Era

By the early teens of the twentieth century, adoption of athletics-for-all had reached its zenith in most of the boarding schools. Testimony to this status came from an unlikely source. Sedgwick,[9] editor of the *Atlantic Monthly*, wrote in February 1914, "Among the impersonal forces which mould the character of boys at boarding-school athletics takes first rank." When a student at Groton, Sedgwick had written about his hatred for athletics and his own lack of talents in that field of competition. Yet, as a mature young professional, Sedgwick held a positive but realistic view of the value athletics carried for young schoolboys. He recognized the dishonest practices of the day and the brutalities of football in some quarters, yet he could assert, "In all the questioning regarding athletics, one thing must never be forgotten, and that is its great, its almost essential importance in education. . . . Among boys to-day athletics is the only systematic training for the sterner life, the only organized 'moral equivalent of war.' . . . Athletics must be purified, for athletics must stay" (Sedgwick 1914, 145–47).

The evolution of schoolboy sport, begun in pre-Victorian times, had come to fruition as America looked at world war in Europe and headed into a new era. Playing the game had become a way of life for American boys just as it had for Tom Brown and his schoolmates. So we can give three cheers for those gritty lads of more than a century ago, who opened up to American boys sports-playing with the best of Victorian manliness traditions. Though at times failing, they still pressed forward with courage, enthusiasm, and teamwork. The epitaph of a British cricketer provides their fitting tribute:

> And when the Last Great Scorer comes
> To write against your name,
> He'll ask not if you won or lost,
> But how you played the game. (Leake 1938, 254)

---

9. The author is cited as E. S. on page 145, "Index by Titles."

11

An Ending and a New Beginning

IN THE BEGINNING, little did academy boys think about what their simple games of bat and ball would come to. Nor did they ponder why they played. Youth tends to play in and for the moment, not to philosophize or plan for the future. Similarly, it is unlikely that early headmasters who permitted or encouraged play could have anticipated the eventual highly organized games and schedules that became commonplace by the early twentieth century. Undergirding the boarding schools' program of sports competition lay a male-oriented philosophy, which justified athletics as integral to the total development of young men. Originating in England, the notion of athletics developing character, or manliness, via team sports eventually permeated American boarding schools. It was a compelling notion for the Victorian headmasters. By the teens of the twentieth century, instead of prohibiting or merely tolerating play, boarding schools had become active sponsors of sport. The decade served as an ending to more than a century of struggle over the necessity and importance of play, games, and sports; the teens of the new century also served as a beginning for a new era of expansion.

Unlike many social movements, which gain momentum and then eventually die out, American school sports only accelerated in the twentieth century. In the late nineteenth century, nearby public high schools had sometimes competed with individual boarding schools. Ultimately, athletic competition became almost universal in public high schools throughout the country. One may well wonder why athletics have exhibited such staying power on the American educational landscape over the past century.

Surely one critical factor is the sport ideology that developed in the Victorian era. In England, the Great War brought many changes, not least some disabusing of the manliness via athletics creed. In this country, no such abatement occurred. Although the language changed over decades, the fundamental creed that sports develop character remained the core of the ideology, which eventually undergirded all of school sports. Whereas boarding school headmasters of the nineteenth century talked of developing "manly" qualities, educators of the early twentieth century began to speak about training for citizenship. But the key conviction remained, viz., the belief that well-run and highly organized athletic competition, controlled by educators, carried positive benefits for the development of character in schoolboys. Experience, anecdotal evidence, and the power of the belief resulted in the tradition being established and maintained. Indeed, as recently as November 30, 2003, an editorial in the *Minneapolis Star Tribune* about sports in the schools declared that "Sports help build community and character; . . . they're an important part of the American essence" (*Minneapolis Star Tribune* 2003). Character development through athletics legitimized school sponsorship of sports and games. No one was going to argue that good character was unimportant.

Periodically during the twentieth century, a few lone voices questioned the truth of the creed. As early as 1928, John Tunis declared, "Why not stop talking about the noble purposes which sport fulfills and take them for what they are. . . . In short, let us cease the elevation of [sport] to the level of a religion" (Edwards 1973, 317). Most recently, Andrew Miracle Jr. and Roger Rees, both social scientists and former athletes, analyze and challenge what they call the myth of character development through sports in their book, titled *Legends of the Locker Room* (Miracle and Rees 1994). Even the average reader of the twenty-first-century sports pages in daily newspapers could question the traditional assertions of character development as article after article details incidents of alleged and actual rape, drunkenness, and illegal receipt of monies by professional and Division I college athletes.

Yet one cannot completely refute the truth of the creed for the early boarding schools. Critical to the development of manly character was the fact that the boarding schools operated on a common set of values, which, for the most part would have been shared by the parents of the boys and much of American society at the time. A common context and masters committed to the ideal meant that boys would have had gentlemanly values reinforced constantly in school, where they lived twenty-four hours a day, nine months of every year. Frederick Gunn put it simply in his address to a teacher's convention in Hartford, Connecticut: "be yourself that which you would train your boys to be" (Korpalski 1977, 40). Horace Taft made the point of context and example in his *Memories and Opinions*:

> Two things more precious than these [physical courage, obedience, honor, self-sacrifice, and endurance] can be developed in athletic games, but only under leaders with high ideals of ethics and sport. . . . One is fair play, a chivalrous regard for the rules of the game. . . . The other is habit of mind which makes him

take the decision of the umpire, a habit on which democracy itself is built. The spirit that produces these two cannot come from mere didactic preaching. It must run through the whole school and the teams, and its nourishment must be the constant aim of headmasters and coaches. The two mental habits go together. It is hard for a boy to play fair if he constantly puts his judgment up against the umpire's. The zeal of the headmaster or coach, however hotly it burns, must be held in control or the partisanship of the boys will get out of hand. If these vitally important matters are disregarded, sport becomes a training in crookedness, insubordination, and bad manners. (Taft 1942, 271)

Although Taft and other headmasters remained cognizant of the evils that had encroached upon athletics of the day, nonetheless, they, like Taft, argued that athletics remained the key to character development for schoolboys. In the words of Alfred Stearns, headmaster of Phillips Andover, writing in the *Atlantic Monthly* for February 1914, "Were athletics, and especially football, taken out of the life of our schools we should search long, and probably in vain, for a suitable substitute." Stearns recognized the problems that could arise from having a ruthless coach. He spelled out infractions plaguing football, including, "tripping, momentary holding, unfair use of arms in blocking, and needless roughness of various kinds." He stated unequivocally that such practices, "forbidden by the rules, injurious to wholesome sport and clean sportsmanship, and utterly mean and contemptible in themselves, flourish and are generally encouraged wherever rival school and college elevens meet to test their skill. This is not a theory, but a fact." Despite this realistic acknowledgment of the current state of affairs, Stearns remained a stalwart believer in the value of athletics for molding boys' character. The importance of character for him, as for Peabody and other headmasters, remained unassailable. In Stearns's words, "If we cannot put knowledge into the minds of our coming citizens while fortifying that knowledge with rugged honesty and sound morals, it will be better for our country, and better for the world, that we close altogether the doors of our institutions of learning" (Stearns 1914, 149, 152).

For all their claims of character-building, the headmasters and masters do not define their concept of character or manliness. The absence of a definition seems clearly to result from the fact that they all knew what they meant by the terms. However, one can find elements of character definition scattered throughout the headmasters' and masters' writing and speaking. When analyzing these constituent traits, the list falls into two general categories: what to avoid and what to acquire. Central to the ideal of character was the emphasis on self-control. On the one hand this meant avoiding vice, especially sexual sins, gambling, betting, cheating, loafing, rowdyism, loud coarseness, and softness. On the other hand, self-control meant acquiring particular virtues, all of which could, presumably, be developed through athletics. In the view of headmasters, a gentleman of character—that is, a manly gentleman—would be honest, courteous, courageous, and unselfish. He would play fairly, play by the rules, play hard, bear defeat gracefully, display a "pure heart and a clean tongue," demonstrate loyalty and helpfulness, think and act for himself, and see his duty and do it. Headmasters do not talk as frequently about teamwork, although their emphasis on team sports for building character certainly implied the necessity of teamwork. Exeter's Amen uses the phrase "the power of unified action" with reference to the values that football can teach. At the same time, he also lauds the "manly virtues of self-reliance, self-control, and self direction" (Amen 1905, 42–43; 1913, 8). While self-reliance and self-direction could be construed as antithetical to teamwork, such comparisons and contrasts do not appear in the literature. Headmasters' emphasis on self-control as character also included a vigorous physique, although they do not seem to have talked as much about this element as about the more obviously moral virtues. Yet, self-control clearly implied building and maintaining health and strength. To play hard and demonstrate courage on the football field, one had to be physically fit. That meant, among other disciplines, avoiding sexual sins, especially masturbation, and eschewing loafing as well as softness.

The emphasis on self-control proved to be part of a larger trend among American males to find their roles during nineteenth-century cultural changes. Historian Michael Kimmel asserts that the "Doctrine of Self-Control" arose from a feeling among middle-class men in the middle of the century that their world was "spinning out of control, rushing headlong towards an industrial future." Advice books and health advertisements in abundance attempted to tell young men how to begin by gaining control of themselves. In Kimmel's characterization, the American "Self-Made Man was a control freak" (Kimmel 1996, 44–50). The label did not apply to nineteenth-century women.

The boarding schools' emphasis on the value of athletics in developing character emerged out of a societal context in which gender roles or "spheres" were separate and distinct. Men ran sports, government, business, and war. Women became the moral teachers and guardians of hearth and home. They had a civilizing influence on men. Therefore, women were to develop desired character traits among children. But headmasters like Peabody believed that their boarding schools functioned in loco parentis. Accordingly, the school could and should develop character in its boys. In this regard, contemporary historian E. Anthony Rotundo makes the point that "advocates of sport were claiming new cultural and social ground away from women. For a century, moral instruction had been regarded as a woman's task, but now men asserted that all-male competition could do the job. Beneath this assertion lay an implied complaint that young males were reaching their teens and twenties without the moral training that they should have received from their mothers" (Rotundo 1993, 242). It seems likely, however, that boarding school headmasters thought less about nineteenth-century gender politics and more about their moral imperative to develop character, derived from Christianity and their own social class of American gentlemen.

The ideal of character emphasized by the headmasters did not originate with them nor was it unique to their philosophy. As historian Gail Bederman notes, Victorians tended to use the term *manly* throughout the century to refer to "admirable men." The noun *manliness* carried "all the worthy, moral attributes which the Victorian middle class admired in a man." For example, in Noah Webster's terms, *manly* and *manliness* encompassed traits including "firm, brave, undaunted" and "dignified, noble, stately," as well as "bravery" and "boldness." Two terms, therefore, that the headmasters frequently used to convey their ideal of character held widespread currency in American society until the end of the nineteenth century. The other term that the headmasters used, *gentleman*, held a centuries-old and continuing connotation of courtesy and moral conduct, denoting a man who sought virtue and shunned vice. Further, as Edwin Cady noted, throughout much of the nineteenth century, the widespread belief "held most strongly at the popular level, that the true gentleman began by being a Christian" (Bederman 1995, 18; *Noah Webster's* 1970; Cady 1949, 55). By the end of the century, the term encompassed the traits listed in *The Century Dictionary*: "good breeding, courtesy and kindness; hence, a man distinguished for fine sense of honor, strict regard for his obligations, and consideration for the rights and feelings of others" *(Century Dictionary* 1889–1904). Moreover, theories about health through exercise and about character's relation to will also circulated in American culture by the late nineteenth century. According to Roberta Park, mind was understood to be the "seat of the 'will.' " The latter was thought to be critical in the development of character. Because mind and body were closely related, "it was assumed that by strengthening the body one could also strengthen the will" (Park 1987, 9). Also encompassing the close relationship of mind, body, and will was the inheritance from England of the ideal of muscular Christianity. Not surprisingly, therefore, Groton, Woodberry Forest, and other boarding schools could seek the development of "manly, Christian character." The goal proved laudable and desirable for prospective parents who thought American schools were too feminized.

Although the boarding schools aimed to send their graduates to college and into society as leaders in government and the professions, the headmasters' ideal of character, for the most part, appeared to be its own end. The headmasters undoubtedly talked privately about the instrumental value of athletics in maintaining social control, that is, in preventing idleness and attendant vices and providing an outlet for surplus energy. At the other end of the spectrum, some headmasters like Stearns would link the values of character to the maintenance of a vibrant democracy. But, for the most part, the value of character as described above was important in and of itself for the class of boys aspiring to be the men of the future. Notably, headmasters do not talk about winning as a part of this character development. One did not develop courage and moral toughness in order to be a winner. While, for example, an Endicott Peabody liked to win, the value he emphasized to Grotonians was playing by the rules. The latter was the ultimate ideal for the gentleman, not merely a means to another end.

But for all the conviction with which headmasters preached about developing gentlemanly qualities through athletics, the evidence does not indicate that they seriously analyzed the actual truth of what they were preaching. In that regard, several questions emerge. For example, the headmasters and masters studied did not talk about substitutes. Does the boy who sits on the bench and plays only one minute in a game develop the same qualities of courage, perseverance, and the like as the lad who plays the entire game? A school like Groton, which fielded at one observation, eleven football teams, could legitimately argue that all boys benefited from playing. But not all schools had so many teams. Moreover, if a lad made the varsity squad but not the starting team, did he acquire the same qualities as the youth who started every game and played almost all the time?

Another question that requires probing is the issue of, "What's at stake?" In other words, does the intensity of the contest affect the degree to which boys learn positive character traits? Certainly more may have been at stake in games between traditional rivals, Andover and Exeter, or between Woodberry Forest and Episcopal, than in a game between on-campus club teams. Size of audience and media coverage all add to the sense of this being "the big game." Does a boy learn to respect and live with an official's judgment better in a game of high stakes than in a less-intense intraclub game? A further question that remained unaddressed by headmasters pertains to practice. They do not talk about the benefits of practice with respect to developing character. One may well ask whether or not courage and teamwork are developed equally as well in practice as in a real game situation.

With the expansion of sports and attempts to implement athletics-for-all, little mention is made of the greater merits of one sport over another in terms of developing character. Clearly many, if not most, headmasters preferred football as the most valuable sport for building character. It was the most combative team sport. But, could baseball or cricket develop the same virtues just as well? What virtues came from track and field or tennis? Finally, the literature studied does not address the question of whether required sports participation could develop manliness as well as voluntary participation.

Thorough reflection could reveal yet more questions. The purpose here is not to resolve the who and what and when with regard to character development but simply to point out that the headmasters preached a generalization that they believed but that they do not seem to have seriously analyzed in depth. However, their lack of such philosophical analysis or sociological study does not negate the likelihood that many boys did indeed acquire the ideal of gentlemanly character sought because of the total environmental emphasis on it. What remains in question is the extent to which all the boys acquired the ideal and the degree to which it was inculcated in them.

Early in 2001, despite those who have debunked the creed of character development through athletics, Headmaster Dennis Campbell of Woodberry Forest School made the same point as did Horace Taft more than one-half a century earlier, though Campbell's language reflects contemporary times and thinking. In his article "Moral Education," Campbell makes a point about what total community emphasis on a common goal, which a boarding school, unlike a public high school, can achieve:

> One of the key features of a boarding school is that the community becomes the major component of the educational mission. Certainly the classroom, the library, and the curriculum are important, but I am convinced that the learning that takes place in the dorms, the dining room, the chapel, the gym, and the faculty homes is just as important. It is in these places of community life that students put their academic learning into context. The shape of the total community of the school is therefore key to all else. (Campbell 2001, 2)

WORKS CITED

INDEX

Works Cited

Abbreviations

EHSA	Episcopal High School Archives
GSA	Groton School Archives
Holyoke DT-T	*Holyoke Daily Transcript-Telegram*
Horae	*Horae Scholasticae*
PAA	Phillips Andover Archives or Academy
PEA	Phillips Exeter Archives or Academy
Philo Mirror	*The Mirror* of the Philomathean Society
Record	*Rural Record*
SPSA	St. Paul's School Archives
WFA	Woodberry Forest Archives
WNSA	Williston Northampton School Archives

School Publications

The Academy	Worcester Academy
The Academy Weekly	Worcester Academy
The Exonian	Phillips Exeter Academy (PEA)
The Grotonian	Groton School (GS)
Horae Scholasticae	St. Paul's School (SPS)
The Log	Williston Northampton School (WNS)
Mercersburg	Mercersburg Academy
The Mirror	Phillips Andover Academy (PAA)
The Mirror	Williston Northampton School (WNS)
The Oracle	Williston Northampton School (WNS)
The Oracle	Woodberry Forest School (WFS)
The Phillipian	Phillips Andover Academy (PAA)
The Phillips Bulletin	Phillips Andover Academy (PAA)

201

Phillips Exeter Bulletin	Phillips Exeter Academy (PEA)
Phillips Exeter Literary Monthly	Phillips Exeter Academy (PEA)
Philo Mirror	Phillips Andover Academy (PAA)
The Rural Record	St. Paul's School (SPS)
The Senior	Suffield School
Willistonian	Williston Northampton School (WNS)
Williston Seminary Catalogue	Williston Northampton School (WNS)

Published, Unpublished, and Archival Sources

Adams, Charles Francis. 1916. *Charles Francis Adams, 1835–1915: An Autobiography.* Boston: Houghton Mifflin.

Ahlstrom, Sidney E. 1975. *A Religious History of the American People.* Vol. 1. New York: Doubleday.

Albertson, Roxanne M. 1975. "Sports and Games in New England Schools and Academies 1780–1860." Paper presented at North American Society for Sport History Conference, Apr. 16–19, Boston.

———. 1976. "The 1831 Athletic Controversy: New England Educators' Dilemma." Paper presented at the North American Society for Sport History Conference, June 16–19, Eugene, Ore.

Allis, Frederick S., Jr. 1979. *Youth from Every Quarter.* Andover, Mass.: Phillips Andover Academy.

Amen, Harlan Page. 1895. "The Exeter Spirit." *Phillips Exeter Literary Monthly* 10, no. 1. PEA.

———. 1905. "Principal Amen's Attitude Toward Football." *Bulletin of the Phillips Exeter Academy* 1, no. 1: 42–43. PEA.

———. 1913. "The Spirit of the Place." *Life at Phillips Exeter,* special issue of *Bulletin of the Phillips Exeter Academy* 5. PEA.

American National Biography. 1999. New York: Oxford Univ. Press.

Amory, Cleveland. 1940. "Goodbye, Mr. Peabs." *Saturday Evening Post* 213, Sept. 14: 16.

Ashburn, Frank. D. 1934. *Fifty Years On: Groton School, 1884–1934.* New York: Printed Privately at the Sign of the Gosden Head.

———. 1967. *Peabody of Groton: A Portrait.* Cambridge, Mass.: Riverside Press.

Baker, William J. 1982. *Sports in the Western World.* Totowa, N.J.: Rowman and Littlefield.

Bamford, T. W. 1975. "Thomas Arnold and the Victorian Idea of a Public School." In *The Victorian Public School,* edited by Brian Simon and Ian Bradley, 58–71. Dublin: Gill and Macmillan.

Barnhart, Robert K., ed. 1988. *The Barnhart Dictionary of Etymology.* N.p.: H. W. Wilson Co.

Bederman, Gail. 1995. *Manliness and Civilization.* Chicago: Chicago Univ. Press.

Beecher, Henry Ward. 1846. *Lectures to Young Men, On Various Important Subjects.* Salem, Mass.: John P. Jewett and Co.

Bell, Charles H. 1883. *Phillips Exeter Academy.* Exeter, N.H.: Wm. B. Morrill.

Bennett, Bruce L. 1965. "The Making of Round Hill School." *Quest* 4, Apr.: 53.

Benson, Albert Emerson. 1925. *History of Saint Mark's School.* Southborough, Mass.: Privately Printed for the Alumni Association.

Betts, John Rickards. 1974. *America's Sporting Heritage: 1850–1950.* Reading, Mass.: Addison-Wesley.

Blair, Frank W. 1940. "Curve Pitching at Williston." Remarks at Williston Alumni Luncheon, June 8. WNSA.

Brailsford, Dennis. 1969. *Sport and Society: Elizabeth to Anne.* London: Routledge and Kegan Paul.

———. 1991. *Sport, Time, and Society.* New York: Routledge.

Bridenbaugh, Carl. 1938. *Cities in the Wilderness.* New York: Ronald Press.

Brooks, Van Wyck. 1937. *The Flowering of New England, 1815–1865.* N.p.: E. P. Dutton.

Butts, R. Freeman. 1978. *Public Education in the United States.* New York: Holt, Rinehart, and Winston.

Cady, Edwin H. 1949. *The Gentleman in America.* Syracuse, N.Y.: Syracuse Univ. Press.

Camp, Walter. 1909. Letter to Endicott Peabody, Nov. 26. File C3 Drawer A-F. GSA.

Campbell, Dennis. 2001. "Moral Education and Popular Culture." *Woodberry Forest Magazine and Journal* 40, no. 1: 2.

Carter, Burnham. 1976. *So Much to Learn: The History of Northfield Mount Hermon School in Commemoration of the 100th Anniversary 1980.* N.p.: Northfield Mount Hermon School.

Century Dictionary and Encyclopedic Lexicon of the English Language. 1889–1904. New York: Century Co.

Chancellor, Paul. 1976. *The History of The Hill School, 1851–1976.* Pottstown, Pa.: The Hill School.

Chandos, John. 1984. *Boys Together.* New Haven, Conn.: Yale Univ. Press.

Cogswell, Joseph G., and George Bancroft. [1823]. *Prospectus of a School to Be Established at Round Hill, Northampton, Massachusetts.* Cambridge, Mass.: Hilliard and Metcalf.

Coit, Henry A. 1891. "An American Boys' School—What It Should Be." *The Forum* 12, Sept.

[Coit, Joseph Howland]. 1891. "Subsequent History." In *Memorials of St. Paul's School,* 27–148. New York: D. Appleton and Co.

Conover, James P. 1906. *Memories of a Great Schoolmaster (Dr. Henry A. Coit).* Boston: Houghton, Mifflin, and Co.

Crocker, Reverend John. 1981. Interview by Axel Bundgaard with former Groton headmaster, June 3.

Crosbie, Laurence M. 1924. *The Phillips Exeter Academy: A History.* Norwood, Mass.: Plimpton Press. Privately printed, Exeter, N.H.: The Academy, 1923.

Crowther, Samuel, and Arthur Ruhl. 1905. *Rowing and Track Athletics.* New York: Macmillan Co.

Cunningham, Frank H. 1883. *Familiar Sketches of the Phillips Exeter Academy and Surroundings.* Boston: James R. Osgood and Co.

Dandridge, Ned. N.d. "I Remember." File: General School Year 1896–97. File 37: Baseball Archives 1896–1900. WFA.

de S. Honey, J. R. 1977. *Tom Brown's Universe.* New York: Quadrangle/New York Times Book Co.

Deming, Clarence. 1887. "Gunnery Sports." In *The Master of the Gunnery: A Memorial of Frederick William Gunn by His Pupils,* edited by William H. Gibson, 81–102. New York: Gunn Memorial Association.

Dictionary of American Biography. New York: Charles Scribner's Sons.

Douglas, Ann. 1977. *The Feminization of American Culture.* New York: Avon Books.

Dubbert, Joe L. 1979. *A Man's Place.* Englewood Cliffs, N.J.: Prentice-Hall.

Dunning, Eric. 1975. "The Origins of Modern Football and the Public School Ethos." In *The Victorian Public School,* edited by Brian Simon and Ian Bradley, 168–76. Dublin: Gill and Macmillan.

Edmonds, Franklin Spencer. 1902. *History of the Central High School of Philadelphia.* Philadelphia: J. B. Lippincott.

Edwards, Harry. 1973. *Sociology of Sport.* Homewood, Ill.: Dorsey Press.

Elson, Ruth Miller. 1959. "American Schoolbooks and 'Culture' in the Nineteenth Century." *Mississippi Valley Historical Review* 46, no. 3: 411.

Elyot, Sir Thomas. [1531] 1962. *The Book Named the Governor.* Edited by S. E. Lehmberg. Reprint. New York: Dutton.

Frank, Douglas Alan. 1992. *The History of Lawrence Academy at Groton, 1792–1992.* Groton, Mass.: Lawrence Academy.

Fredrickson, George M. 1965. *The Inner Civil War: Northern Intellectuals and the Crisis of the Union.* New York: Harper and Row.

Fuess, Claude M. 1917. *An Old New England School: A History of Phillips Academy Andover.* Boston: Houghton Mifflin Co.

———. 1935. *Amherst: The Story of a New England College.* Boston: Little, Brown, and Co.

Gathorne-Hardy, Jonathan. 1977. *The Old School Tie.* New York: Viking Press.

Geiger, Carl. 1961. *The Peddie School's First Century.* Hightstown, N.J.: The Peddie School.

Geldbach, Erich. 1976. "The Beginning of German Gymnastics in America." *Journal of Sport History* 3, no. 3: 236.

"The Gentlemanly Side of Athletics." 1895. *Phillips Exeter Literary Monthly* 10, no. 1: 23. PEA.

Goodlett, Nicholas M. 1928. Letter to Professor Sidney N. Morse, Williston Academy, Nov. 1. WNSA.

Gordon, Malcolm Kenneth. 1908. "School Athletics: What They Are; What They Should Be." *Addresses and Proceedings of the National Education Association*, 616–22.

———. 1910. "The Reform of School Athletics." *Century Magazine* 79, no. 3: 469.

Hale, Edward Everett. 1893. *A New England Boyhood*. Boston: Little, Brown, and Co.

Haley, Bruce E. 1968. "Sports and the Victorian World." *Western Humanities Review* 22, no. 2: 115.

———. 1978. *The Healthy Body and Victorian Culture*. Cambridge, Mass.: Harvard Univ. Press.

Hardy, Stephen. 1982. *How Boston Played the Game*. N.p.: Northeastern Univ. Press.

Harrison, Fred H. 1983. *Athletics for All: Physical Education and Athletics at Phillips Academy, Andover, 1778–1978*. Andover, Mass.: Phillips Academy.

Heckscher, August. 1980. *The Life of a New England School*. New York: Charles Scribner's Sons.

Henderson, Robert. 1947. *Bat, Ball, and Bishop*. New York: Rockport Press.

Higginson, Thomas Wentworth. 1858. "Saints, and their Bodies." *Atlantic Monthly* 1, Mar.: 582.

Holliman, Jennie. 1931. *American Sports, 1789–1935*. Durham, N.C.: Seaman Press.

Holmes, Oliver Wendell. 1858. "The Autocrat of the Breakfast Table." *Atlantic Monthly* 1, May: 871.

Houghton, Walter. 1957. *The Victorian Frame of Mind, 1830–1870*. New Haven, Conn.: Yale Univ. Press.

Hoxton, A. R. 1910. Letter to J. Carter Walker, May 11. File 11: WFS and EHS 1905–25. WFA.

———. 1911. Letter to J. Carter Walker, Nov. 13. File 11: WFS and EHS 1905–25. WFA.

[Hughes, Thomas]. 1863. *School Days at Rugby*. By an Old Boy. Boston: Ticknor and Fields.

Kimmel, Michael. 1996. *Manhood in America*. New York: Free Press.

Kirsch, George. 1984. "American Cricket: Players and Clubs Before the Civil War." *Journal of Sport History* 11, no. 1: 28.

Korpalski, Adam, ed. 1977. *The Gunnery, 1850–1975: A Documentary History of Private Education in America*. Washington, Conn.: The Gunnery School.

Ladd, Tony, and James A. Mathisen. 1999. *Muscular Christianity: Evangelical Protestants and the Development of American Sport*. Grand Rapids, Mich.: Baker Books.

Laws of Football Played at Rugby School. 1845. Rugby: J. S. Crossley, Printer.

Leake, W. R. M. 1938. *Gilkes and Dulwich, 1885–1914*. London: The Allyn Club.

Leonard, Fred E., and George B. Affleck. 1947. *A Guide to the History of Physical Education*. Philadelphia, Pa.: Lea and Febiger.

Lewis, Guy M. 1969. "Theodore Roosevelt's Role in the 1905 Football Controversy." *The Research Quarterly* 40, no. 4: 717–24.

Lillard, W. Huston. 1911. "Andover's New Athletic System." *The Mirror* 7, no. 1: 1. PAA.

Lovett, James D'Wolf. 1906. *Old Boston Boys and the Games They Played*. Boston: Riverside Press.

Lucas, John A., and Ronald A. Smith. 1978. *Saga of American Sport*. Philadelphia, Pa.: Lea and Febiger.

Macleod, David I. 1983. *Building Character in the American Boy: The Boy Scouts, YMCA, and Their Forerunners, 1870–1920*. Madison: Univ. of Wisconsin Press.

Mangan, J. A. 1975a. "Athleticism: A Case Study of the Evolution of an Educational Ideology." In *The Victorian Public School*, edited by Brian Simon and Ian Bradley, 147–67. Dublin: Gill and Macmillan.

———. 1975b. "Play Up and Play the Game: Victorian and Edwardian Public School Vocabularies of Motive." *British Journal of Educational Studies* 23, no. 3: 324.

———. 1981. *Athleticism in the Victorian and Edwardian Public School*. Cambridge, Mass.: Cambridge Univ. Press.

Marr, Harriet Webster. 1954. "Amusements and Athletics in the Old New England Academies." *Old-Time New England* 44, winter: 84.

Martin, George W. 1944. "Preface to a Schoolmaster's Biography." *Harper's Magazine* 188, no. 1124: 156.

Mather, Cotton. 1702. *Magnalia Christi Americana: Or the Ecclesiastical History of New-England*. Book 5. London: Thomas Parkhurst.

McIntosh, P. C. 1957. "Games and Gymnastics for Two Nations in One." In *Landmarks in the History of Physical Education*, edited by J. G. Dixon, P. C. McIntosh, A. D. Munrow, and R. F. Willetts, 177–209. London: Routledge and Kegan Paul.

McLachlan, James. 1970. *American Boarding Schools*. New York: Charles Scribner's Sons.

McPhee, John. 1966. *The Headmaster: Frank L. Boyden of Deerfield*. New York: Farrar, Straus, and Giroux.

Menke, Frank, ed. 1978. *The Encyclopedia of Sports*. 6th rev. ed. New York: A. S. Barnes.

Minneapolis Star Tribune. 2003. "High School Sports." Nov. 30, editorial page.

Miracle, Andrew W., Jr., and C. Roger Rees. 1994. *Legends of the Locker Room: The Myth of School Sports*. Amherst, N.Y.: Prometheus Books.

Money, Tony. 1997. *Manly and Muscular Diversions*. London: Duckworth.

Moore, John Hammond. 1967. "Football's Ugly Decades, 1893–1913." *Smithsonian Journal of History* 2, fall: 49.

Morgan, M. C. 1968. *Cheltenham College: The First Hundred Years*. N.p.: Richard Sadler.

Morris, William, and Mary Morris. 1977. *Morris Dictionary of Word and Phrase Origins*. New York: Harper and Row.

Mulford, Roland J. 1935. *History of the Lawrenceville School, 1810–1935*. Princeton, N.J.: Princeton Univ. Press.

Newsome, David. 1961. "Public Schools and Christian Ideals." *Theology* 64, Dec.: 486.

Newsweek. 1940. "56 Years of Whipcracking End with Dr. Peabody's Retirement." July 1.

Newsweek. 1944. "Groton's Bullying Coaxing Peabody, Patrician Preacher and Educator." Oct. 30.

Noah Webster's Original 1828 Edition of an American Dictionary of the English Language. 1970. New York: Johnson Reprint Corp.

Norfleet, Elizabeth Copeland. 1955. *Woodberry Forest: A Venture in Faith.* New York: Georgian Press, Inc.

———. 1997. *Woodberry Forest in 1889: The Sense of Place.* N.p.

Ogilvie, Vivian. 1957. *The English Public School.* London: B. T. Batsford.

Outline of the System of Education at the Round Hill School, with a List of the Present Instructors and of the Pupils from Its Commencement until This Time. 1831. Boston: N. Hale's Steam Power Press.

Oxford English Dictionary. 1989. Oxford: Clarendon Press.

Park, Roberta J. 1987. "Biological Thought, Athletics, and the Formation of a 'Man of Character': 1830–1900." In *Manliness and Morality: Middle Class Masculinity in Britain and America, 1800–1940,* edited by J. A. Mangan and James Walvin, 7–34. New York: St. Martin's Press.

Peabody, Endicott. Various years. Headmaster's Reports to Trustees. 2 vols. GSA.

———. 1888. "Parochial vs. Public Schools." Speech before Eastern Convention, Feb. 1, Haverhill, Mass. File: Headmaster's Speeches. GSA.

———. 1899. "The Continuous Moral Influence of the School Through College and Through Life." *School Review* 7, Oct.

———. 1901. "Basic Reflections upon the Training of Boys." Speech before the Clericus Society, A Club of Clergy, May 6. File: Headmaster's Speeches. GSA.

———. 1903. Headmaster's Letter to Parents, Dec. 10. GSA.

———. 1906. "Football," Speech to Harvard Teacher's Association., Mar. 3. File: Headmaster's Speeches. GSA.

———. 1909a. "The Aims, Duties, and Opportunities of the Head-Master of an Endowed Secondary School." *School Review* 17, no. 8.

———. 1909b. "English Public Schools." Speech before the Headmaster's Association, Nov. 23. File: Headmaster's Speeches. GSA.

———. 1911. Letter to Walter Camp, Nov. 29. File C3 Drawer A-F. GSA.

———. 1914. "The Ideals of Sport in England and America." *American Physical Education Review* 19, no. 4: 277.

———. 1932. Speech to Groton Masters at Opening of School Year, Sept. 19. File: Headmaster's Speeches 1914–34. GSA.

———. 1934a. Letter to W. Redmond Cross, Dec. 11. File: School By Laws and Act of Inc., Drawer A-F. GSA.

———. 1934b. Speech to Groton Masters at Opening of School Year, Sept. 17. File: Headmaster's Speeches 1914–34. GSA.

———. 1935. Speech to Board of Regents of the Univ. of the State of New York, Oct. 17. File: Headmaster's Speeches 1935–40. GSA.

———. 1940. "St. Mark's Anniversary." Speech, May 25. File: Headmaster's Speeches 1935–40. GSA.

———. N.d. "School Football." Envelope: E. P. Misc. Talks and Football Chapter, Drawer 1916-End. GSA.

Perkins, William. [1606] 1966. *The Whole Treastise of the Cases of Conscience*. In *William Perkins 1558–1602 English Puritanist*, edited and introduction by Thomas Merrill. Reprint. Nieuwkoop, The Netherlands: B. Degraaf.

———. [1608] 1966. *A Discourse of Conscience*. Reprint in *William Perkins 1558–1602, English Puritanist*, edited and introduction by Thomas Merrill. Nieuwkoop, The Netherlands: B. De Graaf.

Perry, Lewis. 1945. "In Memoriam Endicott Peabody." Appended to Letter to Members of the Headmaster's Association from President Perry Dunlap Smith. GSA.

Pier, Arthur Stanwood. 1934. *St. Paul's School, 1855–1934*. New York: Charles Scribner's Sons.

Putney, Clifford. 2001. *Muscular Christianity: Manhood and Sports in Protestant America*. Cambridge, Mass.: Harvard Univ. Press.

Quinby, Frank L. 1920. *Phillips Academy Andover on Diamond, Track, and Field*. Andover, Mass.: Andover Press.

Quincy, Edmund. 1867. *Life of Josiah Quincy of Massachusetts*. Boston: Ticknor and Fields.

Rader, Benjamin. 1983. *American Sports*. Englewood Cliffs, N.J.: Prentice-Hall.

Ragle, John W. 1963. *Governor Dummer Academy History, 1763–1963*. South Byfield, Mass.: Governor Dummer Academy.

Roosevelt, Theodore. 1893. "Value of an Athletic Training." *Harper's Weekly* 37, no. 1931: 1236.

———. 1904. "The Address of the President on Prize Day." *Grotonian* May: 211. GSA.

———. 1926. *American Ideals: The Strenuous Life Realizable Ideals*. New York: Charles Scribner's Sons.

Ross, Howard A. 1935. Obituary. *Phillips Exeter Bulletin* Jan.: 5, 7. PEA.

Rossiter, Ehrick K. 1887. "Mr. Gunn as the Citizen." In *The Master of the Gunnery*, edited by William H. Gibson. New York: The Gunn Memorial Association.

Rotundo, E. Anthony. 1993. *American Manhood: Transformations in Masculinity from the Revolution to the Modern Era*. N.p.: Basic Books.

Sawyer, Joseph Henry. 1917. *A History of Williston Seminary*. Norwood, Mass.: The Plimpton Press.

Scott, Patrick. 1975. "The School and the Novel: Tom Brown's Schooldays." In *The

Victorian Public School, edited by Brian Simon and Ian Bradley, 34–57. Dublin: Gill and Macmillan.

Scudder, Horace E. 1877. "A Group of Classical Schools." *Harper's New Monthly Magazine* 55, no. 328: 704.

Scudder, Winthrop. 1924. "The First Organized Football Club in the United States." *Old-Time New England* 15, July: 7.

[Sedgwick, Ellery]. 1914. "Athletics and Morals." *Atlantic Monthly* 113, no. 2: 145.

Sedgwick, Ellery. 1946. "Three Men of Groton." *Atlantic Monthly* 178, July-Dec.: 65.

Shattuck, George E. 1896. "The Founding." In *Memorials of St. Paul's School*, 5–23. New York: D. Appleton and Co.

Sherman, David. 1893. *History of the Wesleyan Academy at Wilbraham, Massachusetts.* Boston: McDonald and Gill Co.

Simpson, J. B. Hope. 1967. *Rugby since Arnold.* London: Macmillan.

Sizer, Theodore, ed. 1964. *The Age of Academies.* New York: Bureau of Publications, Teachers College, Columbia Univ.

Small, Cloyd. 1968. "Athletics in the Early Years on the Hill." *Worcester Academy Bulletin* autumn: 12.

———. 1979. *Achieving the Honorable: Worcester Academy, 1834–1978.* Worcester, Mass.: Worcester Academy.

Smith, Perry Dunlap. 1945. Letter to Members of the Headmaster's Association, May 7. GSA.

Smith, Ronald A. 1988. *Sports and Freedom.* New York: Oxford Univ. Press.

Spaulding, Randall. 1899. Letter to Edward G. Coy, Secretary of the Headmaster's Association., Dec. 29. PAA.

St. John, George. 1959. *Forty Years at School.* New York: Henry Holt and Co.

Stearns, Alfred E. 1914. "Athletics and Morals." *Atlantic Monthly* 113, no 2: 148.

Stearns, Peter N. 1979. *Be a Man: Males in Modern Society.* New York: Holmes and Meier.

Stevens, Ronnett. 1908. Letter to Endicott Peabody, Feb. 29, on behalf of the Secondary Education Club, thanking him for speaking at Teachers College, Columbia Univ. GSA.

Struna, Nancy. 1977. "Puritans and Sport: The Irretrievable Tide of Change." *Journal of Sport History* 4, no. 1: 1.

———. 1994. "Sport and the Awareness of Leisure." In *Of Consuming Interests*, edited by Gary Carson, Ronald Hoffman, and Peter J. Albert, 406–43. Charlottesville: Univ. Press of Virginia.

———. 1996. *People of Prowess.* Urbana: Univ. of Illinois Press.

Taft, Horace D. 1942. *Memories and Opinions.* New York: MacMillan.

Taverner, Gilbert Y. 1987. *St. George's School: A History, 1896–1986.* Newport, R.I.: St. George's School.

Teller, Rick. 2000. "Legends." Assembly presentation to Williston students, Feb. 24.

Tocqueville, Alexis de. 1945. *Democracy in America.* Vol. 2. New York: Vintage Books.

Wagner, Ann. 1980. "The Significance of Dance in Sixteenth-Century Courtesy Literature." Ph.D. diss., Univ. of Minnesota.

Walker, J. Carter. 1908. "The Fight for Purity in the School: The Moral Welfare of Students in the Secondary Schools." File 5: J. Carter Walker Personal Correspondence 1888–1948. WFA.

——. 1910. Letter to A. R. "Archie" Hoxton, Episcopal High School, May 6. File 11: WFS and EHS 1905–25. WFA.

Ward, George Otis. 1918. *The Worcester Academy: Its Location and Its Principals, 1834–1882.* Worcester, Mass.: Davis Press.

Wertenbaker, Lael Tucker, and Maude Basserman. 1966. *The Hotchkiss School: A Portrait.* Lakeville, Conn.: Hotchkiss School.

Weston, Arthur. 1962. *The Making of American Physical Education.* New York: Appleton-Century-Crofts.

White, John. 1989. *Chronicles of the Episcopal High School in Virginia, 1839–1989.* Dublin, N.H.: William L. Bauhan.

Whitehill, Walter M. 1968. *Boston: A Topographical History.* Cambridge: Belknap Press.

Williams, Edwin Sidney. 1866. *Christian Amusements: A Discourse Delivered at the Annual Meeting of the Young Men's Christian Association.* St. Paul, Minn.: Davidson and Hall, Pioneer Office.

Williams, Myron. 1957. *The Story of Phillips Exeter.* Exeter, N.H.: Phillips Exeter Academy.

Winn, William E. 1960. "Tom Brown's Schooldays and the Development of 'Muscular Christianity.'" *Church History* 29, no. 1: 64.

Wood, James P. 1971. *New England Academy: Wilbraham to Wilbraham and Monson.* Brattleboro, Vt.: R. L. Dothard Association.

Wright, Paul. 1981. Interview by Axel Bundgaard with former Groton master, June 4.

——. 1982. Letter to Axel Bundgaard, Mar. 20.

Ziff, Larzer. 1973. *Puritanism in America: New Culture in a New World.* New York: Viking Press.

Index

Italic page number denotes illustration.